Essential Literary Terms

A Brief Norton Guide with Exercises

Essential Literary Terms

A Brief Norton Guide with Exercises

Sharon Hamilton, Ph.D.

W • W • NORTON & COMPANY

New York • London

Peoples Education

W. W. Norton & Company has been independent since its founding in 1923, when William Warder Norton and Mary D. Herter Norton first published lectures delivered at the People's Institute, the adult education division of New York City's Cooper Union. The Nortons soon expanded their program beyond the Institute, publishing books by celebrated academics from America and abroad. By mid-century, the two major pillars of Norton's publishing program—trade books and college texts—were firmly established. In the 1950s, the Norton family transferred control of the company to its employees, and today—with a staff of four hundred and a comparable number of trade, college, and professional titles published each year—W. W. Norton & Company stands as the largest and oldest publishing house owned wholly by its employees.

Composition by Matrix Publishing Services
Manufacturing by the Maple-Vail Book Manufacturing Group
Book design by Anna Palchik
Production manager: Diane O'Connor

Library of Congress Cataloging-in-Publication Data
Hamilton, Sharon, 1943-
    Essential literary terms : a brief Norton guide with exercises / Sharon Hamilton.
        p. cm.
Includes index.
ISBN-13: 978-0-393-92837-2 (pbk.)
ISBN-10: 0-393-92837-3 (pbk.)

1. Literature—Terminology. 2. Criticism—Terminology. I. Title.

PN44.5.H28 2006
803—dc22

                                                                        2005058540

W. W. Norton & Company, Inc., 500 Fifth Avenue, New York, N.Y. 10110
www.wwnorton.com

W. W. Norton & Company Ltd., Castle House, 75/76 Wells Street, London W1T 3QT

    2 3 4 5 6 7 8 9 0

Contents

PREFACE *XIII*

ACKNOWLEDGMENTS *XVII*

Literary Forms *1*

DRAMA 1

Comedy 3
 High and low comedy 3
 Farce 3
 Romantic comedy 4
 Comedy of manners 4
  Stock characters 4
 Tragedy 4
 Classical tragedy 4
 Senecan tragedy 4
 Revenge tragedy 4
 Domestic tragedy 5
Tragicomedy 5
Theater of the Absurd 6
Periods of Drama 7
 Ancient Greek 7
 Roman 7
 English medieval 7
  Morality plays 7
  Mystery plays 7
 Elizabethan and Jacobean 7
 Restoration and Eighteenth Century 7
 Modern 7

FICTION 8

Novel 8
 Novel of incident 9
 Novel of character 9
 Realistic novel 9
 Romance 9
 Bildungsroman 10
 Historical novel 10
 Epistolary novel 10
 Antinovel 10
 Metafiction 10

Short Story   *11*
Novella   *12*

POETRY   13

Verse   *13*
Epic Poetry   *13*
Dramatic Poetry   *14*
Lyric Poetry   *14*

SPECIALIZED FORMS   15

Dramatic Monologue   *15*

EXERCISE: DRAMATIC MONOLOGUE   *16*

Epigram   *19*
Aphorism   *20*

EXERCISE: EPIGRAM   *20*

Satire   *21*
Direct (formal) satire   *21*
Indirect satire   *22*
Horatian satire   *22*
Juvenalian satire   *22*

EXERCISE: SATIRE   *24*

Figurative Language   32

FIGURES OF THOUGHT (TROPES)   32

Simile   *32*
Metaphor   *33*
Tenor   *33*
Vehicle   *33*
Mixed metaphor   *34*
Extended metaphor   *35*
Subtext   *36*

EXERCISES: SIMILES AND METAPHORS   *36*

Personification   *39*
Allegory   *39*
Pathetic fallacy   *40*
Synecdoche   *41*
Metonymy   *41*

EXERCISE: PERSONIFICATION, PATHETIC FALLACY, SYNECDOCHE,
AND METONYMY   *42*

Irony   *44*
  Verbal irony   44
    Sarcasm   *44*
  Structural irony   45
    Unreliable narrator   *45*
  Dramatic irony   46
  Tragic irony   46
  Cosmic irony   46
EXERCISES: IRONY   *47*

TROPES DEPENDENT ON CONTRASTING LEVELS OF MEANING   54

Hyperbole   *54*
Understatement   *55*
Paradox   *56*
Oxymoron   *57*
Litotes   *57*
Periphrasis   *58*
Pun   *59*
  Equivoque   60
EXERCISE: TROPES DEPENDENT ON CONTRASTING LEVELS OF MEANING   *60*

FIGURES OF SPEECH (SCHEMES)   62

Apostrophe   *62*
  Invocation   63
Rhetorical Question   *63*
Anaphora   *64*
Antithesis   *64*
Chiasmus   *65*
EXERCISE: FIGURES OF SPEECH (SCHEMES)   *66*

Rhetorical Strategies   68

Diction   *68*
  Formal vs. colloquial language   68
  Abstract vs. concrete language   70
  Poetic diction   72
Allusion   *74*
Analogy   *76*
EXERCISES: ALLUSION, ANALOGY, AND DICTION   *78*

Imagery   *83*
Symbolism   *86*

Atmosphere *89*

EXERCISES: IMAGERY, SYMBOLISM, AND ATMOSPHERE *92*

Repetition *98*
Selection and Order of Details *99*
Epiphany *102*

EXERCISES: REPETITION, SELECTION AND ORDER OF DETAILS,
   AND EPIPHANY *104*

Narration 112

VOICE **112**

Narrator *112*

POINT OF VIEW **113**

First-Person *113*
Third-Person *114*
   Third-person omniscient *114*
      Intrusive narrator *115*
      Objective narrator *116*
      Narrator in drama *117*
   Third-person limited *118*
      Stream of consciousness *118*
Second-person *120*

EXERCISE: POINT OF VIEW *122*

CHARACTERIZATION *125*

Flat Characters vs. Round Characters *126*
Showing vs. Telling *127*

EXERCISES: CHARACTERIZATION *127*

ROLES IN THE PLOT **129**

Protagonist *129*
   Hero, heroine *129*
Antagonist *130*
   Villain *130*
Foil *131*

EXERCISES: ROLES *132*

DIALOGUE *132*

   Verisimilitude *137*
   Speech headings *137*
   Stage directions *137*

Direct and indirect discourse   *139*

Repartee   *140*

Soliloquy   *141*

Aside   *143*

EXERCISE: DIALOGUE   *144*

SETTING   150

EXERCISES: SETTING   *152*

THEME   154

TONE   156

Pathos   *161*

EXERCISES: THEME AND TONE   *162*

Structure   167

In Medias Res   *167*

Exposition   *168*

Flashback   *168*

Narrative Pace   *170*

Parenthetical Observation   *172*

Subplot   *174*

Shift in Style   *176*

EXERCISES: STRUCTURE   *178*

Syntax   184

Independent clause   *184*

Dependent clause   *184*

Subject   *184*

Simple subject   *184*

Complete subject   *184*

Predicate   *184*

Simple predicate   *184*

Complete predicate   *184*

Direct object   *184*

Indirect object   *185*

Appositive   *185*

Sentence Fragments   *185*

Kinds of Sentences   *186*

Simple sentence   *186*

▼

Compound sentence   *186*
  Coordinating conjunction   *186*
Complex sentence   *186*
  Subordinate clause   *186*
Means of Linkage   *186*
  Coordination   *186*
  Subordination   *187*
  Parallelism   *188*
Syntactical Order   *189*
  Loose sentence (cumulative sentence)   *189*
  Periodic sentence   *190*
  Inversion   *190*
Sentence Variety   *191*

EXERCISES: SYNTAX   *194*

Prosody   198

METER   198

Quantitative meter   *198*
Syllabic meter   *198*
Stress   *198*
Accentual meter   *198*
Accentual-syllabic meter   *198*
Foot   *199*
Metrical Feet   *199*
  Iamb   *199*
  Anapest   *200*
  Trochee   *200*
  Dactyl   *200*
Number of Feet in a Line   *200*
  Monometer   *200*
  Dimeter   *200*
  Trimeter   *201*
  Tetrameter   *201*
  Pentameter   *201*
  Hexameter   *201*
  Heptameter   *201*
Naming the Meter   *201*
  Iambic pentameter   *201*
  Trochaic trimeter   *202*
  Dactylic tetrameter   *202*

Common Substitutions   *202*
  Spondee   *202*
  Catalexis   *203*
  Masculine and feminine endings   *203*
Pauses within and between Lines of Verse   *204*
  End-stopped lines   *204*
  Enjambed lines   *204*
  Caesura   *205*
Scansion   *205*
EXERCISES: METER   *207*

RHYME   210

End Rhyme   *211*
  Double rhyme   *211*
  Triple rhyme   *211*
  Masculine rhyme   *211*
  Feminine rhyme   *211*
Internal Rhyme   *211*
Rhyme Scheme   *212*
Perfect and Imperfect Rhyme   *213*
  Eye rhyme   *213*
  Half-rhyme (off-rhyme, slant rhyme, imperfect rhyme)   *213*
EXERCISE: RHYME   *215*

SOUND AND SOUND PATTERNS   217

Alliteration   *217*
  Internal alliteration   *218*
Consonance   *219*
Assonance   *220*
Onomatopoeia   *221*
EXERCISES: SOUND AND SOUND PATTERNS   *223*

Poetic Forms   226

STANZAS   226

Couplet   *226*
  Heroic couplet   *226*
  Closed couplet   *226*
  Open couplet   *227*
Tercet (Triplet)   *228*
  Terza rima   *228*

▼

Quatrain   *229*
   In Memoriam *stanza*   *229*
   Ballad meter (common meter)   *229*
Refrain   *230*
Sonnet   *231*
   Italian (Petrarchan)   *231*
   English (Shakespearean)   *231*
     Volta (turn)   *231*
   Sonnet sequence   *233*
   Curtal sonnet   *234*
Blank Verse   *234*
   In poetry   *234*
   In drama   *236*
Free Verse (Open Form Verse)   *239*

EXERCISES: POETIC FORMS   *242*

Appendix: MLA Style   247
MLA In-Text Documentation   *249*
Notes   *254*
MLA List of Works Cited   *254*
Sample Research Paper, MLA Style   *268*

PERMISSIONS ACKNOWLEDGMENTS   275

INDEX OF TERMS   277

Preface

Many students in introductory literature courses are instinctively able to sense the effect of a poem or story: to say if it is uplifting or depressing, satirical or serious, dull or riotous. They can tell whether a character is good or evil, conflicted or self-righteous, unpredictable or conforming. What is not instinctive—what must be taught—is *how* a writer creates these effects, the techniques that he or she uses to convey ideas and to elicit responses from the reader. *Essential Literary Terms: A Brief Norton Guide with Exercises* defines and explains the most essential of those techniques in clear, straightforward prose, providing along the way numerous examples and exercises to help students develop and test their understanding. With its emphasis on application—how writers use these techniques and how students can identify and analyze them—*Essential Literary Terms* guides introductory students to a more sophisticated understanding of literature.

On the most basic level, students need to learn the major ways that the style of fiction and poetry differs from that of ordinary prose. The most workaday prose—for example, a manual for operating an appliance or a description of the early signs of a heart attack—is generally composed of literal statements intended to inform or explain. Other kinds of writing fall on the continuum between workaday prose and literature, borrowing devices common to literary style to persuade as well as inform. Examples include political speeches, ads, and editorials.

Another way of describing the distinctions is that literature is comprised not simply of literal statements but also of implied perspectives on such statements, and of nuances in their meaning. In literature, how something is said is crucial to what it means. The old dictum defines poetry as the genre in which style is inseparable from content; the same might be said of fiction and drama. Good readers recognize that meaning resides in form as well as content, but they must be encouraged to identify and explain their perceptions, to go back to a piece that they have responded to instinctively and look for the elements that influence the overall effect. It is in the nuances, the subtext created by word choice, structure, rhythm, and sound, that full meaning resides.

▼

Literary terms have emerged over the ages in order to describe such elements; an understanding of those terms, therefore, is crucial to a deep, critical response to literature. They not only provide a common vocabulary for discussing poetry and fiction, but also help students to see patterns, to get past a superficial "I like it" or "It's funny" response and begin to divine the art behind the work. A good understanding of literary terms can encourage students to categorize and to compare, which is the essence of critical thinking. Once introduced to the concept of metaphor, for example, students have a basis for understanding how one poet's use of it differs from another's; or, once they learn to identify a sonnet, they are prepared to see how that poetic form can serve multiple subjects and express totally disparate tones. Finally, another purpose of this guidebook is to provide a sense of heritage by presenting the major techniques and approaches with which authors and informed readers have written and read books in the past.

Most books that define literary terms are erudite and encyclopedic. *Essential Literary Terms* instead aims for brevity, clarity, and selectivity. It covers the literary terms that are most likely to benefit introductory students and provides a clear and substantial explanation of each one. Students and teachers can turn to the guidebook for an understanding of key terms needed to read and analyze the classics and their modern heirs. At the same time, with carefully chosen examples accompanying each entry, *Essential Literary Terms* offers more than dictionary-style definitions. Students are encouraged to identify and discuss, for instance, how a poetic line offers an example of alliteration and why the use of that device matters to the line's meaning. In other words, the purpose of each entry is to go beyond simply assigning a label—the what—to speculate on the how and the why.

The study of the terms is reinforced by exercises that both test and augment the student's understanding of and ability to apply the terms in context. The exercises are in three tiers. The first tier focuses on brief passages and asks students to explain how each passage uses a particular device, as well as how that device affects the line's meaning and literary effect. The second, more complex tier asks students to identify and analyze several different literary devices in a longer passage. The third, culminating tier is a set of poems and prose passages for which students are asked to analyze the literary elements, and are given suggestions about matters to address in their responses. In order to help students reference lines in their answers to the exercises, the editors have numbered the long passages of poetry according to the lines quoted. That is, the numbers begin with 1 for the first line of the excerpt rather than with the line number that would apply to the entire poem. A pamphlet of answers to the exercises is available to instructors on request.

Like any complex skill, critical analysis comes to seem graceful and fluid only after long practice. In the learning, it must be broken down into its component parts and practiced in stages, then reassembled into a fluent whole. The exercises in *Essential Literary Terms* give students practice in identifying the techniques that are key to understanding the tone and meaning of any literary passage. In addition, the analyses of passages that accompany the explanations serve as models, offering students examples of how the terms may be used in writing focused, precise, and detailed literary analysis. For instructors, the book presents such material in organized, easily accessible form, and so can serve as a systematic reminder of information and skills that they will want their students to master.

Essential Literary Terms is designed for quick and easy reference. Terms are grouped topically, beginning with those that are broadly applicable to imaginative writing in all genres (Literary Forms, Figurative Language, Rhetorical Strategies), then moving to topics that are more specific to prose (Narration, Structure, Syntax), and then to those that are more specific to poetry (Meter, Rhyme, Sound and Sound Patterns, and Poetic Forms). Within these groupings, terms are arranged to help students see patterns and connections. A reader may look up either an individual term, like **simile**, or an entire group of terms—for example, all the entries under the category **figurative language**. If one term is more prominent or accessible than the others, it is listed first. For example, the most easily understood category of **figures of thought, simile**, is given first, followed by the related, more complex class, **metaphor**. Those major **tropes** are followed by such subsets as **personification** and **synecdoche**. If two terms are related—for example, **couplet** and **tercet**—the table of contents lists them in consecutive order. If no order of importance applies, as in the terms associated with **structure**, the listing within the category is alphabetical. The one exception to this arrangement is Prosody, the section on **meter**, which is clearest if read as a whole, although each term can still be studied on its own. The discussions of individual terms also cross-reference related terms, which are indicated by SMALL CAPITALS. An index in the back of the book allows students to locate a particular term quickly.

An essential part of academic writing is understanding the conventions for documenting sources. The documentation style set by the Modern Language Association has long been the standard for literature and humanities students, and *Essential Literary Terms* includes a brief but comprehensive guide to MLA style. Both in-text documentation and works-cited entries are treated with clear explanations and examples. A sample student paper showcases how documentation is used within an essay; it also gives students a full-length example of the type of literary analysis that they will do in their courses.

Essential Literary Terms benefits from a long and rich heritage. Authors have employed these literary concepts and techniques for thousands of years, before literature had even assumed a written form, to convey the worlds of their imaginations. For nearly as long, scholars, feeling the need to order and describe their responses to that art, have labeled, classified, and analyzed these concepts and techniques. For those who wish to study a larger set of terms than this book provides, inclusive literary dictionaries abound. Meanwhile, this book will offer students the chance not simply to memorize literary terms but to apply them in context, and to explore ways in which knowledge of how they work can clarify tradition and enrich meaning. Ultimately, *Essential Literary Terms* is meant as a means to ends that go beyond the classroom: to enhance literary sensibility and to foster skills that can lead to a lifetime of critical and pleasurable reading.

Acknowledgments

I would like to thank Jim Peoples for his proposal that I write this book; my editors at Peoples Education, Tom Maksym and Steven J. Griffel, for their encouragement of my initial efforts; W. W. Norton's Julia Reidhead for her astute oversight and Erin Granville for her thoughtful direction of the editing process during its many stages; and Francine Weinberg, who composed the MLA documentation guidelines in the appendix. I also want to recognize the countless teachers, colleagues, and students who have provided not only the experience but also the inspiration behind this book. Finally, I want to express special gratitude to M. H. Abrams, whose vast learning, humane sensibility, and wise guidance were crucial to shaping and informing the contents of these pages.

Essential Literary Terms

A Brief Norton Guide
with Exercises

Literary Forms

Imaginative literature may be divided into three major **literary forms**: POETRY, FICTION, and DRAMA. POETRY is usually categorized into three main types: EPIC, DRAMATIC, and LYRIC. All three subcategories share such common traits as specific patterns of RHYTHM and SYNTAX, frequent use of FIGURATIVE language, and emphasis on the effects of the arrangement of the words on the page. Although some works of FICTION and DRAMA also display many of these traits, they are particularly characteristic of POETRY.

FICTION is, broadly speaking, any NARRATIVE about invented characters and events, whether in VERSE or prose. The narrower meaning of the term, however, refers to works written in prose. The major genres of fiction are the **novel**, the **short story**, and the **novella**.

DRAMA differs from POETRY and FICTION in that it does not typically contain a NARRATOR and is usually intended for performance. The form may be divided into the broad categories of COMEDY and TRAGEDY, each of which contains several subcategories, such as ROMANTIC COMEDY or CLASSICAL TRAGEDY. A third and smaller category, TRAGICOMEDY, combines features of each of the major genres.

DRAMA

Drama (from the Greek verb for "to do" or "to act") is the major LITERARY FORM that presents characters directly to the audience, usually without the intermediary of a NARRATOR. Most drama is written to be performed in the theater by live actors, who speak the DIALOGUE and move in accordance with the STAGE DIRECTIONS written by the **playwright**—literally, the maker of the **play**, the term for an individual **dramatic** work. The exception to that mode of presentation is **closet drama**, which is intended to be read rather than performed. ("Closet" is an antiquated term for "study" or "private chamber.") Some examples of closet drama are John Milton's *Samson Agonistes* (1671) and Lord Byron's *Manfred* (1817).

Drama is classified according to the effect intended on the audience, as well as the choice and rendering of the materials in order to achieve that effect: The broadest division is that between COMEDY and TRAGEDY, but these broad categories also contain specialized subgroups.

Some plays, comic and tragic, are written in VERSE, in accordance with the theatrical conventions of a particular literary period. For example, most ELIZABETHAN and JACOBEAN dramas are written almost entirely in BLANK VERSE—that is, UNRHYMED IAMBIC PENTAMETER—while tragedy of the Neoclassical Age (1660–1785), such as John Dryden's *The Conquest of Granada* (1672), is written in RHYMED IAMBIC PENTAMETER COUPLETS, called HEROIC COUPLETS, to accord with their lofty subject matter.

In practice, most students encounter plays in their written form. That medium has several advantages, such as the opportunity to reread a key piece of DIALOGUE, to review the cast of characters, and to see the STAGE DIRECTIONS that the playwright has provided to indicate the actions and the vocal inflections of the characters. At the same time, it can be difficult for a reader to distinguish among the voices of the characters—to avoid the tendency to read a play as an extended monologue—or to envision the physical movements that accompany the words. Seeing a performance of the play, ideally on stage but even on film, can be enlightening. It is important to remember, however, that every performance represents a series of choices, by the director and the actors, about such factors as which lines to cut or to emphasize; how the various roles are cast; how the actors should move, gesture, and deliver their lines; and how the SETTING, the time and place in which the action occurs, is represented. Because theater is by its nature responsive to social tastes and mores, new stagings are constantly reshaped for different audiences. The choices involved are influenced by the theatrical conventions of the period in which the drama was written, as well as by those of the current day, and by the performance history of the play.

Nowhere is the array of possibilities open to directors and actors so clear as in productions of Shakespeare's plays. Because of their long performance history—most have continued to be staged since their composition some four hundred years ago—and the relatively few stage directions that they contain, productions of Shakespeare have inspired a wide variety of choices about styles and settings. For example, the TRAGEDY *Romeo and Juliet* has been set everywhere from Elizabethan England to Renaissance Italy to modern-day Verona to contemporary Sarajevo to Verona Beach, California. The last setting, in the film version directed by Baz Luhrmann (1997), was complete with rival teenage gangs driving hotrods, wearing punk outfits, and armed with switchblades and guns. Not surprisingly, each of the versions threw a different light on the characters and the actions in the text. No production of a play, staged or filmed, however, can be definitive. Even if a production is strikingly effective or innovative for its day, its effect is inevitably ephemeral. The written text, however, remains to inspire future visions of the play, on stage and in readers' imaginations.

See also NARRATION, CHARACTERIZATION, DIALOGUE, SOLILOQUY, and ASIDE.

Comedy

In **comedy**, the TONE is for the most part light, the main effects are to engage and amuse the audience, the situations and characters tend to be drawn from ordinary daily life, as opposed to world-shaking events and noble or royal characters, and the resolution is happy, at least for the major characters. Many traditional comic plots conclude with the marriage of one or more couples. Although the term "comedy" applies primarily to drama, it is also used to describe the type of plot in PROSE FICTION and NARRATIVE POETRY.

Comedy may be divided, according to a classification proposed by the novelist and critic George Meredith in *The Idea of Comedy* (1877), into "high" and "low" types. **High comedy** depends primarily on verbal wit, particularly REPARTEE among sophisticated, clever characters, and it appeals to the tastes of a cultivated audience. **Low comedy**, of which **farce** is the primary type, is characterized by physical humor, such as slapstick and pratfalls, fast paced action, including split-second timing of key exits and entrances; ridiculous caricatures, and broad, often crass verbal humor.

Farce was a major component of such medieval mystery dramas as *The Second Shepherds' Play*, in which, for example, a ne'er-do-well couple disguise a stolen sheep as their newborn son in a clumsy attempt to conceal the theft, and the rascally father is punished by being tossed in a blanket. Farce is often a component of subtler comedies that depend primarily on verbal wit for their effects. For example, Shakespeare's *The Taming of the Shrew* (1593–94) contains such **farcical** elements as Petruchio's various schemes to trick and browbeat his rebellious wife, which include tempting her with food and new clothes that are snatched away just as she is about to take them. The play's deeper effects, however, derive from the battle of wits and the growing regard between Petruchio and Kate, which prove them an ideal match. The plot of Wilde's *The Importance of Being Earnest* hinges on the ludicrous prop of an officious nanny's handbag, which contains an infant that was put in her charge, and that she loses in a London railway station. Several films also partake of both farce and high comic wit—for example, Charlie Chaplin's *Modern Times*, the Marx Brothers' *A Night at the Opera*, Woody Allen's *Sleeper*, and *Monty Python and the Holy Grail*.

Comedy also includes several other forms. **Romantic comedy** was developed by Elizabethan dramatists such as Shakespeare in *As You Like It* (1599) and *Twelfth Night* (1600). Romantic comedies center on a love affair between a beautiful and resourceful maiden, often in male disguise, and a worthy suitor, who must overcome social and personal obstacles to arrive at a joyous resolution. The **comedy of manners** also depicts young lovers, but the TONE tends to be more sophisticated and sometimes cynical and the outlook more worldly. The cast typically includes **stock characters**, such as the interfering father, the clever servant, and the rival suitor, which were first introduced in the ancient Greek comedies of Menander and developed more fully by the Roman playwrights Plautus and Terence. Some classic examples of the genre include Shakespeare's *Much Ado About Nothing* (1598–99), William Congreve's *The Way of the World* (1700), Richard Brinsley Sheridan's *The School for Scandal* (1777), and Oscar Wilde's *The Importance of Being Earnest* (1895). For another prominent category of comedy, see SATIRE.

Tragedy

In **tragedy**, the *tone* is serious, and often somber; the effect is to involve and strongly move the audience; and the outcome is disastrous for the PROTAGONIST and, often, also for those associated with him or her. The resolution of the tragic situation often involves one or more deaths, in particular that of the PROTAGONIST, whose fate is the more moving if the initial faults of character that bring it about are disproportionate to the suffering incurred.

Tragedy is also divided into subtypes. **Classical tragedies**, from ancient Greece, center on a highborn tragic hero who commits an irreversible error of judgment, often resulting from **hubris** (HYOO-bris), or excessive pride. One example is Sophocles' *Antigone*, in which both the heroine—the title character—and her uncle, Creon, the new king of Thebes, refuse to compromise on a principle of honor and end up being destroyed. **Senecan tragedy**, developed by Seneca, the Roman dramatist after whom it is named, inspired the development of **revenge tragedy** by ELIZABETHAN and JACOBEAN playwrights. The plays are full of such sensationalist elements as ghosts, grisly murders, nefarious schemes, and ruthless villains; the violent events occur off-stage in Seneca, but are presented with gory and graphic immediacy in the dramas of his English successors. The earliest English revenge tragedy, Thomas Kyd's melodramatic *The Spanish Tragedy* (1586), is thought to be an inspiration for the outstanding example of the form, Shakespeare's *Hamlet* (1600). JACOBEAN examples include John Marston's *The Malcontent* (1604) and John Webster's *The Duchess of Malfi* (1612–13).

With the rise of the middle classes, dramatists in the eighteenth century depicted a new kind of tragic PROTAGONIST, whose origins were not noble or aristocratic but humble, and whose preoccupations were not with lofty, noble causes but with mundane issues, such as financial debt and marital strife. Such **domestic tragedy** was the predecessor of the kind of tragedy that has predominated since the end of the nineteenth century. Some examples are Henrik Ibsen's *Ghosts* (1881) and *Hedda Gabler* (1890), Arthur Miller's *Death of a Salesman* (1949), and Tennessee Williams's *A Streetcar Named Desire* (1947).

Tragicomedy   ◄

Some plays, called **tragicomedies**, fall in the middle of the tragic/comic spectrum, in that they focus on both high and low characters and situations and that they bring a potentially tragic plot to a happy resolution, at least for the PROTAGONIST, through a sudden reversal of fortune or the reformation of the protagonist's opponent. This hybrid form was especially popular in ELIZABETHAN and JACOBEAN drama. Examples include Shakespeare's *Measure for Measure* (1604) and *All's Well that Ends Well* (1602–03), sometimes called "dark comedies" or "problem comedies," and Beaumont and Fletcher's *Philaster* (1608–10), which has the telling subtitle "Love Lies A-Bleeding."

At the end of *Measure for Measure*, for example, the ruling duke, who has disguised himself as a friar, reveals his true identity and rescues Isabella, the beset heroine, from the attempted seduction of the corrupt deputy who has ruled in his place. The duke then proposes marriage to her. The use of disguise, the last-minute reprieve, and the projected marriage are traditional COMIC elements. On the other hand, several dark aspects of the play lean toward TRAGEDY. The duke's worthiness as a match for the virtuous Isabella is undermined by his conduct. It was he who appointed the deputy, Angelo, knowing of his past corruption, in order to escape the responsibility

▼

of dealing with the moral chaos that his lax reign had created in his dukedom. The duke's religious disguise is blasphemous, since he uses it to administer such sacraments as confession and final rites in order to gain information and manipulate events. He also tricks Isabella into believing that Angelo has had her brother executed in order to test her capacity for empathy and courage. Isabella, who has been preparing to take her final vows as a nun, tellingly remains silent after the duke's proposal, and the play provides no STAGE DIRECTIONS to indicate her response, whether delighted or appalled.

Theater of the Absurd

Drama may be classified according to certain movements that it has inspired. A prominent example in twentieth-century drama is the **theater of the absurd**, which questions the meaning of life in a universe seen as godless and which has overthrown such accepted conventions as a well-established setting, logical dialogue, and a fully resolved conflict. Representative playwrights of the theater of the absurd are Eugene Ionesco, Samuel Beckett, and Harold Pinter, whose work in this genre tends to challenge its audience on philosophical and stylistic levels. For example, Beckett's *Endgame* (1957) is set in a desolate room that looks out from two windows onto a barren landscape, which may represent either the last surviving shelter in a world devastated by a nuclear holocaust, a stage set, a chess board, or the mind of Hamm, its solipsistic PROTAGONIST. Hamm, who is blind and paralyzed, browbeats and torments the other major character, his hapless servant, Clov, who may or may not be Hamm's son. The only other characters are Hamm's parents, Nagg and Nell, who inhabit a pair of trashcans at the front of the stage and are reduced to childish senility. The play begins with Clov removing the sheets that cover the "furniture," which includes Hamm in his wheelchair and the closed trashcans, and saying, "Finished." Immediately, however, he qualifies that assertion by completing the sentence with a decreasingly certain series of statements: "it's finished, nearly finished, it must be nearly finished." At the end, despite Clov's efforts to leave the sadistic Hamm, he remains staring silently at him, while Hamm calls out to him and to his father. Getting no answer, he addresses himself: "You . . . remain"; then as the STAGE DIRECTIONS indicate, he covers his face with his handkerchief. The echo of Clov's opening action suggests that the agonizing "endgame" has not ended, and that both characters are set to play it all over again at the next performance.

Periods of Drama ◀

Drama may be classified according to the literary period in which it was written, which include the following major categories and representative dramatists:

- **Ancient Greek drama**, whose major playwrights were Aeschylus, Sophocles, and Euripides in tragedy (fifth century B.C.E.) and Menander and Aristophanes in comedy (fifth to third centuries B.C.E.)

- **Roman drama**, in which Seneca (first century C.E.) was the chief tragedian and Plautus and Terence (third to first centuries B.C.E.) the major comic dramatists

- **English medieval drama**, divided into **morality plays** such as *The Castle of Perseverance* (ca. 1420) and *Everyman* (ca. 1510), which were ALLEGORIES that depicted abstractions of human qualities, usually engaged in a struggle for the soul's salvation, and **mystery plays**, such as *The Second Shepherds' Play* (ca. 1450), designed to illustrate narratives from the Old and New Testaments; the authors of medieval plays are anonymous

- **Elizabethan** (1558–1603) and **Jacobean** (1603–25) drama, whose major authors were William Shakespeare in both tragedy and comedy, Christopher Marlowe and John Webster in tragedy, and Ben Jonson in comedy

- **Restoration** (1660–1700) and **eighteenth century** (1700–85) drama, represented by John Dryden in tragedy and William Congreve and Richard Brinsley Sheridan in comedy

- **Modern drama**, which began with the Norwegian playwright Henrik Ibsen and the Russian Anton Chekhov and includes such diverse authors as the Irishmen Oscar Wilde, John Millington Synge, George Bernard Shaw, Samuel Beckett, and, recently, Martin McDonough; Americans Eugene O'Neill, Tennessee Williams, Arthur Miller, August Wilson, and Sam Shepard; and English playwrights Harold Pinter, Tom Stoppard, and Caryl Churchill

▼

FICTION

In a broad sense, **fiction** is any narrative, whether written in verse or in prose, about invented characters and events, as opposed to an account of actual happenings. The latter category, which includes such subheadings as history and biography, is called **nonfiction**. The narrower and more common definition of fiction, however, refers to invented narratives written in prose. Fiction encompasses three major genres: the NOVEL, an extended narrative of varying lengths but usually long enough to warrant separate publication; the SHORT STORY, nearly always published in a collection of such pieces or in a magazine or journal; and the NOVELLA, a narrative whose length falls between those of the other two genres and which may or may not be published in an individual volume. All three genres share certain traits. They focus on a character or characters that interact in a given social SETTING, they are narrated from a particular POINT OF VIEW, and they are based on some sort of PLOT, a sequence of events leading to a resolution that is designed to reveal aspects of the characters. The predominant tone may be comic, tragic, satiric, or romantic.

▶

Novel

The **novel**, because of its greater length and scope, has much more complexity than the SHORT STORY. Its plot is typically more involved and multifaceted, its description of the social milieu more complete, and its depiction of characters' motives, feelings, and experiences more complex than the concise SHORT STORY form allows. A major forerunner of the novel is usually said to be the Spanish writer Miguel de Cervantes's *Don Quixote* (1605), which recounted the adventures of a madly idealistic PROTAGONIST who lives under the delusion that he is a knight errant and consequently attempts to perform what he believes are chivalric deeds. Both the book's episodic structure and the sustained ironic contrast between the hero's illusions and the actual, often corrupt society in which he lives have exerted an enormous influence on the novel form. In English literature, the novel as we know it was introduced in the eighteenth century, in such distinctive works as Daniel Defoe's *Robinson Crusoe* (1719), an adventure tale about a resourceful mariner who is marooned for decades on a desert island; Samuel Richardson's *Pamela* (1740), an EPISTOLARY NOVEL written as a series of letters recounting the experiences of a serving maid who succeeds in preserving her virtue despite her worldly master's attempts to seduce her; and Henry Fielding's *Tom Jones* (1749), a rollicking SATIRE about the amorous adventures of a handsome young servant who rises to happiness and prosperity through the aid of a benevolent mentor, his own unquenchable optimism, and some lucky turns in fortune.

Since this vigorous beginning, the novel has assumed an enormous variety of forms in subject matter, style, and structure. Some attempts to categorize the genre may suggest its range and complexity. One major distinction is between the **novel of incident**, in which the main focus is on the course and outcome of events in the PLOT, and the **novel of character**, in which the primary interest is in the PROTAGONIST'S thoughts, feelings, and motives and in the ways that the characters develop. Of the examples listed above, *Robinson Crusoe* and *Tom Jones*, with their episodic structure and their emphasis on the protagonists' ingenuity in surmounting various obstacles, are novels of incident, while *Pamela*, with its focus on the psychological workings of the heroine, is a novel of character. Most successful novels, however, display the characteristics of both forms. For example, Fyodor Dostoevsky's *Crime and Punishment* (1867), while based on a sensational double murder and a suspenseful criminal investigation, draws its power from its exploration of the murderer's disturbed psyche and the anguish that the crime causes him. In contrast, Jane Austen's *Emma* (1816), on the surface a novel of character that focuses on a privileged, complacent young woman who undergoes a process of spiritual and emotional growth, has a plot as intricate as that of the most ingenious detective novel.

Another major distinction is between the **realistic novel** and the **romance**. The realistic novel, which is the predominant type, depicts a fictional world that closely resembles the events, social interactions, settings, motivations, and feelings encountered in everyday life. Examples include books as diverse as Jane Austen's *Pride and Prejudice* (1813), George Eliot's *Middlemarch* (1872), Leo Tolstoy's *Anna Karenina* (1877), James Joyce's *Ulysses* (1922), Ernest Hemingway's *The Sun Also Rises* (1925), Saul Bellow's *The Adventures of Augie March* (1954), and Jhumpa Lahiri's *The Namesake* (2003). The *romance*, in contrast, focuses on characters that are less three-dimensional and more likely to be depicted as either heroic or villainous. Often, the PROTAGONIST is isolated and outside the mainstream because of his or her iconoclastic convictions or extraordinary goals, and inhabits a setting that is either heightened or distanced in a way that distinguishes it from the ordinary and the familiar. The plot of a romance usually revolves around a quest, undertaken to achieve an ideal or to promote the triumph of good over evil. The events may be exaggerated or melodramatic, often with a symbolic aspect that makes them analogous to those in a

▼

dream or a myth. Some examples of the romance include Mary Shelley's *Frankenstein* (1818), Emily Brontë's *Wuthering Heights* (1847), Zora Neale Hurston's *Their Eyes Were Watching God* (1937), J. R. R. Tolkien's *The Lord of the Rings* (1954–55), and Toni Morrison's *Beloved* (1987).

Novels may also be categorized according to subtypes, which depend on any one of a number of distinguishing features. One category is based on the focus of the characterization. For example, the **Bildungsroman** (BIL-doongs-roh-mahn, German for a novel about character formation) depicts the intellectual and emotional development of the PROTAGONIST from childhood into adulthood. Some examples include Charlotte Brontë's *Jane Eyre* (1847), Charles Dickens's *David Copperfield* (1849–50), and Somerset Maugham's *Of Human Bondage* (1915). Other novels are categorized according to the setting that they depict. For example, the **historical novel** is set in a time and, often, a place removed from the period and location in which it is written. Typically, it describes the atmosphere and mores of the past setting in vivid detail and depicts the influence of those historical factors on the characters and events. Some prominent examples include Leo Tolstoy's *War and Peace* (1869), set during the Napoleonic invasion of Russia; Charles Dickens's *A Tale of Two Cities* (1859), set during the French Revolution; Stephen Crane's *The Red Badge of Courage* (1895), set during the American Civil War; and E. L. Doctorow's *Ragtime* (1975), which follows the fortunes of three American families from distinctly different cultural milieus during the first two decades of the twentieth century. Another means of categorizing the novel is based on the mode of its narration. For example, the **epistolary novel** (eh-PIŚ-toh-laree) is comprised of a series of letters between characters, of which Richardson's *Pamela*, mentioned above, was the first English example. Others have included Richardson's *Clarissa* (1747–48), Tobias Smollett's *Humphry Clinker* (1771), and, in recent times, Alice Walker's *The Color Purple* (1982).

Since the mid-twentieth century, experimental variations on the traditional form and subject matter of the novel have abounded. The innovations include the **antinovel**, a work that derives its effects from eschewing such standard features of the genre as coherent plot, established setting, and sustained character development. Authors writing in that form have included a group of French novelists, Alain Robbe-Grillet, Michel Butor, and Nathalie Sarraute. Another experimental movement is **metafiction**, which incorporates into the narrative the process by which the author creates the work and the ways that the reader responds to it. Some prominent practitioners have included John Barth, Donald Barthelme, and Robert Coover. An early predecessor of both of these experimental forms was Laurence Sterne's *Tristram Shandy* (1759–67), which uses such antinovel devices as a page comprised back and front of a black rectangle, to represent the narrator's grief over a friend's death; innumerable digressions between past and present and one topic and another, separated by dashes; and such typographical irregularities as lines comprised of asterisks, imprints of an index finger pointing at particular passages, and crude linear graphs of the story's narrative line. It also incorporates such metafictional aspects as persistently addressing the reader as a confidante, and introducing such issues as the incoherent order in which the narrator is telling his tale and a comparison between the length of time it takes him to record events and the amount of time needed to read about them.

Perhaps because of its diversity and flexibility, the novel has emerged as the most popular of the major literary genres, more widespread than either POETRY or DRAMA.

Short Story ◀

The **short story** shares with the novel several characteristics of fiction, but its more concentrated form results in some crucial differences: a smaller cast of characters, often focusing on the PROTAGONIST; a simpler plot, usually centered on a single major conflict; a limited depiction of SETTING; and a more concentrated format, with descriptive details and DIALOGUE selected for maximum significance and effect. Edgar Allan Poe, one of the early masters of the short story form, defined it as a work that could be read in one session of no more than two hours and that was focused on creating "a single effect."

The short story had predecessors in such Old Testament narratives as the stories of Jonah and Ruth, as well as in such New Testament parables as those of the prodigal son and the good Samaritan. It was also inspired by such oral forms as the folktale and the fable and by collections of tales, such as the anonymous medieval work *The Arabian Nights* (written in Arabic and first translated into European languages in the nineteenth century) and Geoffrey Chaucer's *Canterbury Tales* (1387–1400). The modern short story emerged in the early nineteenth century, when the growing popularity of magazine publishing stimulated the need for a form that was shorter than the novel and that allowed for the inclusion of several different pieces under the same cover.

The short story has flourished especially in the United States, which has produced numerous accomplished practitioners with highly distinctive voices, for example: REALISTS such as Henry James,

Ernest Hemingway, Eudora Welty, J. D. Salinger, John Cheever, and Tillie Olsen, and ROMANCE writers such as Poe, Nathaniel Hawthorne, Washington Irving, and Edith Wharton. Still another group of Americans, such as F. Scott Fitzgerald, William Faulkner, Flannery O'Connor, and Raymond Carver have straddled the line between REALISM and ROMANCE, writing stories, realistic on the surface, that assume symbolic, and at times even apocalyptic force. The short story is by no means solely an American province, however. Writers from other English-speaking countries, and many whose stories have appeared in English translation, have been masters of the short-story form, for example: James Joyce, Frank O'Connor, and William Trevor (Ireland); Katherine Mansfield (New Zealand); D. H. Lawrence (England); Guy de Maupassant (France); Leo Tolstoy, Anton Chekhov, Ivan Turgenev, and Isaac Babel (Russia); Thomas Mann (Germany); Nadine Gordimer (South Africa); and Alice Munro (Canada). Other short-story writers have emerged as important practitioners of experimental forms, including authors of METAFICTION such as Donald Barthelme, Margaret Atwood, Robert Coover, and Joyce Carol Oates. As the authors listed above suggest, many novelists have proven equally adept at both the extended and the concise fictional forms.

▶   ## Novella

The **novella** falls between the novel and the short story in both length and complexity. A particular novella may be substantial enough to be published in a separate volume, like a NOVEL, or, in other circumstances, concise enough to be included in a collection of other relatively short pieces. Some masterpieces of the form include Herman Melville's *Billy Budd* (1890), Kate Chopin's *The Awakening* (1899), Joseph Conrad's *Heart of Darkness* (1902), James Joyce's *The Dead* (1914), Franz Kafka's *The Metamorphosis* (1915), Nella Larsen's *Passing* (1929), and Saul Bellow's *Seize the Day* (1954).

POETRY

Poetry, along with FICTION and DRAMA, is one of the three major categories of literary forms. Poetry has been frequently and variously defined—for example, as the form in which style is inseparable from content and, in Emily Dickinson's whimsical description in a letter to Thomas Wentworth Higginson, her first editor and publisher, as the form recognizable by its effect of making her "feel physically as if the top of [her] head were taken off." In *The Norton Anthology of Poetry* the poet and critic Jon Stallworthy offers a helpful definition: "A poem is a composition written for performance by the human voice." He notes that responding to a poem fully requires not only understanding the sense of the words but also perceiving the ways that their sounds, rhythms, and arrangement interact. Because a poem's aural qualities are so essential to its meaning, one of the most valuable means of access is to hear the poem, either by reading it aloud or by listening to it read by the poet or by a performer. At least, one should try to hear it in one's imagination—let the poem, in Keats's paradoxical description in "Ode to a Nightingale," "pipe to the spirit ditties of no sound." Although attentive listening may not yield the entire meaning, especially of a complex poem, it can emphasize aspects of the sound that give important insights into the sense of the words.

Poetry is usually divided into three main types: EPIC, DRAMATIC, and LYRIC. All three types of poetry share certain common traits: an emphasis on the connections between the sound and sense of words; controlled patterns of rhythm and syntax; vivid, often figurative language; and close attention to the visual and other sensory effects of the arrangement of words on the page. Although many of these characteristics also apply to FICTION and DRAMA, and even to ordinary prose, they are particularly concentrated in poetry. That literary form is often used to express heightened feeling or subtle thought, even though in some instances the tone may be comic or the subject matter mundane. In such cases as the last, some critics use the term "**verse**," to distinguish light or trivial pieces from the more serious and highly developed works of "poetry."

Epic Poetry

An **epic** is a long narrative poem on a serious and exalted subject, such as man's fall from heavenly grace in John Milton's *Paradise Lost*. Ancient and medieval epics, such as Homer's *Iliad* and the anonymous *Beowulf* in the West and *Gilgamesh* and *The Mahabharata* in the East, recount the exploits of a cultural hero. They combine legend, oral history, and moral exemplum to inspire and guide future generations. Such epics began as oral performances, chanted or sung to the accompaniment of an instrument like the lyre. During generations of performance, they were shaped and refined by multiple bards and were finally recorded in written form. The more recent epics that these early works inspired, such as Milton's *Paradise Lost*, were composed in written form by a single author.

Dramatic Poetry

Dramatic poetry is that in which the writer creates the voice of an invented character or characters. In its simplest form, it is a monologue, such as Robert Browning's "My Last Duchess," in which the narrator is an egocentric and unscrupulous Italian duke, or Langston Hughes's "Mother to Son," in which the speaker is a resilient black woman giving counsel to a young son. The most complex form of dramatic poetry is the full-length verse play, in which multiple speakers are given distinctive voices. Some examples are the plays of such Elizabethan writers as Christopher Marlowe and the master of the form, William Shakespeare, and, in the twentieth century, of T. S. Eliot, Archibald MacLeish, Christopher Fry, and Tony Harrison.

Lyric Poetry

Lyric poetry, the most varied and widespread kind, is that in which an individual speaker expresses what he or she feels, perceives, and thinks. This mode includes poems as diverse as Shakespeare's sonnets, Keats's odes, and Sylvia Plath's "Daddy." Although the usual point of view is first person, it is important to distinguish the "I" of the speaker from that of the actual poet; however close the speaker may seem to be to the poet's point of view, he or she is always in some part an invented character. **Lyrics** are usually short, especially in comparison to the other forms of poetry, but some, such as Walt Whitman's "Song of Myself" and Adrienne Rich's "Snapshots of a Daughter-in-Law," may extend to several pages.

SPECIALIZED FORMS

The major literary forms of poetry and fiction contain specialized forms with distinctive elements and styles. The dramatic monologue is a specialized form of poetry, for example, and the epigram and satire are specialized forms of both poetry and fiction.

Dramatic Monologue ◀

A **dramatic monologue** is a poem that is spoken by a FICTIONAL NARRATOR who is clearly different from the author in age, situation, or gender. It is set at some significant point in the speaker's life, and it is often addressed to another character, whose presence is implied by what the speaker says. The major purpose of a dramatic monologue is for the speaker to reveal, often unwittingly, significant aspects of his or her qualities, values, and experiences, which are inferred by the reader. The form came to prominence in the work of the Victorian poet Robert Browning, whose "My Last Duchess," "Fra Lippo Lippi," and "Porphyria's Lover" are classic examples.

In "My Last Duchess," for example, the speaker is an arrogant and vain, but scrupulously polite, Italian Renaissance duke who is showing a visitor around his palazzo, which contains an extensive collection of artworks. Among them is a portrait of his late wife, "looking as if she were alive." As the duke speaks, he reveals that he is irritated by the animated look that the painter has captured, seeing it as evidence of "a heart . . . too soon made glad, / Too easily impressed." To have called the duchess's attention to what he saw as a fault—her universal good will and gratitude, rather than an exclusive preference for his "gift of a nine-hundred-years-old name"— would have been to "stoop" to her simple level, and, the duke proclaims imperiously, "I choose / Never to stoop." The consequence was that he "gave commands" and then "all smiles stopped together." His meaning is slyly ambiguous: Did his oppressive treatment drive his young wife to melancholy and fatal despair? Or were the "commands" of a more violent nature: an order to stop her smiles by ending her life? In any case, the last section of the monologue reveals the identity of the visitor: an emissary from a count whose "fair daughter"—or, rather, whose "dowry"—the duke is interested in pursuing. The poem ends with his off-handed recommendation that the messenger look at another artwork as they descend the stairs, a bronze sculpture of the god "Neptune . . . taming a sea-horse." The implication is that his "last duchess" was nothing more to the ruthless duke than another pretty object in his collection.

Other examples of dramatic monologues are T. S. Eliot's "The Love Song of J. Alfred Prufrock," in which the NARRATOR is a prudish, self-conscious guest at a cocktail party, and several poems in which the speakers are literary characters, whom the poet imagines outside the confines of the work in which they originally appear. For example, many dramatic monologues have been inspired by Homer's *The Odyssey*, including Tennyson's "Ulysses," spoken by the hero, called here by his Latin name, in old age, and Margaret Atwood's "Siren Song," narrated by a modern version of one of the harpies who tries to lure Odysseus to his death with her song, but here a sly temptress who preys on men's egotism. See also UNRELIABLE NARRATOR.

EXERCISE: Dramatic Monologue

For each of the following DRAMATIC MONOLOGUES:

- Describe the point in the speaker's life at which it is set.
- Explain the nature of the implied audience.
- Discuss the revelations that the speech provides about the NARRATOR'S personality traits, values, and experiences.

1. Well, son, I'll tell you:
    Life for me ain't been no crystal stair.
    It's had tacks in it,
    And splinters,
    And boards torn up,   5
    And places with no carpet on the floor—
    Bare.
    But all the time
    I'se been a-climbin' on,
    And reachin' landin's,   10
    And turnin' corners,
    And sometimes goin' in the dark
    Where there ain't been no light.
    So boy, don't you turn back.
    Don't you set down on the steps   15
    'Cause you finds it's kinder hard.
    Don't you fall now—
    For I'se still goin', honey,
    I'se still climbin',
    And life for me ain't been no crystal stair.   20

                          —LANGSTON HUGHES, "Mother to Son"

▼

2. *The speaker of the following poem is Tithonus, a Trojan prince with whom the Roman goddess of the dawn, Aurora, fell in love. She pleaded with Jupiter, father of the gods, to grant Tithonus eternal life, which he did, but she forgot to ask at the same time for the gift of eternal youth.*

The woods decay, the woods decay and fall,
The vapors weep their burthen[1] to the ground,
Man comes and tills the field and lies beneath,
And after many a summer dies the swan.
Me only cruel immortality   5
Consumes: I wither slowly in thine arms,
Here at the quiet limit of the world,
A white-haired shadow roaming like a dream
The ever-silent spaces of the East,
Far folded mists, and gleaming halls of morn.   10

Alas! For this gray shadow, once a man—
So glorious in his beauty and thy choice,
Who madest him thy chosen, that he seemed
To his great heart none other than a God!
I asked thee, "Give me immortality."   15
Then didst thou grant mine asking with a smile,
Like wealthy men who care not how they give.
But thy strong Hours indignant worked their wills,
And beat me down and marred and wasted me,
And though they could not end me, left me maimed   20
To dwell in presence of immortal youth.
Immortal age beside immortal youth,
And all I was in ashes. Can thy love,
Thy beauty, make amends, though even now,
Close over us, the silver star,[2] thy guide,   25
Shines in those tremulous eyes that fill with tears
To hear me? Let me go: take back thy gift:
Why should a man desire in any way
To vary from the kindly[3] race of men,
Or pass beyond the goal of ordinance[4]   30
Where all should pause, as is most meet for all?

---

1. Burden.
2. The morning star.
3. Natural.
4. What is ordained as human fate.

A soft air fans the cloud apart: there comes
A glimpse of that dark world where I was born.
Once more the old mysterious glimmer steals
From thy pure brows, and from thy shoulders pure,   35
And bosom beating with a heart renewed.
Thy cheek begins to redden through the gloom,
Thy sweet eyes brighten slowly close to mine,
Ere yet they blind the stars, and the wild team[5]
Which love thee, yearning for thy yoke, arise,   40
And shake the darkness from their loosened manes,
And beat the twilight into flakes of fire.
    Ever thus thou growest beautiful
In silence, then before thine answer given
Departest, and thy tears are on my cheek.   45

Why wilt thou ever scare me with thy tears,
And make me tremble lest a saying learnt,
In days far-off, on that dark earth, be true?
"The Gods themselves cannot recall their gifts."
    Ay me! ay me! with what another heart   50
In days far-off, and with what other eyes
I used to watch—if I be he that watched—
The lucid outline forming round thee; saw
The dim curls kindle into sunny rings;
Changed with thy mystic change, and felt my blood   55
Glow with the glow that slowly crimsoned all
Thy presence and thy portals, while I lay,
Mouth, forehead, eyelids, growing dewy-warm
With kisses balmier than half-opening buds
Of April, and could hear the lips that kissed   60
Whispering I knew not what of wild and sweet,
Like that strange song I heard Apollo[6] sing,
While Ilion[7] like a mist rose into towers.

Yet hold me not for ever in thine East:
How can my nature longer mix with thine?   65
Coldly thy rosy shadows bathe me, cold
Are all thy lights, and cold my wrinkled feet
Upon thy glimmering thresholds, when the steam
Floats up from those dim fields about the homes

---

5. The horses that draw her chariot.
6. God of music.
7. Troy: according to Ovid, created by Apollo's song.

Of happy men that have the power to die,   70
And grassy barrows[8] of the happier dead.
Release me, and restore me to the ground.
Thou seëst all things, thou wilt see my grave:
Thou wilt renew thy beauty morn by morn;
I earth in earth forget these empty courts,   75
And thee returning on thy silver wheels.

> —ALFRED, LORD TENNYSON, "Tithonus"

Epigram

An **epigram** (from the Greek word for "inscription") has come to
mean a witty saying in either verse or prose, concisely phrased and
often SATIRIC. In "Epigram," Samuel Taylor Coleridge cleverly defines
the form in a verse that exemplifies it:

> What is an Epigram? A dwarfish whole,
> Its body brevity, and wit its soul.

The epigram originated in ancient Greece, where it was a brief verse
intended for inscription on a monument, such as a tombstone or a
building. The Roman poet Martial (first century C.E.) gave the form its
characteristic SATIRIC turn in a collection of biting, often obscene verses.
Epigrams have been popular in English poetry since the late sixteenth
century, when they appeared in the works of such writers as Ben Jonson, Robert Herrick, and John Donne. The neoclassical period,
1660–1785, with its emphasis on witty style, was particularly rich in
writers of epigrams. The acknowledged master of the form was Alexander Pope, who wrote in HEROIC COUPLETS that may often be excerpted
from his longer poems as self-contained epigrams. For example, Pope's
"An Essay on Criticism" contains such **epigrammatic** precepts as the
following, on the importance of terseness to a lucid writing style:

> Words are like leaves; and where they most abound,
> Much fruit of sense beneath is rarely found.

Later wits, such as Mark Twain, Oscar Wilde, and George Bernard
Shaw in the nineteenth century and Dorothy Parker, Robert Frost, and
Ogden Nash in the twentieth, have also been notable for the clever-
ness and plentitude of their epigrams. A well-known prose example is

---

8. Burial mounds.

▼

Wilde's definition of a cynic from *Lady Windermere's Fan:* "A man who knows the price of everything, and the value of nothing."

The epigram should be distinguished from the **aphorism** (AF-or-izm), a terse statement on a serious subject. Both the Old and New Testaments of the Bible are full of aphorisms—for example, Proverbs 15.1 on the means of defusing anger by changing the tone of a potential quarrel: "A soft answer turneth away wrath." Another aphorism, from 1 Timothy 6.10, on the moral dangers of greed, is: "The love of money is the root of all evil." One of the many aphorisms to be found in the plays of William Shakespeare is King Lear's denunciation of his daughter Cordelia, who refuses to accord him the public show of flattery that he craves: "How sharper than a serpent's tooth / It is to have a thankless child."

EXERCISE: Epigram

For each of the following examples:

- Specify whether it is an EPIGRAM or an APHORISM.
- Paraphrase it.
- Explain the basis of its wisdom and/or wit.

1. Relations are simply a tedious pack of people who haven't got the remotest knowledge of how to live, nor the smallest instinct about when to die.   —OSCAR WILDE, *The Importance of Being Earnest*

2. Neither a borrower nor a lender be,
    For loan oft loses both itself and friend.
                                        —WILLIAM SHAKESPEARE, *Hamlet*

3. In much wisdom there is much grief: and he that increaseth knowledge increaseth sorrow.   —ECCLESIASTES 1.18

4. Bore: A person who talks when you wish him to listen.
                                        —AMBROSE BIERCE, *The Devil's Dictionary*

5. Candy
    Is dandy
    But liquor
    Is quicker.   —OGDEN NASH, "Reflections on Ice-Breaking"

6. Necessity never made a good bargain.
                                        —BENJAMIN FRANKLIN, *Poor Richard's Almanac*

7. Man is the only animal that blushes. Or needs to.
   —MARK TWAIN, *Following the Equator, volume 1,*
   Pudd'nhead Wilson's New Calendar

8. It was a delightful visit;—perfect, in being much too short.
   —JANE AUSTEN, *Emma*

9. The course of true love never did run smooth.
   —WILLIAM SHAKESPEARE, *A Midsummer Night's Dream*

10. Oh, she is the antidote to desire!
    —WILLIAM CONGREVE, *The Way of the World*

Satire

◄

Satire is a genre of COMEDY that is directed at ridiculing human foibles and vices, such as vanity, hypocrisy, stupidity, and greed. It differs from pure comedy in that the aim is not simply to evoke laughter, but to expose and censure such faults, often with the aim of correcting them. The target of the satire may vary. In some works, it is a particular individual, as in John Dryden's "Mac Flecknoe" (1682, 1684), directed at a contemporary playwright, Thomas Shadwell, whom Dryden depicts as fatuous and self satisfied. Other satires target a group or set of people, such as the members of the American military establishment in Joseph Heller's *Catch-22* (1961), or an institution, such as totalitarianism in George Orwell's *Animal Farm* (1946). Some satires even aim at the whole of humanity—for example, Book IV of Jonathan Swift's *Gulliver's Travels* (1726). That section of the novel is set on an imaginary island, which is inhabited by two radically opposed species: the brutish Yahoos, who have the outward form of human beings, and their masters, the Houyhnhnms, talking horses who embody the humane intelligence that the Yahoos entirely lack.

A useful means of categorizing satire is into "direct" and "indirect" modes of presentation. In **direct satire**, also called **formal satire**, the FIRST-PERSON NARRATOR addresses a specific audience, either the reader or an invented listener, whom he or she expects will sympathize with the views expressed. For example, in Lord Byron's mock epic, *Don Juan* (1824), the urbane narrator confides to the reader the amorous adventures of Don Juan, a legendary rake, in his youth; Byron depicts him as naïve and irresistibly attractive. Alexander Pope's "Epistle to Dr. Arbuthnot" (1735) is a formal satire on members of the eighteenth-century London literary establishment, such as talentless versifiers who appeal to Pope for praise of their works, spiteful rival poets, and easily flattered patrons. In the poem, Pope represents himself as addressing his physician and friend, Dr. John Arbuthnot; he begins with a mock-desperate plea for sanctuary from such gadflies: "Shut, shut the door, good John! (fatigued I said), / Tie up the knocker, say I'm sick, I'm dead." Arbuthnot serves largely as the audience to the narrative, attempting to calm the indignant speaker and to mitigate his ridicule, though occasionally he, too, joins in the skewering process.

Indirect satire, the usual mode of ridicule in satiric PLAYS and works of PROSE FICTION, is not cast in the form of a direct address to the audience. Rather, the indictment of the characters' vices and follies is implied by simply representing their thoughts, words, and actions. Sometimes that presentation is abetted by the commentary of an INTRUSIVE THIRD-PERSON NARRATOR, as in William Makepeace Thackeray's *Vanity Fair* (1847). The oldest known indirect satires are those of the ancient Greek playwright Aristophanes (c.450–c.385 B.C.E.), who wrote such satiric depictions of Athenian society as *The Frogs* and *The Clouds*. Other examples include Ben Jonson's satire on vanity and greed, *Volpone* (1606); Richard Brinsley Sheridan's witty exposure of licentiousness and hypocrisy in London high society, *The School for Scandal* (1777), and Evelyn Waugh's *The Loved One* (1948), a clever depiction of shallowness, rapacity, and mawkish sentimentality, set at a pet cemetery in Hollywood.

Although satire began with the plays of Aristophanes, the main founders of the form were two Roman poets, Horace (65–68 B.C.E.) and Juvenal (c.65–c.135 C.E.). Each wrote a distinctive type of satire that has given its name to and inspired the two major categories of subsequent satiric works. **Horatian satire** is tolerant and urbane, indulgently mocking faults with the aim of evoking wry amusement rather than repulsion or indignation in the audience. Some examples include Pope's "The Rape of the Lock" (1712), which gently ridicules the vanity and idleness of the British upper classes in the form of a mock epic on the supposed tragedy of the lovely Belinda, a lock of whose hair is ravished by the scissors of a wicked Baron; Lord Byron's *Don Juan* (1819), mentioned above; and the Emmeline Grangerford episode in Mark Twain's *Adventures of Huckleberry Finn* (1884), in which Twain pokes fun at the preoccupation with death in the mawkish drawings and bathetic verse of an adolescent would-be poet. **Juvenalian satire**, in contrast, is harsh and censorious, bitterly condemning vices and foibles and inciting the audience to feelings of indignation and even disgust. Examples of Juvenalian satire include Samuel Johnson's "The Vanity of Human Wishes" (1749), and Mark Twain's *Pudd'nhead Wilson* (1894), an acerbic denunciation of the injustices of slavery. A supreme example of the form is Jonathan Swift's "A Modest Proposal" (1729), in which the author denounces the exploitation of Catholic peasants in his native Ireland by absentee British landlords, who were indifferent to the suffering they were causing and who were abetted by the apathy of the British Parliament and monarchy. Swift's NARRATOR is an imperturbably rational social commentator, who advocates combating overpopulation and hunger by what he perceives as the inspired plan of using the babies of the poor as food.

Satire has been popular throughout the history of English literature, from the ridicule of vanity, promiscuity, and impiety in Chaucer's "The Miller's Tale" and "The Pardoner's Tale" (1386–1400) to the mockery of racial, religious, and class divisions in modern-day London in Zadie Smith's *White Teeth* (2000). The great period of satire, however, was the Restoration and eighteenth century, notably in the witty heroic couplets of John Dryden and Alexander Pope, the REPARTEE among the profligate members of high society in the Restoration comedies of William Congreve, and, later in the century, of Richard Brinsley Sheridan; and the sociopolitical satires of Jonathan Swift and Samuel Johnson. In later ages, the satiric works of such writers as Lord Byron, William Makepeace Thackeray, Mark Twain, and Ambrose Bierce in the nineteenth century, and George Bernard Shaw, Evelyn Waugh, Dorothy Parker, James Thurber, and Kurt Vonnegut in the twentieth have continued to sustain the vitality of the literary form.

In some cases, a satirical episode constitutes part of a longer literary work rather than makes up the whole. For example, in William Shakespeare's *Twelfth Night* (1601), the gulling of Malvolio is a satiric SUBPLOT in the midst of the ROMANTIC COMEDY. ("Gulling" is Elizabethan slang for "duping," based on antiquated bird lore that termed the gull a stupid bird.) Malvolio, the self-centered and humorless steward (head servant) to the Countess Olivia, is convinced by a counterfeit letter that the lady returns his infatuation. He attempts to court her, dressing and acting in the ridiculous styles advocated in the hoax letter. Were Malvolio a sympathetic character, genuinely in love, his inevitable rejection might excite PATHOS rather than mockery. Shakespeare assures that he is a valid satiric target, however, by showing us Malvolio's true character in scenes before he finds the letter: he curries favor with Olivia by berating the clown, prudishly refuses to tolerate the merrymaking of her guests, and, most tellingly, fantasizes not about the lady herself but about the rank and power he would achieve were she to favor him with her hand. Such faults provoke Maria, a quick-witted gentlewoman-in-waiting, into devising the diabolically clever scheme, which she justifies with satiric glee in a contemptuous description of her intended victim:

> [He is nothing but] a time-pleaser; an affectioned[1] ass,
> that cons state without book[2] and utters it by great
> swathes; the best persuaded of himself; so crammed, as
> he thinks, with excellencies that it is his grounds of faith[3]
> that all that look on him love him; and on that vice in
> him will my revenge find notable cause to work.

For the most part, Shakespeare's satire of Malvolio is Horatian. The tricks go too far for most modern audiences, however, when Malvolio's attempts to conform to the letter's directives establish grounds for the pranksters' charge that he has gone mad, and he is imprisoned in a dark cell. At the end, when he is freed and the truth is revealed to him, he remains incapable of either perspective or humor. Although Olivia offers him the chance for restitution, he rejects her generous offer and storms off, vowing, "I'll be revenged on the whole pack of you." The overall mode of *Twelfth Night*, however, is COMIC rather than satiric; accordingly, it ends with the projected celebration of three marriages, so that the emphasis is not on the satire but on the happy romantic fortunes of the main characters.

EXERCISE: Satire

For each of the following examples:

- State whether the satire is FORMAL (DIRECT) or INDIRECT. If it is direct, describe the nature of the audience to whom it is addressed.
- Identify the type of SATIRE that it exemplifies, HORATIAN or JUVENALIAN, and justify that choice of category.
- Explain the targets of the SATIRE: the human vice[s] or foible[s] and the person, institution, or group at which it is aimed.

1.   All human things are subject to decay,
   And when fate summons, monarchs must obey.
   This Flecknoe[1] found, who, like Augustus, young
   Was called to empire, and had governed long;
   In prose and verse, was owned, without dispute,   5
   Through all the realms of Nonsense, absolute.

---

1. Affected. *Time-pleaser:* sycophant.
2. Memorizes high-flown speeches.
3. Creed.
1. Richard Flecknoe, an Irish poet Dryden considered dull.

This agèd prince, now flourishing in peace,
And blest with issue of a large increase,[2]
Worn out with business, did at length debate
To settle the succession of the state;   10
And, pondering which of all his sons was fit
To reign, and wage immortal war with wit,
Cried: "'Tis resolved; for Nature pleads that he
Should only rule, who most resembles me.
Sh——[3] alone, of all my sons, is he   15
Who stands confirmed in full stupidity.
The rest to some faint meaning make pretense,
But Sh—— never deviates into sense."

–JOHN DRYDEN, "Mac Flecknoe"

2. By the time you swear you're his,
    Shivering and sighing,
And he vows his passion is
    Infinite, undying—
Lady, make a note of this.   5
    One of you is lying.

–DOROTHY PARKER, "Unfortunate Coincidence"

3. In this section of Adventures of Huckleberry Finn, Huck, the NARRATOR, has just seen Buck Grangerford, his new friend and the son of his generous host, shoot at "a splendid young man" from the other prominent local family, the Shepherdsons. Buck's father, Col. Grangerford, clearly approves of the attack. Huck takes the first opportunity to question the other boy about the situation.

> "Did you want to kill him, Buck?"
> "Well, I bet I did."
> "What did he do to you?"
> "Him? He never done nothing to me."
> "Well, then, what did you want to kill him for?"
> "Why nothing—only it's on account of the feud."
> "What's a feud?"
> "Why, where was you raised? Don't you know what a feud is?"
> "Never heard of it before—tell me about it."
> "Well," says Buck, "a feud is this way. A man has a quarrel
with another man, and kills him; then that other man's brother kills

---

2. Children; also, Flecknoe's practice of republishing old works under new titles.
3. Thomas Shadwell, a playwright and rival of Dryden.

▼

him; then the other brothers, on both sides, goes for one another;
then the *cousins* chip in—and by and by everybody's killed off, and
there ain't no more feud. But it's kind of slow, and takes a long
time."

"Has this one been going on long, Buck?"

"Well I should *reckon*! it started thirty year ago, or som'ers
along there. There was trouble 'bout something and then a lawsuit
to settle it; and the suit went agin one of the men, and so he up
and shot the man that won the suit—which he would naturally do,
of course. Anybody would."

"What was the trouble about, Buck?—land?"

"I reckon maybe—I don't know."

"Well, who done the shooting?—was it a Grangerford or a
Shepherdson?"

"Laws, how do *I* know? it was so long ago."

— MARK TWAIN, *Adventures of Huckleberry Finn*

4. "next to of course god america i
    love you land of the pilgrims' and so forth oh
    say can you see by the dawn's early my
    country 'tis of centuries come and go
    and are no more what of it we should worry   5
    in every language even deafanddumb
    thy sons acclaim your glorious name by gorry
    by jingo⁴ by gee by gosh by gum
    why talk of beauty what could be more beau-
    tiful than these heroic happy dead   10
    who rushed like lions to the roaring slaughter
    they did not stop to think they died instead
    then shall the voice of liberty be mute?"

He spoke. And drank rapidly a glass of water

— E. E. CUMMINGS, "'next to of course god america i'"

5. MRS. CANDOUR My dear Lady Sneerwell, how have you been this
    century? Mr. Surface, what news do you hear?—though indeed it
    is no matter, for I think one hears nothing else but scandal.
    JOSEPH SURFACE Just so, indeed, madam.
    MRS. CANDOUR Ah, Maria! child,—what, is the whole affair off
    between you and Charles? His extravagance, I presume—the
    town talks of nothing else.
    MARIA I am very sorry, ma'am, the town has so little to do.
    MRS. CANDOUR True, true, child: but there is no stopping people's
    tongues. I own I was hurt to hear it, as indeed I was to learn,

---

4. A mild oath; also, jingoism: extreme nationalism.

from the same quarter, that your guardian, Sir Peter, and Lady
Teazle have not agreed lately so well as could be wished. . . .

MARIA Such reports are highly scandalous.

MRS. CANDOUR So they are, child—shameful, shameful! But the
world is so censorious, no character escapes. Lord, now who
would have suspected your friend, Miss Prim, of an indiscretion?
Yet such is the ill-nature of people, that they say her uncle
stopped her last week, just as she was stepping into the York
Diligence[5] with her dancing-master.

MARIA I'll answer for't there are no grounds for the report.

MRS. CANDOUR Oh, no foundation in the world, I dare swear; no
more, than for the story circulated last month, of Mrs. Festino's
affair with Colonel Cassino;—though, to be sure, that matter was
never rightly cleared up.

JOSEPH SURFACE The license of invention some people take is monstrous indeed.

MARIA 'Tis so.—But, in my opinion, those who report such things
are equally culpable.

MRS. CANDOUR To be sure they are; tale-bearers are as bad as the tale-
makers—'tis an old observation, and a very true one—but what's to
be done, as I said before? how will you prevent people from talking?

—RICHARD BRINSLEY SHERIDAN, *The School for Scandal*

6. *In the following scene from* Hamlet, *Polonius, the Lord Chamberlain at the
court of Denmark, is attempting to discover the cause of Prince Hamlet's supposed madness. Polonius is convinced that Hamlet has gone mad because of
his daughter Ophelia's rejection, done at Polonius's own command, because
he feared wrongly that Hamlet was merely toying with her affections. Hamlet, who is only feigning insanity, is all too aware that Ophelia acted on her
father's orders and that Polonius is spying on him in order to curry favor with
the corrupt king, Hamlet's despised uncle.*

POLONIUS How does my good Lord Hamlet?

HAMLET Well, God-a-mercy.

POLONIUS Do you know me, my lord?

HAMLET Excellent well, you are a fishmonger.[6]

POLONIUS Not I, my lord.

HAMLET Then I would you were so honest a man.

POLONIUS Honest, my lord?

HAMLET Ay, sir, to be honest as this world goes, is to be one man
picked out of ten thousand.

POLONIUS That's very true, my lord.

---

5. Coach to York.
6. Elizabethan slang for pimp, a glance at Polonius's exploitation of Ophelia.

HAMLET For if the sun breed maggots in a dead dog, being a good
  kissing carrion—Have you a daughter?
POLONIUS I have, my lord.
HAMLET Let her not walk i' th' sun. Conception[7] is a blessing, but as
  your daughter may conceive—friend, look to't.
POLONIUS [*Aside.*] How say you by that? Still harping on my daughter. Yet he knew me not at first. 'A[8] said I was a fishmonger. 'A
  is far gone. And truly in my youth I suffered much extremity for
  love, very near this. I'll speak to him again.— What do you read,
  my lord? . . .
HAMLET Slanders, sir; for the satirical rogue says here that old men
  have grey beards, that their faces are wrinkled, their eyes purg-
  ing thick amber and plum-tree gum, and that they have a plenti-
  ful lack of wit, together with most weak hams[9]—all which, sir,
  though I most potently and powerfully believe, yet I hold it not
  honesty to have it thus set down, for yourself, sir, shall grow old
  as I am, if like a crab you could go backward.[1]
POLONIUS [*Aside.*] Though this be madness, yet there is method in't.
                              —WILLIAM SHAKESPEARE, *Hamlet*

7.   But scarce observed, the knowing and the bold
     Fall in the general massacre of gold;
     Wide-wasting pest! That rages unconfined,
     And crowds with crimes the records of mankind;
     For gold his sword the hireling ruffian draws,   5
     For gold the hireling judge distorts the laws;
     Wealth heaped on wealth, nor truth nor safety buys,
     The dangers gather as the treasures rise.
                      —SAMUEL JOHNSON, "The Vanity of Human Wishes"

8.   **26**

     Don José and the Donna Inez led
         For some time an unhappy sort of life,
     Wishing each other, not divorced, but dead;
         They lived respectably as man and wife,
     Their conduct was exceedingly well-bred,   5
         And gave no outward signs of inward strife,

---

7. Thought, but also pregnancy.
8. He.
9. Thighs.
1. In time.

Until at length the smothered fire broke out,
And put the business past all kind of doubt.

27

For Inez called some druggists and physicians,
     And tried to prove her loving lord was *mad*,   10
But as he had some lucid intermissions,
     She next decided he was only *bad*;
Yet when they asked her for her depositions,
     No sort of explanation could be had,
Save that her duty both to man and God   15
Required this conduct—which seemed very odd.

28

She kept a journal, where his faults were noted,
     And opened certain trunks of books and letters,
All which might, if occasion served, be quoted;
     And then she had all Seville for abettors,   20
Besides her good old grandmother (who doted);
     The hearers of her case became repeaters,
Then advocates, inquisitors, and judges.
Some for amusement, others for old grudges.

29

And then this best and meekest woman bore   25
     With such serenity her husband's woes,
Just as the Spartan ladies did of yore,
     Who saw their spouses killed, and nobly chose
Never to say a word about them more—
     Calmly she heard each calumny that rose,   30
And saw *his* agonies with such sublimity,
That all the world exclaimed, "What magnanimity!"
                   –George Gordon, Lord Byron, *Don Juan*

9. *In the following scene, Dennis Barlow, an Englishman employed by
The Happier Hunting Ground, a posh pet cemetery in Hollywood, has been
called to the home of the Heinkels, whose lapdog has been hit by a car.
The dog belonged primarily to Mrs. Heinkel, who is sitting in the hall,
drinking.*

     "This way," said Mr. Heinkel. "In the pantry."
     The Sealyham lay on the draining board beside the sink. Dennis
lifted it into the container. "Perhaps you wouldn't mind taking a
hand?"

Together he and Mr. Heinkel carried their load to the wagon.

"Shall we discuss arrangements now, or would you prefer to call in the morning?"

"I'm a pretty busy man mornings," said Mr. Heinkel. "Come into the study."

There was a tray on the desk. They helped themselves to whisky.

"I have our brochure here setting out our service. Were you thinking of interment or incineration?"

"Pardon me?"

"Buried or burned?"

"Burned, I guess."

"I have some photographs here of various styles of urn."

"The best will be good enough."

"Would you require a niche in our columbarium or do you prefer to keep the remains at home?"

"What you said first."

"And the religious rites? We have a pastor who is always pleased to assist."

"Well, Mr.—?"

"Barlow."

"Mr. Barlow, we're neither of us what you might call very church-going people, but I think on an occasion like this Mrs. Heinkel would want all the comfort you can offer."

"Our Grade A service includes several unique features. At the moment of committal, a white dove, symbolizing the deceased's soul, is liberated over the crematorium."

"Yes," said Mr. Heinkel, "I reckon Mrs. Heinkel would appreciate the dove."

"And every anniversary a card of remembrance is mailed without further charge. It reads: *Your little Arthur is thinking of you in heaven and wagging his tail.*"

"That's a very beautiful thought, Mr. Barlow."

"Then, if you will just sign the order. . . ."

—Evelyn Waugh, *The Loved One*

10. If thou beest born to strange sights,
         Things invisible to see,
     Ride ten thousand days and nights,
         Till age snow white hairs on thee,
     Thou, when thou return'st, wilt tell me   5
     All strange wonders that befell thee,
             And swear
             Nowhere
     Lives a woman true, and fair.[2]

     If thou find'st one. Let me know,   10
         Such a pilgrimage were sweet;
     Yet do not, I would not go,
         Though at next door we might meet;
     Though she were true when you met her,
     And last till you write your letter,   15
             Yet she
             Will be
     False, ere I come, to two, or three.

                                        —JOHN DONNE, "Song"

———————————

2. Beautiful.

Figurative Language

Figurative language is the inclusive term for words that are used in ways that depart conspicuously from their *literal* applications, so as to achieve special meanings or effects. (**Literal language** designates what most speakers would perceive as the standard meaning of words, or as their standard order or syntactical sequence.) Figurative language is used most often in poetry, but it is essential to all literary genres, in VERSE or prose, as well as to ordinary discourse.

Figurative language is usually divided into two broad classes: FIGURES OF THOUGHT and FIGURES OF SPEECH.

FIGURES OF THOUGHT (TROPES)

Figures of thought, or **tropes** (from the Greek word meaning "a turn") are words or phrases used in ways that effect an obvious change (or "turn") in their standard meaning. One kind of trope depends on a comparison between two very different objects, or else on a transference of qualities associated with an object, experience, or concept to another not literally connected with it. Such figures of thought include SIMILE, METAPHOR, PERSONIFICATION, PATHETIC FALLACY, SYNECDOCHE, and METONYMY. A second kind of trope depends on a contrast between two levels of meaning, or a shift from one level of meaning to another. IRONY is the most prominent example of this type; others are PARADOX, OXYMORON, UNDERSTATEMENT, LITOTES, HYPERBOLE, and PERIPHRASIS.

Simile

A **simile** is a FIGURE OF THOUGHT in which one kind of thing is compared to a markedly different object, concept, or experience; the comparison is made explicit by the word "like" or "as": "Jen's room is like a pig sty." (This definition is suggested by the Latin root of simile, which means "similar" or "like.") The simile can be carried further and specify some feature of the comparison: "Jen's room is as dirty as a pig sty." In either case, the effect is that the subject and the analogy are pictured in quick sequence, side by side.

Similes occur in both poetry and prose, and they may be short and simple or long and extended. They provide an important indication of an author or speaker's TONE; that is, implied attitude toward the subject. As with a METAPHOR, the means is to use a comparison that reflects some key quality of the literal subject. For example, the tone of a simile may be exalted, as in Robert Burns's lyrical tribute: "O, my luve's like a red, red rose." Here, the image evoked is of a fresh, vibrant, and lovely object of adoration. The tone may be wry and scornful, as in James Joyce's more extended simile from the SHORT STORY "Two Gallants" describing a self-satisfied wastrel: "His head was large, globular and oily; . . . and his large hat, set upon it sideways, looked like a bulb which had grown out of another." The adjective "globular" is extended to the roundness of the double "bulb" of hat and head. The image is made ludicrous by equating the item of clothing with the supposed locus of human intellect and by the contrast between the man's head and the humble onion to which it is compared.

To take a third example, from *Romeo and Juliet*, the tone may indicate heartbreak, as in Lord Capulet's grief at what he believes is his dead daughter: "Death lies on her like an untimely frost / Upon the sweetest flower of all the field." Here Juliet's death is compared to an early frost that kills a rare and lovely flower. The simile describes the effect of the blighting cold on the frozen but still beautiful plant. By extension, we are made aware of the deathly pallor of the stricken young woman who has so recently looked blushing and vibrant. Although Juliet is not in fact dead at this point, her father's expression of the devastating loss of vitality and hope foreshadows the tragedy to come.

Metaphor

In a **metaphor**, a word or phrase that in literal use designates one kind of thing is applied to a conspicuously different object, concept, or experience, without asserting an explicit comparison. In the last point, it differs from a SIMILE. For example, in "Jen's room is a pig sty," the metaphorical word, "sty," is applied to the literal subject, "room," without using "like" or "as." The critic I. A. Richards posed a helpful conception of the metaphorical relationship in *Philosophy of Rhetoric*: he called the literal subject the **tenor**, the aspect that "holds" (alluding to the Latin root) the meaning, and he termed the analogy the **vehicle**, the part that "conveys" the comparison. In this example, the sty is the vehicle used to convey certain impressions of the room, the tenor. Unlike a SIMILE, in which the tenor and the vehicle are shown side by side, a metaphor describes them as though they were superimposed on each other. It appeals to the reader or listener's imagination—the image-making capacity of the "mind's eye," to use Hamlet's metaphor—by expressing the analogy in terms of sensory impressions. Metaphor is the most comprehensive category of TROPE, or FIGURES OF THOUGHT, all of which use words in ways that depart markedly from their standard literal meanings. (See also SIMILE, PERSONIFICATION, PATHETIC FALLACY, SYNECDOCHE, and METONYMY.)

The effect of a metaphor (derived from the Greek word for "carry over" or "transfer") is to transfer to the tenor qualities closely associated with the vehicle. In the simplest metaphors, the analogy may be plain and direct: in the example above, the implication is that Jen's room is dirty and disheveled, as one might expect an enclosure for swine to be. The figurative spectrum, however, is broad, and in more complex metaphors the associations between vehicle and tenor may be multifaceted and surprising. For example, when Romeo, hiding under Juliet's balcony, says, "But soft, what light from yonder window breaks? / It is the east, and Juliet is the sun," the tenor is the light shed by the open window; the vehicle is the brightness and warmth of his young love's beauty, which seem to him as powerful as those of the rising sun. At the same time, the vehicle may be taken to convey, subtly, an unexpected and ominous aspect of the tenor: the implication that Juliet is not literally the solar body but a human being, vulnerable to the forces of time and violence. Romeo's exalted vision suggests how much he ignores or denies as he falls recklessly in love with the daughter of his family's enemy.

A metaphor may be short or long, a quick linking or a series of sustained comparisons. On the simplest level, it is as concise as a single word. That may be a verb (I "wilted," her heart "sang"); an adjective ("leaden" thoughts, a heart "of gold"); or a noun (calling someone an "angel" or a "dragon"). Sometimes a speaker elaborates on a metaphor to explain its relevance, as in *Hamlet* when Horatio describes the effect of the ghost's appearance on his nerves: "It harrows me with fear and wonder." In order to feel the extent of his disturbance, a city-bred student might well have to look up the meaning of that agricultural verb "harrow": to break up soil with a sharp, heavy implement.

A **mixed metaphor** occurs when two or more incongruous vehicles are applied to the same tenor. Instead of clarifying some aspect of the subject, the figure confuses it by linking images that clash: "She felt a heavy burden of guilt, but she would not let it engulf her resolve." The word "burden" is already a vehicle for the tenor, her guilt; it clashes with the second vehicle, "engulf." The image of being weighed down is confused by the conflicting image of being surrounded and swallowed up, drowned. The solution would be to rethink the qualities of the tenor and choose a single vehicle that reflects them: "She felt a heavy burden of guilt, but she would not let it hinder her resolve." Mixed metaphors often occur because the writer is not thinking clearly, in which case, as in the example above, they sound ludicrous. Sometimes, though, authors use them to suggest that a speaker is so carried away by powerful feelings as to be heedless of the mixed vehicles, as when Ophelia, distraught over what she believes is Hamlet's sudden plunge into madness, contrasts her bereft state with the delight of having "sucked the honey of his music vows." The reference to tasting the sweet honey clashes with that of delighting in the musicality of Hamlet's professions of love, but both express eloquently the young woman's despair over an incalculable loss of something rare and precious. Perhaps the slight unhinging of Ophelia's logic is also meant to foreshadow the complete breakdown of her reason that will shortly follow.

Sometimes a writer uses an **extended metaphor**, a TROPE that is sustained through several lines, ringing changes on the multiple relevance of the vehicle to the tenor. The loquacious old courtier in *Hamlet*, Polonius, relishes any chance to elaborate on a point, as in the scene where he warns his hapless daughter Ophelia not to trust the seductive lies of young men who are "burning" with passion:

> I do know,
> When the blood burns, how prodigal the soul
> Lends the tongue vows. These blazes, daughter,
> Giving more light than heat, extinct in both
> Even in their promise, as it is a-making,
> You must not take for fire.

Polonius is saying that the momentary "blazes"—fervent declarations of aroused suitors hoping to seduce gullible maidens—should not be mistaken for "true fire"—trustworthy and lasting vows. Such false assurances of love "give[ ] more light than heat"—they express the men's flattery but not their sincerity—and are "extinct"—extinguished—even in the moment that they are being made.

Shakespeare also sometimes uses a series of vehicles for the same tenor in order to suggest how rapidly and desperately a speaker's mind is working. In his expression of total despair, for example, the tyrant Macbeth compares life to "a walking shadow," "a poor player that struts and frets his hour upon the stage," and "a tale told by an idiot." His metaphors convey the sense of transience, failure, and futility: the bitter images of meaninglessness. The man who began the play rich in all of the worldly blessings has by this point annihilated every person and value he once treasured. In destroying so many other lives, the metaphors imply, he has done irreparable damage to his own. An extended metaphor may also recur through an entire work, and alter or reinforce the depiction of the characters and the plot. For example, the references to gardens in *Hamlet*, to heavenly bodies—stars, sun, moon—in *Romeo and Juliet*, and to birds and flight in *Jane Eyre* gain power and scope from their recurrence and variety.

At whatever level of complexity, a metaphor offers an indirect commentary on the literal action, a subtle second perspective. It is more engaging than simple direct statement because it invites a silent dialogue with the audience, a partnership between author and reader, or reader and speaker. Implication (the author's or speaker's role) and inference (the reader's or listener's response) are the main sources of **subtext**, the underlying meaning or set of meanings that provide one of the chief challenges and gratifications of literature. Discerning subtext in reading is comparable to having a conversation with a clever, subtle friend. The speaker of Shakespeare's Sonnet 23, a tongue-tied lover, pleads with his love to let his "books" serve as his "eloquence" in expressing his deeply felt thoughts: "O, learn to read what silent love hath writ; / To hear with eyes belongs to love's fine wit." This tribute to the understanding of the perceptive lover might apply as well to the perceptive reader, with metaphor as the quintessential expression of "fine wit."

EXERCISES: Similes and Metaphors

I. For each of the following examples:
- Specify whether it is a SIMILE or a METAPHOR. *Note:* Some excerpts contain more than one SIMILE and/or METAPHOR; in those cases, give responses for both FIGURES OF THOUGHT.
- Identify the TENOR and the VEHICLE.
- Describe the effects—the impressions and feelings—created by this use of FIGURATIVE LANGUAGE.

1. I weep like a child for the past.

    –D. H. LAWRENCE, "Piano"

simile

t : way she stared
v : ice

2. Her eye of ice continued to dwell freezingly on mine.

   metaphor
   —CHARLOTTE BRONTË, *Jane Eyre*

3. *On soldiers during World War I:*   *simile*

   Bent double, like old beggars under sacks,
   Knock-kneed, coughing like hags, we cursed through sludge.
   —WILFRED OWEN "Dulce Et Decorum Est"

4. This bud of love, by summer's ripening breath,
   May prove a beauteous flower when next we meet.

   metaphor —WILLIAM SHAKESPEARE, *Romeo and Juliet*

5. I love thee freely, as men strive for right;
   I love thee purely, as they turn from praise.
   —ELIZABETH BARRETT BROWNING, "How do I love thee?"

   simile

6. She'd come again, and with a greedy ear
   Devour up my discourse.

   metaphor —WILLIAM SHAKESPEARE, *Othello*

7. Her fingers felt like a dead person's, like an old peach I once found
   in the back of the refrigerator; the skin just slid off the meat when I
   picked it up.   *simile* —AMY TAN, "Two Kinds"

8. He watches from his mountain walls,
   And like a thunderbolt he falls.

   metaphor —ALFRED, LORD TENNYSON, "The Eagle"

9. When she paid the coachman, she took the money out of a hard
   steel purse, and she kept the purse in a very jail of a bag which   *simile*
   hung upon her arm by a heavy chain, and shut it up like a bite.

   metaphor —CHARLES DICKENS, *David Copperfield*

10. This is the Hour of Lead—   *simile*
    Remembered, if outlived,
    As freezing persons recollect the Snow—
    First—Chill—then Stupor—then the letting go—
    —Emily Dickinson, "After great pain"

[handwritten top margin: birds have short life / need nourishment / fly south]

II. Extended Metaphors

[handwritten left margin rotated: spin light-hearted toward]

1. In *Jane Eyre,* Jane is summoned by her cruel aunt to meet Mr. Brocklehurst, the clergyman who directs the boarding school to which she is to be sent. Identify the extended metaphor and simile in the following passage, specifying the tenor and the vehicle of each. Then describe what the figures of thought suggest and reveal about both Mr. Brocklehurst and the narrator.

I now stood in the empty hall; before me was the breakfast-room door, and I stopped, intimidated and trembling. What a miserable little poltroon had fear, engendered of unjust punishment, made of me in those days! I feared to return to the nursery; I feared to go forward to the parlour; ten minutes I stood in agitated hesitation: the vehement ringing of the breakfast-room bell decided me: I *must* enter.

"Who could want me?" I asked inwardly, as with both hands I turned the stiff door-handle, which, for a second or two, resisted my efforts. "What should I see besides aunt Reed in the apartment?—a man or a woman?" The handle turned, the door unclosed, and passing through and curtseying low, I looked up at—a black pillar!—such, at least, appeared to me, at first sight, the straight, narrow, sable-clad shape standing erect on the rug: the grim face at the top was like a carved mask, placed above the shaft by way of capital.

–CHARLOTTE BRONTË, *Jane Eyre*

[handwritten left margin: why bird? / indicates life, projects comfort and happiness / flying upward]

2. The following poem by Emily Dickinson presents an extended metaphor. Identify the tenor and the vehicle, and summarize the ways that the details develop the metaphor. Then describe the effects on our impressions and understanding of the literal subject that the extended metaphor suggests.

"Hope" is the thing with feathers—
That perches in the soul—
And sings the tune without the words—
And never stops—at all—

And sweetest—in the Gale—is heard—
And sore must be the storm
That could abash the little Bird
That kept so many warm—

I've heard it in the chillest land—
And on the strangest Sea—
Yet, never, in Extremity,
It asked a crumb—of Me.

5

[handwritten annotations around poem: innate essential to all / not extreme / can't force it / hope in soul essential to being / tenor hope / never ending hope / storm wind / vehicle / metaphor bird / without words needs no translation no analysis / storm trials of life / hope is needed most]

Personification

Personification is a FIGURE OF THOUGHT (or TROPE) in which an abstract concept, animal, or inanimate object is treated as though it were alive or had human attributes. The name refers to the process of conceiving of the literal subject as though it were a person. For example, in "Ode on Melancholy," John Keats represents that feeling as a goddess who coexists, paradoxically, with earthly delights—but delights that by their very nature are transient: "She dwells with Beauty—Beauty that must die; / And Joy, whose hand is ever at his lips / Bidding adieu." Here Keats personifies not only Melancholy but also the worldly gifts of Beauty and Joy by picturing them as her necessarily fleeting companions.

To cite another example: in *Romeo and Juliet*, Lord Capulet uses personification to express his despair at finding Juliet supposedly dead on the morning of her wedding day: "Death is my son-in-law, Death is my heir; / My daughter he has wedded." The grim representation of Death as both his daughter's bridegroom and his own prospective heir conveys the morbid turn of mind of the old father as well as the empty future he envisions now that he has lost his only child. A quite different use of the trope occurs in Charlotte Brontë's *Jane Eyre* when the heroine agonizes over her decision to refuse Mr. Rochester's proposal to run off with him: "Conscience and Reason turned traitors against me and charged me with crime in resisting him." The dilemma is that Jane has just discovered that her beloved is already married, but to a long demented wife whom he cannot legally divorce. He is ardently devoted to Jane and in despair at the prospect of her leaving him, and she is torn by the conflict between standing on moral principles and offering succor to the man she loves. The personification of Conscience and Reason suggests both the complexities of moral decision-making and the irony of Jane's situation: the very forces that would usually underpin hard but righteous decisions—moral principles and rational thought—side with the suffering sinner and chastise the upright moralizer.

An extended form of personification occurs in **allegory**, in which an abstract concept is presented as though it were a character who speaks and acts as an independent being. In the medieval morality play *Everyman*, for example, the personified characters include not only the hero, Everyman, who represents all human beings as they face death and final judgment, but also such abstract qualities as Beauty, Knowledge, and Good Deeds. The play depicts the extent to which each of these abstractions is able and willing to accompany Everyman on his terrifying final journey toward the grave and the

bird provides warmth in own

bird has to stop and wait for ridiculously strong storm

don't need hope until storm taken for granted, bird is heard even thru storm divine reward or punishment that awaits him beyond it. Seeing the abstractions interact with the protagonist serves as a means of conveying the intricacies of the struggle for the medieval Christian to live a life of rectitude and faith and to believe in the rewards, on earth and in the afterlife, of fidelity, humility, and compassion.

Other examples of complex, sustained allegory are Edmund Spenser's sixteenth-century epic, *The Faerie Queen*, and John Bunyan's seventeenth-century work, *The Pilgrim's Progress*; allegoric episodes occur also in many of the novels and short stories of Nathaniel Hawthorne. Jonathan Swift's *Gulliver's Travels* (1726) and George Orwell's *Animal Farm* (1946) use allegory not to exalt a subject but to satirize it.

Pathetic Fallacy

Pathetic fallacy is a special type of PERSONIFICATION, in which inanimate aspects of nature, such as the landscape or the weather, are represented as having human qualities or feelings. The term, which was invented by the Victorian critic John Ruskin, derives from the logical absurdity ("fallacy") of supposing that nature can sympathize with (feel *pathos* for) human moods and concerns. Although Ruskin considered pathetic fallacy a derogatory term because he thought that it showed false or "morbid" feelings, it no longer has that negative connotation and is now merely descriptive. Usually the pathetic fallacy reflects or foreshadows some aspect of the poem or narrative at that point, such as the plot, theme, or characterization, and so intensifies the tone. For example, a mild, sunny day would promise a tranquil, happy scene, while it is no accident that the dire events in *Hamlet* begin with the ghost's appearance on a winter midnight. James Joyce has his prescient young narrator in "Araby" allude to this TROPE when he anticipates the failure of his futile romantic quest: "The air was pitilessly raw and already my heart misgave me."

At times, writers reverse the usual use of the pathetic fallacy for purposes of IRONY. For example, the bloody battle of Chancellorville in Stephen Crane's *The Red Badge of Courage* is set on a lovely summer day. On the eve of the battle, the naive young private Henry Fleming sees nature as attuned to his need for consolation: "There was a caress in the soft winds; and the whole mood of the darkness, he thought, was one of sympathy for himself in his distress." A change in the mood of the weather or the look of the landscape is a favorite means for authors to signal a shift in the fortunes of characters. As Henry encounters the devastation of war, the setting accordingly turns dark and threatening. Only much later, after he has emerged from the battle, scarred by his experiences but grateful to have survived, does the pathetic fallacy return to its usual use. The young soldier is able "to turn with a lover's thirst to images of tranquil skies, fresh meadows, cool brooks—an existence of soft and eternal peace." The weather reflects his newly optimistic mood as "a golden ray of sun [comes] through the hosts of leaden rain clouds."

Synecdoche

part represents whole

Synecdoche (Sin-EK-do-key), derived from the Greek word for "to take up together," is a FIGURE OF THOUGHT in which the term for part of something is used to represent the whole, or, less commonly, the term for the whole is used to represent a part. For example, a fleet of ships may be described as "forty sails," athletes have been nicknamed "Muscles" and "the Toe," manual laborers called "blue collar" workers, and the food needed for sustenance "daily bread." In its basic component, the comparison between a larger and smaller entity, synecdoche is closely allied with METONYMY.

associated represents whole

Metonymy

Metonymy (meh-TAHN-ah-mee) is a TROPE which substitutes the name of an entity with something else that is closely associated with it. For example, "the throne" is a **metonymic** synonym for "the king"; "Shakespeare" for the works of the playwright; the citadel "the Kremlin" for the ruling body of modern Russia; and "England" or "old Norway" as the designation for the king of the country. The word derives from Greek roots that mean "changing a name." See also SYNECDOCHE.

At times, a mingling of SYNECDOCHE and metonymy has been used with ironic effect. For example, the distraught Ophelia, in shock over Hamlet's malicious tirade, says about her heretofore gentle lover: "The courtier's, soldier's, scholar's, eye, tongue, sword . . . Th'observed of all observers, quite, quite down." Here the order of Ophelia's list goes against logic, associating the courtier with the eye, the soldier with the tongue, and the scholar with the sword. Furthermore, only "eye" and "tongue," which represent the whole man by means of the part, are SYNECDOCHES; "sword," which expresses the close association between the soldier and his weapon, is a metonymy. The jumbled PARALLELS provide a poignant foreshadowing of Ophelia's mental breakdown.

▼

EXERCISE: Personification, Pathetic Fallacy, Synecdoche, and Metonymy

For each of the following passages:

- Specify whether it exemplifies PERSONIFICATION, PATHETIC FALLACY, SYNECDOCHE, or METONYMY. *Note:* Some excerpts contain more than one FIGURE OF THOUGHT; in those cases, identify both.
- Describe the effects—the impressions and feelings—that result from this use of FIGURATIVE LANGUAGE.

1. *The moment before the protagonist experiences the horror of finding his first decomposing corpse, this account of his thoughts occurs:*

    He conceived Nature to be a woman with a deep aversion to tragedy. *personification* —STEPHEN CRANE, *The Red Badge of Courage*

2. O Time, thou must untangle this, not I;
    It is too hard a knot for me t'untie.
    personification —WILLIAM SHAKESPEARE, *Twelfth Night*

3. Let not Ambition mock their useful toil,
        Their homely joys, and destiny obscure;
    Nor Grandeur hear with a disdainful smile
        The short and simple annals of the poor.
                    —THOMAS GRAY, "Elegy Written in a Country Churchyard"

4. *Just after Mr. Rochester, who is secretly married to a mad wife whom he cannot legally divorce, proposes bigamous marriage to the unsuspecting Jane Eyre, the following description occurs:*

    But what had befallen the night? The moon was not yet set, and we were all in shadow: I could scarcely see my master's face, near as I was. And what ailed the chestnut tree? It writhed and groaned; while wind roared in the laurel walk, and came sweeping over us.
    pathetic fallacy —CHARLOTTE BRONTË, *Jane Eyre*

    pathetic fallacy / personification / must be direct

5. He seemed a part of the mute melancholy landscape, an incarnation of its frozen woe, with all that was warm and sentient in him fast bound below the surface; but there was nothing unfriendly in his silence. I simply felt that he lived in a depth of moral isolation too remote for casual access, and I had the sense that his loneliness was

pathetic fallacy

not merely the result of his personal plight, tragic as I guessed that to be, but had in it . . . the profound accumulated cold of many Starkfield[1] winters. —EDITH WHARTON, *Ethan Frome*

6. For Mercy has a human heart,
   Pity, a human face:
   And Love, the human form divine;
   And Peace, the human dress.

   personification

   —WILLIAM BLAKE, "The Divine Image"

7. *The prince is reflecting on the deaths of the young lovers, who had been caught in the feud between their families:*

   A glooming peace this morning with it brings;
   The sun for sorrow will not show his head.

   —WILLIAM SHAKESPEARE, *Romeo and Juliet*

   pathetic fallacy

8. The weather added what it could of gloom. A cold stormy rain set in, and nothing of July appeared but in the trees and shrubs, which the wind was despoiling, and the length of the day, which only made such cruel sights the longer visible.

   —JANE AUSTEN, *Emma*

   pathetic fallacy

9. *The ghost of Hamlet's father reveals to his son the circumstances of his assassination:*

   So the whole ear of Denmark
   Is by a forged process[2] of my death
   Rankly abused.

   synechdoche

   false account

   —WILLIAM SHAKESPEARE, *Hamlet*

10. *Rosalind, who has disguised herself as a young man and run away to the forest with her cousin Celia, says:*

    I could find in my heart to disgrace my man's apparel and to cry like a woman; but I must comfort the weaker vessel, as doublet and hose ought to show itself courageous to petticoat.

    —WILLIAM SHAKESPEARE, *As You Like It*

---

1. A fictional town in western Massachusetts.
2. False account.

▼

Irony

Irony is the broadest class of FIGURES OF THOUGHT that depend on presenting a deliberate contrast between two levels of meaning. The word derives from a type of character in Greek drama, the eiron, who pretended to be stupid and unaware. He used that pretense to deceive and triumph over another stock character, the alazon, who was truly stupid, but boastful and complacent. The major types of irony are VERBAL, STRUCTURAL, DRAMATIC, TRAGIC, and COSMIC.

Verbal irony consists of implying a meaning different from, and often the complete opposite of, the one that is explicitly stated. Usually, the irony is signaled by clues in the context of the situation or in the style of expression. For example, the sententious narrator of Robert Frost's "Provide, Provide," lamenting the transience of earthly fame and power, advises: "Die early, and avoid the fate." The irony is implied by the contrast between the mock sagacity of the tone and the cold comfort of the drastic so-called solution. In more complex cases, the detection of irony may depend on values that the author assumes are shared by his or her audience. One of the most famous examples is Jonathan Swift's bitter satire "A Modest Proposal," which purports to present a happy solution to the famine in the author's native Ireland: using the infants of the starving lower classes as a source of food. At no point does the narrator abandon his pretense of cool rationality or complacency: the reaction of horror is left to the reader. The risk, which did in fact affect the reception of Swift's essay, is that an oblivious audience will mistake irony for serious statement and so miss the underlying meaning altogether. In other words, verbal irony depends on the reader's ability to infer meaning that an author implies, rather than directly expresses. For this reason, it flatters the reader's intelligence, implying an accord with the author and superiority to readers or other characters who can perceive only the literal meaning or superficial tone. Thus, irony requires subtle reading comprehension and is always in danger of being misconstrued, and thereby of shocking or offending a naïve audience.

Sometimes the term sarcasm, the taunting use of apparent approval or praise for actual disapproval or dispraise, is mistakenly used as synonymous with verbal irony. The distinctions are that sarcasm is simpler and more crude; in dialogue, it is often signaled by vocal inflection. For example, someone might react to the news that the car is out of gas with the sarcastic retort, "Great! Just what we needed." In another example, Amanda Wingfield, the controlling mother in Tennessee Williams's play The Glass Menagerie, demands to know of her adult son where he has been going at night. Tom, an aspiring writer who feels trapped by having to work in a warehouse *gap between appearance + reality* (handwritten annotation, top)

to support his mother and sister, has been escaping to bars and movies in his free time. When Amanda calls his explanation that he goes to the movies "a lie," Tom reacts with bitter sarcasm:

> I'm going to opium dens, dens of vice and criminals' hangouts, Mother. I've joined the Hogan Gang, I'm a hired assassin, I carry a tommy gun in a violin case! . . . They call me Killer, Killer Wing-field, I'm leading a double-life, a simple, honest warehouse worker by day, by night a dynamic *czar* of the *underworld*, Mother.

Tom's sarcasm is signaled by the exaggerated details, clichés of B-movie gangster plots, which mock Amanda's groundless charges, and by the italicized words that emphasize his frustration and outrage.

Structural irony refers to an implication of alternate or reversed meaning that pervades a work. A major technique for sustaining structural irony is the use of a naïve protagonist or **unreliable narrator who continually interprets events and intentions in ways that the author signals are mistaken**. For example, Voltaire's Candide, despite several experiences of horrendous suffering and corruption, persists in his conviction that "everything is for the best in this best of all possible worlds." Huckleberry Finn, Mark Twain's boy narrator, believes at first that the rascally King and Duke are the brave and erudite noblemen they claim to be, despite signs of their shady past and specious learning. Other narrators may be unreliable not because they are gullible but because they are mentally incapacitated. The narrator of Edgar Allan Poe's short story "The Tell-Tale Heart" is paranoid and hallucinatory. He claims that his preternaturally acute senses and clear motives for murdering an old man—the victim has regarded him with a filmy and thus, he asserts, malevolent eye—are proofs that he is "not mad." A reader who accepts this self-defense at face value is missing the story's well-sustained structural irony.

Another means of creating structural irony is to relate the same events from the perspectives of different narrators. That is a favorite technique of William Faulkner, who uses it to brilliant effect in *The Sound and the Fury*. The novel's narration shifts between two different time periods and among three sons from the same dysfunctional southern family. The ironic contrasts in perception are made more complex because each of the narrators is in some way unreliable: the first is mentally retarded and describes characters and events with a stream-of-consciousness simplicity and literalness, and perceives time sequence in a kaleidoscope of shifting referents; the second is suicidally depressed and is speaking on the day—eighteen years before the events narrated by his afflicted brother—that he drowns himself; and the third narrator, speaking in the same time period as the first, is a sadistic egotist consumed with rage and scorn. The book concludes

(handwritten marginal annotations:)
modest proposal
gap between things appear is about character, NO LIE
may limited things appear is about character
HUCK FINN,
What Maisie Knew
product peoples minds
structure: mental, culture
permanant reason to read reality wrong

▼

with an omniscient third-person narrator who focuses on the perspective of the kind and resourceful black servants who try their best to hold the family together. The challenges and pleasures for the reader are to make sense of what Faulkner called in an appendix the "jigsaw puzzle" of needs, motives, and perceived half-truths.

Dramatic irony occurs when the audience is privy to knowledge that one or more of the characters lacks. The technique may be used for comic or tragic effects. In *Twelfth Night* Shakespeare lets us in from the first scene on the secret that Viola is disguised as a boy and that she is smitten with the duke whom she is serving as page. We can therefore enjoy the humorous dramatic ironies that result when the Countess Olivia, the object of the duke's courtship, falls in love with the charming messenger. In Homer's *Odyssey*, the long-absent Odysseus's disguise as a beggar provides poignant dramatic irony as he encounters various beloved family members and hated rivals but, for the sake of his intended revenge, must refrain from revealing his true identity. Again, the audience is flattered by being allowed to share in the omniscient point of view often reserved for the author.

When dramatic irony occurs in tragedies, it is called **tragic irony**. The audience knows from the opening scene of *Othello*, for example, that the malevolent Iago is plotting the demise of the noble general whom he pretends to serve faithfully, and that his epithet, "honest Iago," is entirely ironic. In *Oedipus Rex*, Oedipus seeks to cleanse his kingdom by finding the murderer of King Laius, only to discover that the culprit is himself, and that the king was his father and the widowed queen, whom he has married, his own mother. In *Romeo and Juliet*, we watch in helpless dismay as the rash Mercutio wholly misconstrues his friend Romeo's motives for refusing to respond to Tybalt's challenge. Unlike Mercutio, we know that Romeo is secretly married to Juliet, the daughter of his family's enemy. Rather than demurring out of fear, he is trying to appease the insolent Tybalt, who has just become his cousin by marriage. Mercutio takes Romeo's courtesy for cowardice, steps into the fray, and inadvertently triggers the series of deaths that devastate both families.

Cosmic irony refers to an implied worldview in which characters are led to embrace false hopes of aid or success, only to be defeated by some larger force, such as God or fate. For instance, Macbeth believes that he is protected by the weird sisters' prophecies, but he is betrayed by their fiendish duplicity, and Arthur Miller's Willy Loman kills himself to secure his family the insurance payment that his suicide will, in fact, make invalid. Shakespeare's *King Lear* is a tour de force of cosmic irony, in which several characters congratulate themselves on a triumph or a narrow escape, only to be destroyed shortly afterward. The Earl of Gloucester, stunned by a series of blows that

[handwritten: Greek oedipus, fate, cannot escape, not master of own fate]

have left him blind, in peril of his life, and, he wrongly believes, betrayed by his favorite son, describes cosmic irony in a bitter simile:

> As flies to wanton boys are we to th' gods,
> They kill us for their sport.

By the end of the play, the stage is littered with corpses, and even the loyal, compassionate Cordelia is murdered despite her father's repentance and courageous effort to save her. In Samuel Beckett's ABSURDIST DRAMA *Waiting for Godot*, the cosmic irony is ambiguous, and even the existence of the larger forces and the finality of the defeat are uncertain. Two tramps wait years for a Godot (in a French/English coinage, the name is the diminutive of "god") who may or may not exist. As the play ends, they begin their futile quest anew, in the same place where they may or may not have waited before.

The establishment of complex, even contradictory, attitudes toward experience, and the interpretation of possible motives or outcomes in more than one way, are major sources of literature's richness. Because life itself is full of contradictions and unexpected turns, irony has long had a special appeal to writers and readers alike. The ability to respond to irony in its myriad forms is a sure sign of a reader's astuteness.

[handwritten: Thomas Hardy]

[handwritten: Situational irony: when something works in two different ways. ex Hinkley + bullet proof]

EXERCISES: Irony

I. For each of the following examples:

- Identify the IRONY as VERBAL, STRUCTURAL, DRAMATIC, TRAGIC, or COSMIC.
- Explain why that type of IRONY applies to the example.
- Describe the effects—the impressions and feelings—created by the IRONY.

1. She thinks that even up in heaven
        Her class lies late and snores,
    While poor black cherubs rise at seven
        To do celestial chores.

    —COUNTEE CULLEN, "For a Lady I Know"

    [handwritten: structural]

2. *In Shakespeare's* King Lear, *Edmund, the illegitimate son of the Earl of Gloucester, falsely accuses his brother, Edgar, of plotting their father's death. The gullible Earl, believing his treacherous son, calls Edgar a "villain" and Edmund a "loyal and natural boy." He gives orders to have Edgar killed and promises to transfer Edgar's entire inheritance to Edmund.*

    [handwritten: tragic irony structural irony]

3. [. . .] I knew the language of the floweret;
        "My fragile leaves," it said, "his heart enclose."
    Love long has taken for his amulet
        One perfect rose.

    [handwritten: dramatic irony]

▼

Why is it no one ever sent me yet   5
    One perfect limousine, do you suppose?
Ah no, it's always just my luck to get
    One perfect rose.

                                                    —DOROTHY PARKER, "One Perfect Rose"

4. In Robert Browning's "Porphyria's Lover," the narrator describes his solution
    to the social barriers that separate him from his wealthy lady love: when
    she comes to his lonely chamber, he strangles her with her long yellow
    hair. The poem concludes:

I propped her head up as before,
    Only, this time my shoulder bore
Her head, which droops upon it still:
    The smiling, rosy little head,
So glad it has its utmost will,   5
    That all it scorned at once is fled,
    And I, its love, am gained instead!
Porphyria's love: she guessed not how
    Her darling one wish would be heard.
And thus we sit together now,   10
    And all night long we have not stirred,
    And yet God has not said a word!

5. In Sophocles' Antigone, Creon, the King of Thebes, attempts to uphold
    order in his kingdom by outlawing the burial of any who have rebelled
    against him. Antigone, who is betrothed to Creon's son, Haemon, defies
    the new law in order to give her brother an honorable burial. In sentencing
    her to death, Creon scorns the following warning from the prophet Teire-
    sias that his harsh interpretation of the law has offended the gods:

All men make mistakes, it is only human.
But once the work is done, a man
can turn his back on folly, misfortune too,
if he tries to make amends, however low he's fallen,
and stops his bullnecked ways. Stubbornness   5
brands you for stupidity—pride is a crime.[1]

Creon repents his excessive pride, but too late: Haemon, his only heir, joins
Antigone in death, and Creon's wife, Eurydice, commits suicide in despair
over the loss of her son.

---

1. From *The Three Theban Plays*, trans. Robert Fagles.

6. *In Oscar Wilde's* The Importance of Being Earnest, *the formidable Lady Bracknell cross-examines the young man who wishes to marry her daughter:*

LADY BRACKNELL I have always been of the opinion that a man who desires to get married should know either everything or nothing. Which do you know?

JACK [*after some hesitation*] I know nothing, Lady Bracknell.

LADY BRACKNELL I am pleased to hear it. I do not approve of any- thing that tampers with natural ignorance. Ignorance is like a delicate exotic fruit; touch it and the bloom is gone. *[handwritten: ✓ verbal]*

7. *In Shakespeare's* Henry V, *the night before the battle of Agincourt, the king disguises himself as one of his own officers and visits his troops, attempting to raise their spirits. He assures some soldiers that he is prepared to fight selflessly in support of King Henry's causes:*

Methinks I could not die anywhere so contented as in the king's company.

[handwritten: cosmic irony (doing right, not going to hell)]

8. *In Mark Twain's* Adventures of Huckleberry Finn, *the narrator, a poor Southern boy living in the days before emancipation, has helped a runaway slave to escape. Huck has acted impulsively, out of compassion for the slave, Jim, but he knows that his actions go against the dictates of his society's legal system and customs. He decides to "do the right thing and the clean thing" and return Jim to his owner. After he has written the telltale letter, he starts reminiscing about their long raft trip down the Mississippi and recalls how Jim "would always . . . do everything he could think of for me, and how good he always was." Huck looks at the letter and says: "I was a trembling, because I'd got to decide, forever, betwixt two things, and I knowed it. I studied a minute, sort of holding my breath, and then says to myself: 'All right, then, I'll go to hell'—and tore it up."*

[handwritten: structural irony]

9. *In Shakespeare's* A Midsummer Night's Dream, *the fairy queen, Titania, is given a drug by her mischievous husband, Oberon, the fairy king, that causes her to fall in love with the next creature that she sees. That happens to be the coarse Athenian workman, Nick Bottom, whom Oberon has magically transformed into an ass. Gazing starry-eyed at her hairy new love, the smitten Titania murmurs, "Thou art as wise as thou art beautiful."*

[handwritten: verbal + dramatic; verbal (donkey not smart or beautiful)]

10. My candle burns at both ends;
    It will not last the night;
    But ah, my foes, and oh, my friends—
    It gives a lovely light!

—EDNA ST. VINCENT MILLAY, "First Fig"

11. *In Shakespeare's* Macbeth, Macduff, *the nobleman whose entire family the king has had murdered, challenges Macbeth to a duel. He responds scornfully with the prophecy that three witches have told him: "I bear a charmed life which must not yield / To one of woman born." Macduff responds with the revelation that he was born by Caesarian section:*

> Despair thy charm
> And let the angel whom thou still hast served
> Tell thee, Macduff was from his mother's womb
> Untimely ripped.

12. *Wilkie Collins's* The Woman in White *is a mystery about a woman's subjection to and escape from an abusive husband, told by a succession of narrators. Some, such as an illiterate cook, are limited in their understanding of events; others, like the woman's former fiancé, are biased in their views. The reader must compare the various narratives in order to judge characters' actions and motives, particularly those of the enigmatic Count Fosco, the husband's accomplice. Fosco's own narrative, which comes near the end of the novel, asserts his uprightness.*

> Is my conduct worthy of any serious blame? Most emphatically, No! . . . Judge me by what I might have done. How comparatively innocent! How indirectly virtuous I appear in what I really did!

The reader must measure these claims against the harsh depiction of the Count by such narrators as the woman's devoted sister.

13. *George Orwell's* 1984 *contains an appendix entitled "The Principles of Newspeak," which describes "the official language" invented by the tyrannical Party ruled by Big Brother. Newspeak, the narrator explains, was designed to replace "Oldspeak, or Standard English," in order to promote the "world-view and mental habits proper to the devotees" of the Party.*

> . . . the Newspeak vocabulary was tiny, and new ways of reducing it were constantly being devised. Newspeak, indeed, differed from almost all other languages in that its vocabulary grew smaller instead of larger every year. Each reduction was a gain, since the smaller the area of choice, the smaller the temptation to take thought. Ultimately it was hoped to make articulate speech issue from the larynx without involving the higher brain centers at all. This aim was frankly admitted in the Newspeak word *duckspeak*, meaning "to quack like a duck." Like various other words in the B vocabulary, *duckspeak* was ambivalent in meaning. Provided that

the opinions which were quacked out were orthodox ones, it implied nothing but praise, and when the *Times* referred to one of the orators of the Party as a *doubleplusgood duckspeaker* it was paying a warm and valued compliment.

14. *In Shakespeare's* Othello, *the devious Iago pretends to console Cassio, whose humiliating dismissal from his post as lieutenant Iago has, in fact, engineered. When Cassio laments that he has "lost his reputation," Iago responds:*

Reputation is an idle and most false imposition, oft got without merit and lost without deserving.

15. *In Jonathan Swift's* Gulliver's Travels, *the narrator relates his voyages to several fantastic countries. The first, Lilliput, is inhabited by tiny, fierce creatures who capture Gulliver and force him to serve in their ceaseless wars. When he inadvertently offends them, they accuse him of high treason, and several members of the court want to sentence him to death. Bitter debates follow, resulting in the following decision, which is reported to Gulliver by one of his supporters:*

In three days your Friend the Secretary will be directed to come to your House, and read before you the Articles of Impeachment; and then to signify the great Lenity and Favour of his Majesty and Council, whereby you are only condemned to the loss of your Eyes, which his Majesty doth not question you will gratefully and humbly submit to; and twenty of his Majesty's Surgeons will attend, in order to see the Operation well performed, by discharging very sharp-pointed Arrows into the Balls of your Eyes, as you lie on the Ground.

Extended examples of irony

1. *In William Makepeace Thackeray's* Vanity Fair, *a pretty, poor young woman, Rebecca (Becky) Sharpe, sets out to charm Joseph Sedley, the brother of a rich school friend whom she is visiting. Joseph has just returned to London from India, where he holds a lucrative but isolated post in the East India Company's Civil Service. How does the following passage establish the irony in the narrator's view of the characters and the situation? Pay particular attention to the contrasts between the self-image that each character tries to present and the implications of the underlying actualities:*

Luckily at this time he caught a liver complaint for the cure of which he returned to Europe. . . . On returning to India, and ever after he used to talk of the pleasures of this period of his existence with great enthusiasm and give you to understand that he and Brummel[1] were the leading bucks of the day. But he was as lonely here as in his jungle at Boggley wollah. He scarcely knew a single soul in the metropolis: and were it not for his Doctor and the society of his blue pill and his liver-complaint he must have died of loneliness. He was lazy, peevish, and a *bon-vivant*;[2] the appearance of a lady frightened him beyond measure . . . His bulk caused Joseph much anxious thought and alarm—now and then he would make a desperate attempt to get rid of his superabundant fat, but his indolence and love of good living speedily got the better of these endeavours at reform, and he found himself again at his three meals a day. He never was well dressed: but he took the hugest pains to adorn his big person: and passed many hours daily in that occupation. . . . His toilet-table was covered with as many pomatums and essences[3] as ever were employed by an old beauty: he had tried, in order to give himself a waist, every girth, stay, and waist-band then invented. Like most fat men he *would* have his clothes made too tight and took care they should be of the most brillant colours and youthful cut. When dressed at length in the afternoon he would issue forth to take a drive with nobody in the park: and then would come back in order to dress again and go and dine with nobody at the Piazza Coffee House. He was as vain as a girl: and perhaps his extreme shyness was one of the results of his extreme vanity. If Miss Rebecca can get the better of *him,* and at her first entrance into life, she is a young person of no ordinary cleverness.

The first move showed considerable skill. When she called Sedley a very handsome man, she knew that Amelia would tell her mother, who would probably tell Joseph, or who at any rate would be pleased by the compliment paid to her son. All mothers are. If you had told Sicorax[4] that her son Caliban was as handsome as Apollo,[5] she would have been pleased, witch as she was. Perhaps too Joseph Sedley would overhear the compliment: Rebecca spoke loud enough: and he *did* hear and (thinking in his heart that he was a very fine man) the praise thrilled through every fiber of his big

---

1. George Bryan ("Beau") Brummel (1778–1840), a London man of fashion and a famous dandy.
2. A person who enjoys good food and drink and lives luxuriously (from the French for "living well").
3. Scented ointments and perfumes.
4. A witch in Shakespeare's romance *The Tempest,* the mother of the monster, Caliban.
5. The Greek god of the sun, prophecy, music, medicine, and poetry, known for his extraordinary beauty.

▼

body, and made it tingle with pleasure. Then however came a recoil. "Is the girl making fun of me?" he thought, and straightaway he bounced towards the bell and was for retreating as we have seen, when his father's jokes and his mother's entreaties caused him to pause and stay where he was. He conducted the young lady down to dinner in a dubious and agitated frame of mind—"does she really think I am handsome," thought he, "or is she only making game of me?" We have talked of Joseph Sedley being as vain as a girl—Heaven help us! the girls have only to turn the tables and say of one of their own sex, "She is as vain as a man," and they will have perfect reason. The bearded creatures are quite as eager for praise, quite as finikin[6] over their toilettes, quite as proud of their personal advantages, quite as conscious of their powers of fascination as any coquette in the world.

2. *The following poem by Sharon Olds depicts a typical event in a child's life. What contrast does it present between the view that a mother might be expected to take and the actual perspective she offers? How do the word choice, details,* FIGURATIVE LANGUAGE, *and* POINT OF VIEW *help to establish the narrator's* IRONY?

Rites of Passage

As the guests arrive at my son's party
they gather in the living room—
short men, men in first grade
with smooth jaws and chins.
Hands in pockets, they stand around   5
jostling, jockeying for place, small fights
breaking out and calming. One says to another
How old are you? Six. I'm seven. So?
They eye each other, seeing themselves
tiny in the other's pupils. They clear their   10
throats a lot, a room full of small bankers,
they fold their arms and frown. *I could beat you
up,* a seven says to a six,
the dark cake, round and heavy as a
turret, behind them on the table. My son,   15
freckles like specks of nutmeg on his cheeks,
chest narrow as the balsa keel of a
model boat, long hands
cool and thin as the day they guided him

---

6. Finicky: highly fussy, difficult to please.

▼

out of me, speaks up as a host   20
for the sake of the group.
We could easily kill a two-year-old,
he says in his clear voice. The other
men agree, they clear their throats
like Generals, they relax and get down to   25
playing war, celebrating my son's life.

TROPES DEPENDENT ON CONTRASTING LEVELS OF MEANING

In addition to IRONY, a number of other TROPES depend on contrasts
in levels of meaning: HYPERBOLE, UNDERSTATEMENT, PARADOX,
OXYMORON, LITOTES, PERIPHRASIS, and PUN. Such FIGURES OF THOUGHT
may or may not be IRONIC: the test is whether or not the speaker
intends to imply an underlying meaning that differs from the literal.

► # Hyperbole

Hyperbole (hi-PER-boh-lee, from the Greek word for "to exceed") is
a TROPE in which a point is stated in a way that is greatly exaggerated. The effect of hyperbole is often to imply the intensity of a
speaker's feelings or convictions by putting them in uncompromising
or absolute terms. In this use, it is the opposite of UNDERSTATEMENT.
For example, in John Donne's "The Sun Rising," the speaker
declares of himself and his lover: "She's all states, and all princes,
I, / Nothing else is." The **hyperbolic** pronouncement suggests the
exclusivity and self-assurance of the impassioned lover's perspective.
    Hyperbole may be comic, as in the tall tales of the American
West, or serious, as in cases where the excessive feeling signals an
ominous imbalance. For example, Othello, greeting his new wife
after surviving a perilous storm, says:

> O my soul's joy!
> If after every tempest come such calms,
> May the winds blow till they have wakened death!

Although he means only to show his overwhelming elation and
relief, the hyperbole is also an instance of TRAGIC IRONY, in that it
foreshadows the loss of control that will later lead Othello to act on
his violently overwrought feelings to the point that they do indeed
"waken[ ] death" for his beloved and himself.

Understatement   ◀

Understatement is a form of IRONY in which a point is deliberately expressed as less, in magnitude, value, or importance, than it actually is. For example, in *Romeo and Juliet*, Mercutio dismisses the fatal wound he has just received as "a scratch." He elaborates on the figure with a second understatement: "Marry, 'tis enough." The effect is to create a sort of double take, with the force of the implied meaning—here, that Mercutio is well aware that he has suffered a death blow—intensified by the restraint with which it is expressed. In this sense, the TROPE is the opposite of HYPERBOLE, in which an attitude or feeling is greatly exaggerated.

Understatement is a favorite device of Old English poetry, in which the enormous odds against the hero or the desperate conditions of everyday life are downplayed in order to achieve a grim irony. (See also LITOTES.) For example, one of the historic battles described in the epic *Beowulf* ends with the description of the funeral pyre for the slain warriors: "Fire swallowed them—greediest of spirits—all of those whom war had taken away from both peoples: their strength had departed."[1] The euphemism of the verb "taken away" for "killed," and the understatement of the final clause—of course "strength" is obliterated by death—suggest the devastating destruction that war has wrought upon the once stalwart warriors. It also serves to underline the unspoken courage with which they have faced the harsh odds against their survival.

Understatement may also be used for comic or satiric effect. For example, Jonathan Swift's ESSAY describing a grotesque plan for alleviating starvation in his native Ireland by using the babies of the poor as food has the seemingly innocuous title "A Modest Proposal."

In more recent times, such writers as Ernest Hemingway and Franz Kafka have made highly effective use of understatement. For example, Hemingway's *The Sun Also Rises* ends with a DIALOGUE between the PROTAGONIST/NARRATOR, Jake Barnes, and Brett Ashley, the promiscuous femme fatale. Jake, who has been left impotent by a war wound, has been futilely in love with Brett for years. At this point, he has just rescued her after her latest disastrous affair and gotten steadily drunker as he has listened to her reminiscences of it. Brett turns to him with one of the flirtatious appeals with which she has tormented him throughout the novel: "Oh, Jake . . . we could have had such a damned good time together." Rather than vent his frustration and anger directly, Jake undercuts her self-serving bathos with a sardonic understatement: "Isn't it pretty to think so?"

---

1. Trans. Talbot Donaldson.

In Kafka's "The Metamorphosis," the PROTAGONIST, Gregor Samsa, a mild-mannered traveling salesman, awakes one morning to discover that he has been turned into a giant insect. Rather than react with the horror and revulsion that such a transformation would be expected to evoke, or even question why it has happened, Gregor complains about the overcast weather. The only anxiety that he expresses is over how to get out of bed. He is on his back and so, like any beetle, cannot turn over, and he is afraid of beinig late for work. The surface calm doubles the shock for the reader and also, perhaps, suggests the philosophical-psychological reasons that so lowly and self-effacing a man might have been subjected to such a horrific transformation. The OMNISCIENT NARRATOR never reveals the reason for Gregor's metamorphosis, however, adding to the shock effect created by the understated TONE.

Paradox

Paradox is a TROPE (TRŌPE) in which a statement that appears on the surface to be contradictory or impossible turns out to express an often striking truth. For example, the **paradoxical** slogan of the Bauhaus School of art and architecture, "Less is more," suggests that spareness and selectivity are more important in achieving aesthetic beauty than expansiveness and inclusiveness. To take another example, John Donne's sonnet "Batter my heart, three-personed God" expresses the speaker's yearning to be forced violently into the pious faith that he feels incapable of attaining on his own. The poem ends with a startling vision of God as a masterful seducer, to whom the speaker pleads: "Take me to you, imprison me, for I / Except You enthrall me, never shall be free, / Nor ever chaste, except You ravish me." In other words, the paradox implies, only in total servitude to the power of the deity can the worshipper achieve genuine autonomy.

Paradox is used to express servitude of a different sort in Shakespeare's *Antony and Cleopatra*, when the usually cynical Enobarbus describes the overpowering charisma of Cleopatra:

> Other women cloy
> The appetites they feed, but she makes hungry
> Where most she satisfies.

The soldier is explaining his commanding general Antony's enthrall-ment by the Egyptian temptress: her seductive powers, rather than jading those who succumb to them, become more addictive with every experience. The implications of the paradox are that even the misogynistic Enobarbus is smitten by Cleopatra's erotic attractions, and that Antony will never break the "strong Egyptian fetters" that keep him from fulfilling his duties to Rome.

Oxymoron

An **oxymoron** (ox-ih-MOR-on) is a compressed PARADOX that closely links two seemingly contrary elements in a way that, on further consideration, turns out to make good sense. Common examples of the TROPE are "bittersweet," "a living death," and "passive aggressive." As with paradox, the effect is to suggest a subtle truth—in the last expression, for example, that refusal to take action can be a means of asserting one's will. The Greek roots of the word are themselves an oxymoron: "sharp" and "dull or foolish"—in other words, "pointedly foolish." Similarly, the **oxymoronic** etymology of "sophomore" means "wise" and "foolish," a reference to the young scholar's shortsighted conviction that he or she knows all.

Often in literature an oxymoron is a sign of a speaker's conflicted feelings. For example, when Juliet discovers that her new husband has just slain her cousin Tybalt, she exclaims: "O serpent heart, hid with a flowering face!   / Beautiful tyrant! fiend angelical!" Juliet is outraged at the seeming rift between Romeo's physical beauty and the moral corruption that she thinks is revealed by his violent act.

Oxymorons can also create humor by exposing a speaker's befuddlement. In Shakespeare's *A Midsummer Night's Dream*, for example, Duke Theseus mocks the ridiculous description of the play that some plodding Athenian workmen propose to present to his court: "Merry and tragical? Tedious and brief? / That is hot ice and wondrous strange snow. / How shall we find the concord of this discord?" The clever nobleman is signaling his delight at the absurd contradictions by describing them with equally silly oxymorons.

Litotes

Litotes (LY-toh-teez, from the Greek word for "simple" or "plain") is a FIGURE OF THOUGHT in which a point is affirmed by negating its opposite. It is a special form of UNDERSTATEMENT, where the surface denial serves, through ironic contrast, to reinforce the underlying assertion. Common examples are: "He's no fool," which implies "He is wise," and "not uncommon," which means "frequent." Litotes occurs frequently in Old English poetry, where the effect is to suggest the stoic outlook adapted toward the perilous way of life depicted. For example, the account of the noble Beowulf's fatal last battle against the dragon uses litotes to describe his incipient death: "That was no pleasant journey, not one on which the famous son of Ecgtheow would wish to leave his land."[2] The litotes, "no pleasant journey," suggests that even this supreme hero feels an all too human anguish over leaving everything that he knows and loves.

Periphrasis

Periphrasis (peh-RIF-rah-sis) is a FIGURE OF THOUGHT in which a point is stated by deliberate circumlocution, rather than directly. One prominent use of periphrasis is in euphemisms, such as "passed away" for "died" and "in his cups" for "drunk." There the aim is to cushion the painful or embarrassing effect of the explicit term. Periphrasis also occurs in the kennings (descriptive phrases that substitute for ordinary words) characteristic of Old English poetry, such as "whale-road" for "sea" and "sword-hate" for warfare. In this case, the **periphrastic** term gives the narration greater variety by avoiding the repetition of common words and makes the concept more vivid by turning it into a virtual metaphor.

Periphrasis can be seen as strained and artificial if carried to excess, a charge that William Wordsworth made against its frequent use in eighteenth-century poetry. It can also signal a deliberate attempt to avoid unpleasant truths, a frequent device of politicians, as in such terms as "ethnic cleansing," for "genocide." George Orwell inveighs against such "consciously dishonest" abuse of diction in his essay, "Politics and the English Language."

A complex use of periphrasis is King Claudius's expedient description, in *Hamlet*, of his controversial marriage to his former sister-in-law. Not only has the wedding occurred with unseemly haste, but in the eyes of the Elizabethans such a match was considered incestuous. In alluding to this event, Claudius resorts in his first public audience to periphrasis. He refers to Gertrude not as his bride but as "th' imperial jointress to this warlike state"—a widow whose inherited property ("jointure"), he claims, is the state of Denmark itself. The sly implication of this periphrasis is that the state

2. Trans. Talbot Donaldson.

can now be shared with Gertrude's new husband and so assure the stability of the succession. The full extent of Claudius's political savvy and corruption become clear only later, when we learn that he has not only succeeded but also murdered his brother in order to procure both his throne and his queen.

Pun

A **pun** is a FIGURE OF THOUGHT that plays on words that have the same sound (homonyms), or closely similar sounds, but have sharply contrasted meanings. The usual effect is a witty or humorous double meaning. For example, Shakespeare was fond of punning on "Will," which was not only his nickname, but in his day meant "desire," especially "carnal desire"; see his Sonnets 135 and 136. A more serious example occurs in *Hamlet*, when the prince answers his despised uncle's public inquiry about his continued melancholy— "How is it that the clouds still hang on you?" with a pun: "Not so, my lord. I am too much in the sun." The retort is a reminder to the listening court and to Claudius, who has succeeded Hamlet's father on the throne, that the prince both dislikes this light of royal favor being shone on him ("sun") and that he feels too strongly his father's loss (as his "son") to celebrate Claudius's ascension. The pun is both ingenious and ominous. It announces the prince's instinctive loathing for the man whom he will soon discover has murdered his father, and it suggests the roundabout, intellectual nature of Hamlet's weapon of choice, "words, words, words."

Puns were especially popular in Renaissance and metaphysical literature; they have also been used extensively by such modern writers as James Joyce, Samuel Beckett, and Tom Stoppard. In fact, Beckett suggests their supreme importance in his work by having his title character in the novel *Murphy* (1952) announce: "In the beginning was the pun," an ALLUSION to the first words of the Gospel of John: "In the beginning was the word." Although the usual tone of puns is humorous, they can also be used with serious intent. For example, Juliet, in agony over the possibility that Romeo has died, turns to the Nurse for the dreaded confirmation: "I am not I, if there be such an 'Ay' / Or those eyes shut that makes thee answer 'Ay.'" The triple level pun ("I" / "Ay" / "eye") expresses Juliet's despairing claim that her very identity would be destroyed if an affirmative answer confirms that her new husband's eyes will never open again. To take another example, in Joyce's last novel, *Finnegans Wake* (1939), the ambiguities of the writer's perception of human experience are given form through elaborate, often multilingual puns. Even the title is a play on words, in the dual meanings of "wake," the peculiarly Irish celebration/vigil for the newly deceased, and also "to awaken."

A special form of the pun is the **equivoque** (EK-wi-vohke), in which a word or phrase that has disparate meanings is used in a way that makes each meaning equally relevant. The term is French, derived from the Latin words for "equal" and "voice"—the adjective in English is "**equivocal**." For example, in Sylvia Plath's bitter poem "Daddy," addressed to her late father, the narrator says that an old photo shows "a cleft in your chin instead of your foot, / But no less a devil for that." The equivoque expresses both the literal look of the man's dimpled ("cleft") chin, and the narrator's condemnatory metaphor of him as a demon, with a "cleft" hoof. A more elaborate example is the warning of the self-important old courtier, Polonius, to his daughter Ophelia that Hamlet is an unscrupulous seducer, whose "tenders" [offers] of affection must not be believed: "Think yourself a baby / That you have ta'en these tenders [legal currency] for true pay / Which are not sterling. Tender [conduct] yourself more dearly, / Or . . . you'll tender me [present me with; or expose me as] a fool" [in the first meaning, a baby, for which "fool" was a common Elizabethan endearment; in the second, that such an illegitimate grandchild would subject Polonius to public ridicule]. The elaborate equivoque suggests both the pleasure that the old courtier takes in displaying his wit and the relentlessness of his onslaught on his vulnerable daughter's sensibilities.

EXERCISE: Tropes Dependent on Contrasting Levels of Meaning

For each of the following passages:

- Name the TROPE—HYPERBOLE, UNDERSTATEMENT, PARADOX, OXYMORON, LITOTES, PERIPHRASIS, or PUN. *Note:* Some passages may exemplify more than one form.
- Explain why that term applies.
- Describe the effects—the impressions and feelings—created by the contrasts in levels of meaning.

1. *The following dialogue takes place between Henry V and Catherine, the French princess he is courting, whose grasp of English is uncertain:*

    KING HENRY   Do you like me, Kate?
    CATHERINE   Pardonnez-moi, I cannot tell what is "like me."
    KING HENRY   An angel is like you, Kate, and you are like an angel.
    —WILLIAM SHAKESPEARE, *Henry V*

▼

2. It is in giving that we receive; *paradox*
    It is in pardoning that we are pardoned.
    —Prayer of St. Francis of Assisi

3. The stars are not wanted now: put out every one; *hyperbole* ?
    Pack up the moon and dismantle the sun;
    Pour away the ocean and sweep up the wood;
    For nothing now can ever come to any good.
    —W. H. AUDEN, "Funeral Blues"

4. *On hearing the report of his daughter's elopement with Othello, Brabantio,*
    who is prejudiced against Moors, says:
    This accident is not unlike my dream. *litotes?*
    Belief of it oppresses me already.
    —WILLIAM SHAKESPEARE, *Othello*

5. *Hamlet, having mistakenly killed an interfering old courtier in the act of*
    spying for the king, addresses the body:
    understatement Take thy fortune.
    Thou find'st to be too busy is some danger.
    —WILLIAM SHAKESPEARE, *Hamlet*

6. Success is counted sweetest *paradox*
    By those who ne'er succeed.
    —EMILY DICKINSON, "Success is counted sweetest"

7. *Romeo reacts to the news that, for the crime of slaying Tybalt, he has been*
    banished from Verona, where his new wife, Juliet, resides:
    There is no world without Verona walls, *hyperbole*
    But purgatory, torture, hell itself.
    —WILLIAM SHAKESPEARE, *Romeo and Juliet*

8. you fit into me *periphrasis* ?
    like a hook into an eye

    a fish hook
    an open eye
    —MARGARET ATWOOD, "You Fit Into Me"

9. *Romeo, dejected by his unrequited infatuation for Rosaline, gives this*
    description of love:
    Feather of lead, bright smoke, cold fire, sick health,
    Still-waking sleep, that is not what it is!
    litotes —WILLIAM SHAKESPEARE, *Romeo and Juliet*

▼

10. Beneath those rugged elms, that yew tree's shade,
      Where heaves the turf in many a moldering heap,
   Each in his narrow cell forever laid,
      The rude[1] forefathers of the hamlet sleep.
                    —THOMAS GRAY, "Elegy Written in a Country Churchyard"

FIGURES OF SPEECH (SCHEMES)

Figures of speech, also called **schemes**, depend upon a change in the standard order or usual SYNTAX of words to create special effects. The term "figures of speech" is sometimes used to refer to the much broader category of TROPES, which depend on changes not in the order or SYNTAX but in the standard meanings of words. More specifically, however, it describes a smaller category of rhetorical figures, including APOSTROPHE, RHETORICAL QUESTION, ANAPHORA, ANTITHESIS, and CHIASMUS.

Apostrophe

An **apostrophe** (a-POS-troh-fee) is an address to a dead or absent person or to an inanimate object or abstract concept. The aim is not, of course, to evoke a response—a logical impossibility—but to elevate the style or to give emotional intensity to the address. For example, Wordsworth's sonnet, "London, 1802," begins with an apostrophe to the narrator's long-dead predecessor, the seventeenth-century poet John Milton: "Milton! thou shouldst be living at this hour: / England hath need of thee." In Shakespeare's *Romeo and Juliet*, the young heroine, awaiting the consummation of her marriage with Romeo, **apostrophizes** a personification of night to guide her through the thrilling and intimidating experience: "Come, civil night, / Thou sober-suited matron all in black, / And learn me how to lose a winning match, / Played for a pair of stainless maiden-hoods." In *A Midsummer Night's Dream*, Shakespeare makes fun of the usual serious use of apostrophe in his absurd play-within-the-play, "Pyramus and Thisbe." The dim-witted Athenian workmen who perform it have a stolidly literal-minded conception of the stage set, and enlist members of their company to represent the Wall that

---

[1]Rustic.

separates the longing lovers and the Moon that shines on their encounter. In one hilarious moment, the vainglorious Bottom, playing Pyramus, pleads: "Thou wall, O wall, O sweet and lovely wall, / Show me thy chink, to blink through with mine eyne." In contrast to the usual unresponsiveness from an inanimate entity that is **apostrophized**, the Wall complies by "*hold[ing] up his fingers.*"

A special form of apostrophe is the **invocation**, in which the poet addresses an appeal to a muse or a god to inspire the creative endeavor. Such epic poems as Homer's *Odyssey* begin with an invocation: "Sing in me, Muse, and through me tell the story / of that man skilled in all ways of contending."[1]

Rhetorical Question

A **rhetorical question** is a FIGURE OF SPEECH in which a question is posed not to solicit a reply but to emphasize a foregone or clearly implied conclusion. The goal is to create a stronger effect than might be achieved by a direct assertion. An everyday example is: "Can you imagine that?" The point is to stress that a surprising or shocking thing has in fact happened. A less courteous example from ordinary conversation—"Are you crazy?" is meant to imply that the person addressed is behaving irrationally. Examples abound in literature. In Wilfred Owen's "Futility," the narrator, contemplating the body of a young soldier who has been killed in the First World War, asks the heart-wrenching rhetorical question: "Was it for this the clay grew tall?" William Blake's "Holy Thursday (II)" is a blistering denouncement of the suffering imposed on poor children in the charity schools of eighteenth-century England. The narrator expresses his outrage in a series of rhetorical questions:

> Is this a holy thing to see
> In a rich and fruitful land,
> Babes reduced to misery,
> Fed with cold and usurous hand?
>
> Is that trembling cry a song?
> Can it be a song of joy?
> And so many children poor?

1. Trans. Robert Fitzgerald (New York: Farrar, Straus and Giroux, 1998), p. 1.

Anaphora

Anaphora (a-NAF-or-ah, from the Greek word for "repetition") is the intentional repetition of words or phrases at the beginning of successive lines, stanzas, sentences, or paragraphs. It is used frequently in both poetry and prose to create emphasis, though the effect differs with the context. Anaphora occurs often in both the Old and New Testaments; a prominent example is the series of Beatitudes ("blessings" promised the faithful) from Jesus' Sermon on the Mount, all of which begin with the phrase "blessed are the . . . ": "Blessed are the merciful, for they shall obtain mercy, / Blessed are the pure in heart, for they shall see God" (Matthew 5.7–8). African American spirituals, inspired by biblical sources, often use anaphora, as in "Go Down, Moses," with its poignant refrain, "Let my people go." Walt Whitman's "Song of Myself" is replete with anaphora. One example is the narrator's response to a child's question—"What is the grass?"—which he answers with a series of whimsical propositions, all of which contain the phrase "I guess": "I guess it must be the flag of my disposition, out of hopeful green stuff woven. / Or I guess it is the handkerchief of the Lord." The effect is a soothing, rhythmic harmony. In contrast, in "The Charge of the Light Brigade," Tennyson uses anaphora to suggest the speed and tension of a fatal battle: "Cannon to right of them, / Cannon to left of them, / Cannon in front of them / Volleyed and thundered."

Antithesis

Antithesis (an-TITH-eh-sis, from the Greek word for "opposition") is a figure of speech in which words or phrases that are parallel in order and syntax express opposite or contrasting meanings. The long opening sentence of Charles Dickens's *A Tale of Two Cities* provides a famous series of **antitheses**: "It was the best of times, it was the worst of times, it was the age of wisdom, it was the age of foolishness, it was the epoch of belief, it was the epoch of incredulity, it was the season of Light, it was the season of Darkness. . . . " Antithesis was a favorite device of eighteenth-century poets, of whom Alexander Pope is the acknowledged master. In the opening stanza of his mock epic, "The Rape of the Lock," for example, the narrator claims as his antithetical subject "What mighty contests rise from trivial things," and follows that tongue-in-cheek assertion with another antithesis: "Slight is the subject, but not so the praise."

William Blake makes a quite different use of the figure of speech in the opening stanza of his moralistic fable, "A Poison Tree":

> I was angry with my friend:
> I told my wrath, my wrath did end.
> I was angry with my foe:
> I told it not, my wrath did grow.

Here the antitheses suggest not Pope's mock grandiosity but the dire effects of repressing rage.

Chiasmus

Chiasmus (ky-AZ-mus, from the Greek word for "criss-cross," a designation based on the Greek letter "chi," written X) is a FIGURE OF SPEECH in which two successive phrases or clauses are parallel in syntax, but reverse the order of the analogous words. Robert Frost's "The Gift Outright," for example, begins with the **chiastic** line: "The land was ours before we were the land's." The pattern of noun, verb, possessive pronoun of the first clause becomes that of pronoun, verb, possessive noun in the second; the figure suggests the connection between Americans' colonization of their new country and the need to prove their claim to it by "the gift outright" of fervent acts of patriotism. In Samuel Taylor Coleridge's "The Rime of the Ancient Mariner," the following chiasmus occurs: "The Sun came up upon the left, / Out of the sea came he!" The word order of the first clause—noun, verb, prepositional phrase—is inverted in the second clause. Here, the effect is to suggest a sense of the eerie setting and fatalistic course of the sailors' voyage. Lord Byron makes quite different use of the technique in his satire *Don Juan*, when he describes his young hero's seduction by an older married woman in a wickedly funny chiasmus: "Pleasure's a sin, and sometimes sin's a pleasure."

EXERCISE: Figures of Speech (Schemes)

For each of the following passages:

- Identify the FIGURE OF SPEECH: APOSTROPHE, RHETORICAL QUESTION, ANAPHORA, ANTITHESIS, or CHIASMUS. *Note:* Some passages may contain more than one *figure of speech.*
- Explain why that term applies.
- Describe the effects—the impressions and feelings—created by the FIGURE OF SPEECH.

1. Bring me my Bow of burning gold:
    Bring me my Arrows of desire:
    Bring me my Spear: O clouds unfold!
    Bring me my Chariot of fire!

    —WILLIAM BLAKE, "And Did Those Feet"

    [handwritten: anaphora]

2. Bright star, would I were steadfast as thou art—

    —JOHN KEATS, "Bright Star"

    [handwritten: Apostrophe]

3. *In Shakespeare's* Hamlet, *Laertes returns from France to discover that his beloved sister, Ophelia, has gone mad with grief over the murder of their father. As he watches her insane antics, he utters the following cry:*

    Do you see this, O God?

    [handwritten: Apostrophe / rhetorical question / Apostrophe]

4. Much Madness is divinest Sense—
    To a discerning Eye—
    Much Sense—the starkest Madness—

    —EMILY DICKINSON, "Much Madness is divinest Sense"

    [handwritten: chiasmus]

5. I have a dream that one day this nation will rise up and live out the true meaning of its creed: 'We hold these truths to be self-evident: that all men are created equal.' I have a dream that one day on the red hills of Georgia the sons of former slaves and the sons of former slave owners will be able to sit down together at a table of brotherhood. . . . I have a dream that my four children will one day live in a nation where they will not be judged by the color of their skin but by the content of their character.

    —MARTIN LUTHER KING, JR., Speech delivered at the Lincoln Memorial, August 28, 1963

    [handwritten: Anaphora]

Apostrophe

6. O wild West Wind, thou breath of Autumn's being,
   Thou, from whose unseen presence the leaves dead
   Are driven, like ghosts from an enchanter fleeing . . .
   —PERCY BYSSHE SHELLEY, "Ode to the West Wind"

7. A honey tongue, a heart of gall,   *antithesis*
   Is fancy's spring, but sorrow's fall.
   —SIR WALTER RALEGH, "The Nymph's Reply to the Shepherd"

8. *In James Joyce's "Counterparts," an imperious boss confronts an employee
   who denies knowing the whereabouts of some missing papers.*

   "You—know—nothing. Of course you know nothing," said Mr.
   Alleyne. "Tell me," he added, glancing first for approval to the lady
   beside him, "do you take me for a fool? Do you think me an utter
   fool?"   *rhetorical question*

9. I love thee freely, as men strive for Right;   *Anaphora*
   I love thee purely, as they turn from Praise.
   —ELIZABETH BARRETT BROWNING, "How do I love thee?"

10. *In the following line from Sonnet 129, Shakespeare describes the conflict-
    ing effects of acting on feelings of "lust":*

    A bliss in proof,[1] and proved, a very woe.   *antithesis ?
                                                     chiasmus?*

    chiasmus

    _____
    1. As experienced.

Rhetorical Strategies

Rhetorical strategy is a loose term for techniques that help to shape or enhance a literary work. Some rhetorical strategies involve DICTION, the relative level of abstraction and formality of the word choice. Others, such as ALLUSION and ANALOGY, describe a reference to some element outside of the text itself. Some rhetorical strategies concern a conceptual pattern that influences a work's TONE—for example, its IMAGERY, SYMBOLISM, and ATMOSPHERE. Still others, such as the REPETITION of ideas and the SELECTION AND ORDER OF DETAILS, describe aspects of the work's content and organization. Finally, some works use an EPIPHANY, a sudden insight or realization, as a means of characterizing the PROTAGONIST and of providing climactic moments of revelation.

▶

Diction

Diction (from the Latin word for "to say") denotes the word choice and phrasing in a literary work. Diction may be described in terms of various qualities, such as the degree to which it is formal or collo-quial, abstract or concrete, LITERAL or FIGURATIVE, or whether it is derived largely from Latin or from Anglo-Saxon. For example, the following passage from *Rambler* No. 5, an essay by the eighteenth-century man of letters Samuel Johnson, describes the unwarranted optimism that each new springtime evoked in an acquaintance. It is written in **formal**, erudite diction:

> The spring, indeed, did often come without any of those effects, but he was always certain that the next would be more propitious; nor was ever convinced that the present spring would fail him before the middle of summer; for he always talked of the spring as coming till it was past, and when it was once past, everyone agreed with him that it was coming.
>
> By long converse with this man, I am, perhaps, brought to feel immoderate pleasure in the contemplation of this delightful season; but I have the satisfaction of finding many, whom it can be no shame to resemble, infected with the same enthusiasm; for there is, I believe, scarce any poet of eminence, who has not left some testimony of his fondness for the flowers, the zephyrs, and the warblers of the spring. Nor has the most luxuriant imagina-tion been able to describe the serenity and happiness of the

golden age, otherwise than by gaining a perpetual spring, as the highest reward of uncorrupted innocence.

The Latinate vocabulary ("propitious" rather than the Anglo-Saxon "lucky," "converse" instead of the Anglo-Saxon "talk," and the sonorous phrase "luxuriant imagination"); lengthy COMPLEX SENTENCES, full of subordinate clauses; and PERIPHRASIS ("zephyrs" and "warblers" rather than the more straightforward "warm winds" and "songbirds") are characteristic of formal diction. Johnson concludes by urging his younger readers, to whom he "dedicate[s] this vernal speculation"—more LATINATE PERIPHRASIS—to see the season in FIGURATIVE TERMS, as a METAPHOR for the "spring of life" and to use it to acquire "a love of innocent pleasures" and "an ardor for useful knowledge," which he calls the "vernal flowers" that are "only intended by nature as the preparation for autumnal fruits." The formal, assured diction creates an air of authority appropriate to the moralist who is the implied writer of the essay.

In contrast, the American novelist and short story writer Ernest Hemingway made a point of writing in **colloquial** diction. The following description of a trip to Spain is from his novel *The Sun Also Rises* (1925):

> The bus climbed steadily up the road. The country was barren and rocks stuck up through the clay. There was no grass beside the road. Looking back we could see the country spread out below. Far back the fields were squares of green and brown on the hillsides. Making the horizon were the brown mountains. They were strangely shaped. As we climbed higher the horizon kept changing. As the bus ground slowly up the road we could see other mountains coming up in the south. Then the road came over the crest, flattened out, and went into a forest. It was a forest of cork trees, and the sun came through the trees in patches, and there were cattle grazing back in the trees. We went through the forest and the road came out and turned along a rise of land, and out ahead of us was a rolling green plain, with dark mountains beyond it. These were not like the brown, heat-baked mountains we had left behind. These were wooded and there were clouds coming down from them. The green plain stretched off.

Several qualities contribute to the colloquial level of the diction: the plain SYNTAX—short, either SIMPLE SENTENCES or COMPOUND SENTENCES made up of clauses linked by "and"; the monosyllabic, Anglo-Saxon vocabulary, with its emphasis on nouns ("rocks stuck up," "squares," "trees"); and the repetition of words ("green," "brown," "mountains") and sentence structures ("These were . . . "). The style creates an impression of candor and objectivity, with a narrator who seems in tight control of his emotions, observant of the landscape but determined not to seem sentimental or effusive.

At times a literary speaker will attempt to sound more erudite than he or she in fact is by using elevated diction that is beyond his understanding. In *Adventures of Huckleberry Finn*, for example, Mark Twain exposes the fraudulent credentials of "the king," a rascal who had at first claimed to Huck that he is descended from French royalty. In the passage below, he is posing as a British clergyman in a scheme to abscond with the fortune left by a man who, he claims, was his brother. In eulogizing the "diseased" (his malapropism for "deceased"), he says how fitting it is for so charitable a person that his "funeral orgies sh'd be public." His fellow con man, "the duke," while equally corrupt, is considerably more learned and is furious at the shallowness of his partner's subterfuge. The duke, however, is posing as a deaf mute, and so he cannot cut off the ignorant oration. Huck, the narrator, describes the scene:

> And so he [the king] went a mooning on and on, liking to hear himself talk, and every little while he fetched in his funeral orgies again, till the duke he couldn't stand it no more; so he writes on a little scrap of paper, "*obsequies*, you old fool," and folds it up and goes to goo-gooing and reaching it over people's heads to him.

The king is not deterred. He misuses the term three more times, and then gives the following explanation:

> "I say orgies, not because it's the common term, because it ain't—obsequies bein' the common term—but because orgies is the right term. Obsequies ain't used in England no more—it's gone out. We say orgies, now, in England. Orgies is better, because it means the thing you're after, more exact. It's a word that's made up out'n the Greek, *orgo*, outside, open, abroad; and the Hebrew *jeesum*, to plant, cover up; hence *inter*. So, you see, funeral orgies is an open er public funeral."

The combination of the contrast between the king's uneducated diction and learned pose, the absurdity of his invented etymology, and his imperturbable effrontery makes for exquisite satire.

A writer's diction may also differ enormously in its relative levels of **abstraction**—that is, the extent to which it deals with general concepts—or of **concreteness**: with physical objects, IMAGERY, and emotive and sensual details. For example, "love," "patriotism," "beauty," and "time" are **abstract** terms, while "lips," "gun," "silky gown," and "shrill cry" are **concrete**. Most literary works contain both abstract and concrete diction, in varying degrees. Often a writer will illustrate an abstract concept with concrete details. For example, in John Keats's "Ode to a Nightingale," the narrator describes with increasingly concrete diction a magical wine that could make him oblivious to life's sufferings:

> O, for a draught of vintage! That hath been
>   Cooled a long age in the deep-delvèd earth,
> Tasting of Flora[1] and the country green,
>   Dance, and Provençal song,[2] and sunburnt mirth!
> O for a beaker full of the warm South,
>   Full of the true, the blushful Hippocrene,[3]
>   With beaded bubbles winking at the brim,
>   And purple-stainèd mouth.

The passage moves from a description of a "vintage" whose taste incorporates such abstractions as "Flora," "the country green," and "dance" to the more specific sensations of the sound of "Provençal song" and the look and feel of "sunburnt mirth." It builds to the concrete details of the "blushful" look of the wine in a glass, its "beaded bubbles winking at the brim," leaving the happy imbiber with "purple-stainèd mouth."

A writer might also imply an abstract concept or theme, which must be inferred from a series of concrete descriptions or images. For example, Christina Rossetti's "Goblin Market," a poem about the dangers of giving way to pleasurable but fatal temptations, gives that THEME concrete form by depicting it as forbidden fruits sold by goblins, who use them to ensnare the souls of innocent maidens. The satanic nature of the "little men" is suggested by the concrete details describing their physical appearance, all features of lowly animals:

> One had a cat's face,
> One whisked a tail,
> One tramped at a rat's pace,
> One crawled like a snail.

The afflicted maiden implies the addictive nature of the goblins' wares as she recalls the temperature, texture, look, and taste of the fruit that she longs to savor again:

---

1. Roman goddess of spring.
2. Of medieval troubadours from southern France.
3. Fountain of the Greek muses.

"What melons icy-cold
Piled on a dish of gold
Too huge for me to hold,
What peaches with a velvet nap,
Pellucid grapes without one seed;
Odorous indeed must be the mead
Whereon they grow, and pure the wave they drink
With lilies at the brink,
And sugar-sweet their sap."

The aptness of a particular level of diction depends partly on
the context in which it is being used—for example, a philosophical
treatise would tend to use words that are formal, often Latinate,
and abstract, while a LYRIC poem would likely be more COLLOQUIAL
and concrete. For those generalizations, too, however, there are
exceptions—for example, Tennyson, a poet whose work is full of
sensuous details and images, also uses abstract diction at times
with great effectiveness. In "Ulysses," he imagines the Greek hero
Odysseus, whom he calls by his Latin name, in old age, frustrated
by inaction and rallying his "mariners" for one last adventure.
Ulysses couches the address in a series of abstract concepts:

Though much is taken, much abides; and though
We are not now that strength which in old days
Moved earth and heaven, that which we are, we are—
One equal temper of heroic hearts,
Made weak by time and fate, but strong in will
To strive, to seek, to find, and not to yield.

The abstractions express both the virtues that the men have brought
to their previous triumphs—"strength" and "heroic hearts"—and the
implacable forces—"time" and "fate"—that Ulysses knows will
inevitably defeat them. Still, he urges that their collective "will"
drive them to continue to "strive . . . and not to yield," so that they
may go out in a moment of glory. While a concrete description of a
specific venture might have exposed the physical limitations and
perhaps the hubris of the old hero, the soaring abstractions elevate
his doomed quest and reflect Ulysses' unflagging valor. A work's diction, then, should reflect the writer's meaning and TONE and suit the
intended audience.

A special kind of formality is created by **poetic diction**, which in
a broad sense means phrasing and vocabulary that are characteristic
of poetry, as distinguished from the informality of everyday speech.
It uses such devices as antiquated words—for example, "lo," "abide,"

and "ere"; poetic contractions, such as "ne'er" for "never," " 'tis" for "it is," and "morn" for "morning"; and an emphasis on FIGURATIVE, rather than LITERAL, language.

In a more limited sense, **poetic diction** refers to the style favored by neoclassical poets of the eighteenth century, such as Alexander Pope and Thomas Gray, who brought its usage to a high art. They believed that the guiding principle for poetic diction was "decorum"—highly formal word choice suitable to a lofty subject and a refined audience. In order to attain that dignified level, they advocated the use of such devices as archaic phraseology, reflecting models in Greek and Roman literature and the poetry of such English predecessors as Edmund Spenser (1552–99) and John Milton (1608–74); a Latinate, rather than Anglo-Saxon, vocabulary; frequent PERSONIFICATION of abstract qualities; and PERIPHRASIS, deliberate circumlocution to avoid what they considered commonplace or vulgar words and expressions. An example of the last device from James Thomson's "Winter" in his long poem *The Seasons* is his PERIPHRASTIC description of sheep as "the bleating kind" and of the grass buried beneath the snow that they seek as "the withered herb." The following lines from Thomas Gray's "Elegy Written in a Country Churchyard" use neoclassical poetic diction:

> Can storied urn[4] or animated[5] bust
>> Back to its mansion call the fleeting breath?
> Can Honor's voice provoke[6] the silent dust,
>> Or Flattery soothe the dull cold ear of Death?
>
> Perhaps in this neglected spot is laid
>> Some heart once pregnant with celestial fire;
> Hands that the rod of empire might have swayed,
>> Or waked to ecstasy the living lyre.
>
> But Knowledge to their eyes her ample page
>> Rich with the spoils of time did ne'er unroll;
> Chill Penury repressed their noble rage,
>> And froze the genial current of the soul.

Typical characteristics are the words derived from Latin, such as "provoke," "celestial," and "repressed"; personifications of abstract moral qualities—"Honor"—and adverse conditions—"chill Penury"; and PERIPHRASIS, for example, "mansion" for the human body and "the living lyre" for the poet in a state of inspiration. Also, the eleva-

---

4. Funeral urn with epitaph.
5. Lifelike.
6. Call forth.

tion of the aspirations and feelings of those buried in the country churchyard—a "heart once pregnant with celestial fire," "hands that the rod of empire might have swayed," people motivated by "noble rage"—is characteristic of the euphemisms and refinements of neoclassical poetic diction.

Poets of the Romantic age (1785–1832), led by William Wordsworth and Samuel Taylor Coleridge, reacted against the poetic diction of the previous period as being too artificial and self-conscious. In Wordsworth's Preface to the second edition of *Lyrical Ballads* (1800), he presented a critical manifesto that advocated that poets choose as their subjects "incidents and situations from common life," and that they write about them in "simple and unelaborated expressions" that represent "a selection of language really used by men." The collection of poems included in *Lyrical Ballads* was meant to illustrate those principles. Although most modern readers would also see in Coleridge and Wordsworth's poems instances of the neoclassical poetic diction of their predecessors that they condemned, their critical principles gave a new sanction to directness, simplicity, and colloquial diction that has exerted a major influence on subsequent poets.

Allusion

An **allusion** (al-LOO-zyun, from the Latin word for "to play with") is a passing reference in a work of literature to another literary or historical work, figure, or event, or to a literary passage. The reference is not explained, so that it can convey the flattering presumption that the reader shares the writer's erudition or inside knowledge. For example, in Andrea Lee's novel *Sarah Phillips* (1984), the narrator describes her Harvard roommate, a chemistry major and "avid lacrosse player" who "adored fresh air and loathed reticence and ambiguity," as having the following surprising predilection: "Margaret, the scientist, had . . . a positively Brontëesque conception of the ideal man." The allusion is to the dark, brooding, enigmatic heroes in the works of Charlotte and Emily Brontë, especially Mr. Rochester in *Jane Eyre* and Heathcliff in *Wuthering Heights*. Only a reader who recognizes the allusion would appreciate the IRONY of the frank, forthright Margaret's preference for men who are far from being either frank or forthright.

The title of William Faulkner's *The Sound and the Fury* (1929) presents a more complex example. It **alludes** to the SOLILOQUY in Shakespeare's *Macbeth* in which the embittered PROTAGONIST dismisses all of life as merely "a tale / Told by an idiot, full of sound and fury, / Signifying nothing." The aptness of the reference becomes evident when the reader discovers that the first part of the novel is told from the perspective of a mentally challenged narrator, who is incapable of intelligible speech. Thus, an allusion can provide a rich network of associations and intensify the effects of a passage.

In other situations, in which the subject is of an inferior stature to the literary or historical source, an allusion may create a sense of IRONIC deflation. T. S. Eliot calls attention to that use of the technique in "The Love Song of J. Alfred Prufrock." The insecure narrator, feeling hopelessly inadequate in polite society, says of his efforts to court women:

> . . . though I have wept and fasted, wept and prayed,
> Though I have seen my head (grown slightly bald) brought in
>   upon a platter,
> I am no prophet—and here's no great matter. . . .

The allusion is to John the Baptist, the prophet in the New Testament who was beheaded after he refused to compromise his moral principles and assent to the advances of the seductress Salome. Prufrock envisions his own severed head, made ludicrous by its balding state, exposed to public scrutiny and his earnest endeavors amounting to "no great matter." Later, Prufrock further denigrates his own worth by alluding to the hero of Shakespeare's *Hamlet*: "No! I am not Prince Hamlet, nor was meant to be." Rather, he claims, he is merely "an attendant lord, . . . deferential, glad to be of use," or even, occasionally, "the Fool," the court jester among the dramatis personae. The comparisons to the heroic figures in the Bible and the Shakespearean tragedy underline Prufrock's sense of pathetic inadequacy.

Some literary works rely heavily on extensive allusions to another source—for example, Tom Stoppard's *Rosencrantz and Guildenstern Are Dead* (1967) provides a running allusion to, and absurdist variation on, aspects of Shakespeare's *Hamlet*; William Faulkner's *Light in August* (1932) contains a sustained allusion to the account of the birth of Jesus in the New Testament, as well as to the iconography (that is, the standard emblematic details) of Renaissance paintings of that story; and John Gardner's NOVELLA *Grendel* (1971) tells the story of Beowulf from the point of view of the first monster that the hero fights, who is in Gardner's version articulate and insightful.

Other allusions may be more obscure, either because they refer to highly specialized areas of knowledge, as is the case with many instances in Eliot's "The Waste Land" and James Joyce's *Ulysses*, or because they describe people and events known to only a small circle of the writer's intimates. For example, the British and American expatriates in Ernest Hemingway's *The Sun Also Rises* (1925) are based on the author's cronies in the Left Bank café society of Paris in the 1920s. Hemingway's biographers have revealed the real-life identities of the characters, including the American humorist, Donald Ogden Stewart, the model for the affable Bill Gorton, and the British novelist Ford Madox Ford, the counterpart of the Englishman Braddocks. In similar fashion, the annotations in a scholarly edition of a work, a source such as a specialized dictionary of mythology, or an anthology of quotations can clarify most allusions.

► # Analogy

An **analogy** (ah-NAL-oh-gee, from the Greek word for "proportionate") is the comparison of a subject to something that is similar to it in order to clarify the subject's nature, purpose, or function. For example, medical science often uses **analogies** to describe bodily processes, such as comparing the liver to a filter to explain its function of removing wastes from the bloodstream. "Shooting an Elephant," George Orwell's autobiographical essay about an incident that occurred when he was a young military policeman in Burma, concerns an agonizing decision about whether to kill an elephant that had gone on a rampage but is now calm. Before delving into the complex moral, political, and emotional ramifications of the situation, the narrator uses an analogy to clarify for his Western audience its simple economic aspect:

> As soon as I saw the elephant I knew with perfect certainty that I ought not to shoot him. It is a serious matter to shoot a working elephant—it is comparable to destroying a huge and costly piece of machinery.

The uncompromising candor of Orwell's analogy prevents any possibility of rationalizing the killing on commercial grounds and so adds weight to the condemnation of his own cowardice toward which the essay will build.

In Joseph Conrad's NOVELLA *Heart of Darkness* (1902), Marlow is about to recount his venture into the "heart" of the Congo as a ship captain in the service of a Belgian trading company. He is speaking to a group of friends, reunited on a yawl moored on the Thames River above London, who have never been to Africa. He broaches his subject with the disconcerting assertion that the peaceful stretch of the Thames on which they are meeting has also been " 'one of the dark places of the earth.' " He explains that statement by drawing a long analogy between his experience in Africa and that of the ancient Romans who first conquered Britain:

"Imagine the feelings of a commander of a fine—what d'ye call 'em—
trireme in the Mediterranean, ordered suddenly to the north; run
overland across the Gauls in a hurry; put in charge of one of these
craft the legionaries . . . used to build, apparently by the hundred, in
a month or two, if we may believe what we read. Imagine him
here—the very end of the world, a sea the colour of lead, a sky the
colour of smoke, a kind of ship about as rigid as a concertina—and
going up this river with stores, or orders, or what you like. Sand-
banks, marshes, forests, savages, precious little fit to eat for a civilised
man, nothing but Thames water to drink. No Falernian wine here,
no going ashore. Here and there a military camp lost in a wilderness
like a needle in a bundle of hay—cold, fog, tempests, disease, exile,
and death—death skulking in the air, in the water, in the bush. They
must have been dying like flies here. Oh yes—he did it. Did it very
well too, no doubt, and without thinking much about it either,
except afterwards to brag of what he had gone through in his time,
perhaps. They were men enough to face the darkness. . . . Or think
of a decent young citizen in a toga—perhaps too much dice, you
know—coming out here in the train of some prefect, or tax-gatherer,
or trader even—to mend his fortunes. Land in a swamp, march
through the woods, and in some inland post feel the savagery. The
utter savagery had closed round him—all that mysterious life of the
wilderness that stirs in the forest, in the jungles, in the hearts of wild
men. There's no initiation either into such mysteries. He has to live
in the midst of the incomprehensible which is also detestable. And it
has a fascination too, that goes to work upon him. The fascination of
the abomination—you know. Imagine the growing regrets, the longing to escape, the powerless disgust, the surrender— the hate."

The analogy serves several purposes: to get the fictional audience for
Marlow's tale, as well as the larger audience of the readers, into the
mindset for understanding the physical and psychological challenges
for so-called "civilized" people of venturing into an utterly primitive
place—"imagine" is the imperative verb that echoes through the
account. Marlow also foreshadows the terror, disorientation, and
corruption that he will discover in the jungle, the human "heart of
darkness" that emerges in such a primal setting. Finally, while he
clearly respects the hypothetical Roman captain who managed in the
midst of all the chaos to do his job and do it "very well too"—a
foreshadowing of Marlow's own competence and courage—he does
not conclude the analogy on a smug note of triumph. Rather, he
warns about the temptations and perils of surrendering to moral and
spiritual darkness—"the fascination of the abomination," which his
encounter with Mr. Kurtz, the "heart" of the story, will depict.

Some SIMILES and METAPHORS are based on analogies between qualities shared by the subject and the thing to which it is compared. Some SUBPLOTS are analogous to aspects of the main plot; for example, in Shakespeare's *King Lear*, the secondary story of the Earl of Gloucester and his sons parallels the main story of Lear and his daughters.

EXERCISES: Allusion, Analogy, and Diction

I. For each of the following passages:
- Identify the ALLUSION or the ANALOGY.
- Explain how that term applies.
- Describe the effects of this RHETORICAL STRATEGY on the meaning and the tone of the passage.

1. *For his fourteenth birthday, the protagonist of Jhumpa Lahiri's* The Namesake, *Gogol Ganguli, whose parents are from India, has received from his father a book of short stories by the Russian writer for whom he was named:*

> At the door [his father] pauses, turns around. "Do you know what Dostoyevsky once said?"
> Gogol shakes his head.
> " 'We all came out of Gogol's overcoat.' "
> "What's that supposed to mean?"
> "It will make sense to you one day. Many happy returns of the day."
> Gogol gets up and shuts the door behind his father, who has the annoying habit of always leaving it partly open. He fastens the lock on the knob for good measure, then wedges the book on a high shelf between two volumes of the Hardy Boys. He settles down again with his lyrics on the bed when something occurs to him. This writer he is named after—Gogol isn't his first name. His first name is Nikolai. Not only does Gogol Ganguli have a pet name turned good name, but a last name turned first name. And so it occurs to him that no one he knows in the world, in Russia or India or America or anywhere, shares his name. Not even the source of his namesake.

2. *This passage from Jonathan Swift's* Gulliver's Travels, *a SATIRE that purports to be an account by one Lemuel Gulliver of his travels, is from the section on Brobdingnag, a country of giants:*

> . . . there suddenly fell such a violent shower of Hail, that I was immediately by the force of it struck to the Ground. And when I was down, the Hail-stones gave me such cruel Bangs all over the Body, as if I had been pelted with Tennis-balls; however I made a shift to creep on all four, and shelter my self by lying flat on my

Face on the Lee-side of a Border of Lemmon Thyme, but so bruised from Head to Foot that I could not go abroad in[1] ten Days.

Neither is this at all to be wondered at, because Nature in that Country observing the same Proportion thro' all her Operations, a Hail-stone is near eighteen hundred times as large as one in EUROPE, which I can assert upon Experience, having been so curious to weigh and measure them.

3. *The narrator of the following passage is recalling an encounter that took place when she was ten years old:*

    . . . when I saw him lift and poise the book and stand in act to hurl it, I instinctively started aside with a cry of alarm: not soon enough, however; the volume was flung, it hit me, and I fell, striking my head against the door and cutting it. The cut bled, the pain was sharp: my terror had passed its climax; other feelings succeeded.

    "Wicked and cruel boy!" I said. "You are like a murderer- -you are like a slave driver—you are like the Roman emperors!" I had read Goldsmith's "History of Rome," and had formed my opinion of Nero, Caligula, &c. Also I had drawn parallels in silence, which I never thought thus to have declared aloud.

    –CHARLOTTE BRONTË, *Jane Eyre*

4. *In this excerpt from Shakespeare's* Henry V, *the Archbishop of Canterbury is trying to persuade the new king that his subjects at home would continue to be obedient and orderly were he to leave England and go to make war on France:*

    For so work the honey-bees,
    Creatures that by a rule in nature teach
    The act of order to a peopled kingdom.
    They have a king,[2] and officers of sorts,
    Where some like magistrates correct at home;   5
    Others like merchants venture trade abroad;
    Others like soldiers, armèd in their stings,
    Make boot upon[3] the summer's velvet buds,
    Which pillage they with merry march bring home
    To the tent royal of their emperor,   10
    Who busied in his majesty surveys
    The singing masons building roofs of gold,
    The civil citizens lading up[4] the honey.

---

1. Leave the house for.
2. The queen bee was thought to be male.
3. Plunder.
4. Weighing.

▼

* * *

    I this infer:
That many things, having full reference   15
To one consent,[5] may work contrariously.[6]
As many arrows, loosèd several ways,
Fly to one mark, as many ways meet in one town,
As many fresh streams meet in one salt sea,
As many lines close in the dial's[7] center   20
So many thousand actions once afoot
End in one purpose, and be all well borne
Without defect. Therefore to France, my liege.
Divide your happy England into four,
Whereof take you one quarter into France,   25
And you withal shall make all Gallia[8] shake.

II. For each of the following passages:
- Identify the level and generality of the DICTION: FORMAL or COLLOQUIAL; ABSTRACT or CONCRETE. Also specify if a passage is written in neoclassical POETIC DICTION. Note that some passages may exemplify more than one kind of DICTION.
- Explain why the term or terms apply.
- Describe the effects of the DICTION on the meaning and TONE.

1. The old lady settled herself comfortably, removing her white cotton gloves and putting them up with her purse on the shelf in front of the back window. The children's mother still had on slacks and still had her head tied up in a green kerchief, but the grandmother had on a navy blue sailor hat with a bunch of white violets on the brim and a navy blue dress with a small white dot in the print. Her collar and cuffs were white organdy trimmed with lace and at her neckline she had pinned a spray of cloth violets containing a sachet. In case of an accident anyone seeing her dead on the highway would know at once that she was a lady.

                        –FLANNERY O'CONNOR, "A Good Man Is Hard to Find"

---

5. United by one purpose.
6. Disparately.
7. Sundial's.
8. France.

2. Ye distant spires, ye antique towers,
       That crown the watery glade,
   Where grateful Science[9] still adores
   Her Henry's[1] holy shade;
   And ye, that from the stately brow   5
   Of Windsor's heights the expanse below
       Of grove, of lawn, of mead[2] survey,
   Whose turf, whose shade, whose flowers among
   Wanders the hoary[3] Thames along
   His silver-winding way.   10

   Ah happy hills, ah pleasing shade,
       Ah fields beloved in vain,
   Where once my careless childhood strayed,
       A stranger yet to pain!
                   –THOMAS GRAY, "Ode on a Distant Prospect of Eton College"

3. The instructor said,
       Go home and write
       a page tonight.
       And let that page come out of you—
       Then, it will be true.   5

   I wonder if it's that simple?
   I am twenty-two, colored, born in Winston-Salem.
   I went to school there, then Durham, then here
   to this college on the hill above Harlem.
   I am the only colored student in my class.   10
   The steps from the hill lead down into Harlem,
   through a park, then I cross St. Nicholas,
   Eighth Avenue, Seventh, and I come to the Y,
   the Harlem Branch Y, where I take the elevator
   up to my room, sit down, and write this page.   15
                   –LANGSTON HUGHES, "Theme for English B"

4. Vanity was the beginning and the end of Sir Walter Elliot's character; vanity of person and of situation. He had been remarkably
   handsome in his youth; and, at fifty-four, was still a very fine man.
   Few women could think more of their personal appearance than he
   did; nor could the valet of any new made lord be more delighted
   with the place he held in society. He considered the blessing of

---

9. Learning.
1. Henry VI, founder of Eton.
2. Meadow.
3. Aged.

beauty as inferior only to the blessing of a baronetcy;[4] and the Sir
Walter Elliot who united these gifts, was the constant object of his
warmest respect and devotion.

His good looks and his rank had one fair claim on his attachment; since to them he must have owed a wife of very superior character to any thing deserved by his own. Lady Elliot had been an
excellent woman, sensible and amiable; whose judgment and conduct, if they might be pardoned the youthful infatuation which made
her Lady Elliot, had never required indulgence afterwards.—She had
humoured, or softened, or concealed his failings, and promoted his
real respectability for seventeen years; and though not the very happi-
est being in the world herself, had found enough in her duties, her
friends, and her children, to attach her to life, and make it no matter
of indifference to her when she was called on to quit them.

–Jane Austen, *Persuasion*

5. Trust thyself: every heart vibrates to that iron string. Accept the
   place the divine Providence has found for you; the society of your
   contemporaries, the connexion of events. Great men have always
   done so and confided themselves childlike to the genius of their
   age, betraying their perception that the Eternal was stirring at their
   heart, working through their hands, predominating in all their
   being. And we are now men, and must accept in the highest mind
   the same transcendent destiny; and not pinched in a corner, not
   cowards fleeing before a revolution, but redeemers and benefactors,
   pious aspirants to be noble clay plastic[5] under the Almighty effort,
   let us advance on Chaos and the Dark.

   –Ralph Waldo Emerson, "Self-Reliance"

6. In the hickory scent
   Among slabs of pork
   Glistening with salt,
   I played Indian
   In a headdress of redbird feathers   5
   & brass buttons
   Off my mother's winter coat.
   Smoke wove
   A thread of fire through meat, into December
   & January. The dead weight   10
   Of the place hung around me,
   Strung up with sweetgrass.   –Yusef Komunyakaa, "The Smokehouse"

---

4. Title below a baron's.
5. Malleable.

Imagery

Imagery is a widely used term that has several distinctive meanings. All, however, refer to the CONCRETE, rather than the ABSTRACT, aspects of a literary work.

In a narrow sense, imagery means a visual description of an object or a scene—an **image** or picture of it, especially one that is particularly detailed and vivid. The opening stanza of Algernon Charles Swinburne's "The Forsaken Garden" fits that definition:

> In a coign[1] of the cliff between lowland and highland,
>   At the sea-down's edge between windward and lee,
> Walled round with rocks as an inland island,
>   The ghost of a garden fronts the sea.
> A girdle of brushwood and thorn encloses
>   The steep square slope of the blossomless bed
> Where the weeds that grew green from the graves of its roses
>   Now lie dead.

Swinburne's details about the location, landmarks, and foliage create a vivid verbal sketch of the "forsaken" spot, an "inland island" formed by a rock wall on the "steep . . . slope" of a cliff. It is so barren that not only the "roses" but even the "weeds" that once lived on the flowers' "graves" have died. Only "brushwood" and "thorn" now grow in the "ghost of a garden."

The broad meaning of imagery, however, includes all of the references to sensory perception that a work contains or evokes, not only in the form of the objects, actions, and scenes depicted in literal descriptions, but also in ALLUSIONS and in the VEHICLES of METAPHORS and SIMILES. Moreover, in this broad sense, the term is not limited to the appeals to sight in a literary work, but also includes descriptions and evocations of sound, touch, taste, smell, temperature, and movement as well.

For example, Li-Young Lee's "Persimmons" uses vivid imagery in this broader sense to describe the narrator's experience of visiting his elderly father, a painter who has gone blind:*

> This year, in the muddy lighting
> of my parents' cellar, I rummage, looking
> for something I lost.
> My father sits on the tired, wooden stairs,

---

1. Corner.
*This excerpt from "Persimmons" is reprinted with the permission of BOA Editions.

black cane between his knees,
hand over hand, gripping the handle.
He's so happy that I've come home.
I ask how his eyes are, a stupid question.
All gone, he answers.

Under some blankets, I find a box.
Inside the box I find three scrolls.
I sit beside him and untie
three paintings by my father:
Hibiscus leaf and a white flower.
Two cats preening.
Two persimmons, so full they want to drop from the cloth.

He raises both hands to touch the cloth,
asks, *Which is this?*

This is persimmons, Father.

Oh, the feel of the wolftail on the silk,
the strength, the tense
precision in the wrist.
I painted them hundreds of times
eyes closed. These I painted blind.
Some things never leave a person:
scent of the hair of one you love,
the texture of persimmons,
in your palm, the ripe weight.

The poet first evokes the image of what the old man looks like, sitting on the worn stairs clutching his cane. He summarizes the son's hopeless question and lets us hear directly the father's candid answer; next he describes the act of untying the Chinese scrolls, and then the CONCRETE details of the painted images: the sight of the hibiscus, the movements of the "cats preening," the look and heft of the ripe persimmons. Then Lee takes us into the perspective of the artist as he relives the kinesthetic experience of creating the paintings, touching the silk canvas with the delicate brush, moving his wrist in controlled, precise strokes. Finally, the poem reveals the startling fact that the father was blind when he painted these last pictures, but, like Beethoven continuing to write symphonies after he had gone deaf, he was able to replicate the perceptions of his physical senses in his imagination. Even now, he can experience the "scent" and "texture" and "weight" of objects to which he once gave visual form.

The term "imagery" is sometimes used to refer to the FIGURATIVE LANGUAGE in a literary work, especially to the VEHICLES of its METAPHORS and SIMILES. That meaning has been extended by such critics as Caroline Spurgeon and Cleanth Brooks to apply to patterns of imagery in Shakespeare's plays, which, they maintain, form a motif that helps to establish the work's ATMOSPHERE or to underline a major THEME. For example, *Romeo and Juliet* contains several images of celestial sources of light which, when considered together, may be seen to suggest both the beauty and the peril of romantic love in the play. To cite a few of the images, the lovers are described in the opening chorus as "star-crossed," that is, doomed by adverse astrological influences. When Romeo, who has just met Juliet and fallen instantly in love with this daughter of his family's bitter enemies, sees her emerge on her balcony, he says: "But soft, what light through yonder window breaks? / It is the east, and Juliet is the sun." He goes on to reject the influence of the moon, the province of Diana, the goddess of chastity, and to praise his beloved's eyes as comparable to "two of the fairest stars in all the heavens." The associations between the heavenly bodies and youthful beauty are clear.

Later, after the lovers have rashly contracted a secret marriage, Juliet unwittingly gives the same images of sun and stars a more ominous turn. Waiting impatiently for Romeo to climb to her chamber so that they can consummate their new marriage, she wishes fancifully that the sun god Phoebus Apollo's "fiery-footed steeds" could be whipped toward sunset by his nimble son Phaeton and so "immediately" bring on "love-performing night." In Greek legend, Phaeton loses control of his father's chariot and must be killed by one of Zeus's lightning bolts in order to save the earth from burning up. That ALLUSION is made the more ominous by DRAMATIC IRONY: the audience knows what Juliet has yet to discover: that, returning from the wedding, Romeo has gotten into a rash duel with Juliet's cousin Tybalt and killed him, rekindling the feud between their families and imperiling still further their already risky marriage. In the same SOLILOQUY, Juliet imagines herself and Romeo after death, and pleads to a PERSONIFICATION of "loving, black-browed night" to give her beloved a whimsical kind of apotheosis:

Take him and cut him out in little stars,
And he will make the face of heaven so fine
That all the world will be in love with night
And pay no worship to the garish sun.

Again, the fanciful vision ironically foreshadows the lovers' tragic deaths.

At the end of the play, after both the young lovers have committed suicide rather than face separation, the families stand helplessly at the side of their graves. The Prince of Verona, who had tried and failed to stop the pointless feud, describes the mournful atmosphere:

> A glooming peace this morning with it brings
> The sun for sorrow will not show his head.

The thematic imagery culminates in the PATHETIC FALLACY of the weather's sympathy with the tragically truncated lives of the brilliant young couple and the PERSONIFICATION of the sun itself, once the image of Juliet's shining beauty and of the headlong heat of their passion, beweeping their fate.

Symbolism

A **symbol** is an object, action, or event that represents something, or creates a range of associations, beyond itself. Some "conventional," or "public," symbols are widespread in a given culture, for example, the hammer and sickle, a monarch's crown, and the Red Cross. Writers may use such symbols as they stand, as well as adapt other conventional concepts or events to give them personal or exclusive meanings. For example, the voyage as a symbol of self-discovery is a motif in such books as *The Odyssey*, *Adventures of Huckleberry Finn*, and *Heart of Darkness*; and in other works, beginning with the Book of Genesis in the Hebrew Bible, the snake is a symbol of entrancing but fatal temptation. In many literary works, however, a symbol is unique in that its meaning is particular to that poem, play, or story and must be inferred by the reader as the work develops.

In the last case, a symbol differs from an ALLEGORY—a sustained and circumscribed analogy between a subject and an image to which it is compared—in being more complex and less specific. For example, Nathaniel Hawthorne's "Young Goodman Brown" is an allegory in which a young Puritan ignores the warning of his wife, who is named Faith, and ventures into a dark forest, where the first person he meets is a mysterious "traveler" who carries a staff "which bore the likeness of a great black snake." Deep in the forest the young man discovers a conclave engaged in satanic worship, which ironically is comprised of those from his village whom he had believed to be most pious. Feeling a sudden "sympathy of all that was wicked in his heart," he is overcome with the temptation to join the "loath-some brotherhood." By the end of the story, he has entirely lost his Faith. The meanings of the allegorical emblems are clear and specific: the dark forest represents temptation, the traveler the devil, and the wife the religious piety that the initially "Good Man" forsakes.

A symbol, in contrast, presents the image but leaves the subject that it represents open to a wide range of possible interpretations. A case in point is the poetry of William Blake, who was trained as an engraver and was by nature a visionary; his poems are full of enigmatic **symbolism**. An example is his enigmatic lyric "The Sick Rose," in which the blighted flower might represent many forms of human suffering and corruption. Often, a longer work will contain a complex symbol that enlarges the LITERAL meaning of the story. Some signs of its **symbolic** weight might be its repeated appearances, especially at key points in the narrative, such as the climax or the conclusion; its close connection with the fate of the protagonist; and its detailed description.

In the course of Shakespeare's *Othello*, the handkerchief emerges as a symbolic object. The hero's first courtship gift to his bride, Desdemona, it is introduced at the midpoint of the tragedy, just after the villainous Iago has begun to convince Othello of the falsehood that Desdemona is having an affair with his junior officer, the handsome Cassio. Desdemona loses the handkerchief in the process of trying to cure a headache that Othello has developed. She offers to "bind [his head] hard," a folk remedy for a migraine. The ache comes ostensibly from getting too little sleep, but in fact is in itself symbolic of Othello's supposed cuckoldry. Popular legend in Shakespeare's day held that a wife's infidelity caused horns to grow on her betrayed husband's head, a painful process. Impatiently, Othello knocks the delicate cloth away with the words, "Your napkin [handkerchief] is too little." This line marks the climax of the play, the point at which Iago's poisonous influence has become too strong to be counteracted by Desdemona's love.

The neglected handkerchief is found by Iago's wife Emilia, Desdemona's lady in waiting, whom her husband has often urged to steal it. She gives it to Iago in a vain attempt to please him, and he then plants it in Cassio's bedchamber. Cassio admires the rich embroidery work and asks his mistress to sew a copy of it before the unknown owner can demand its return. Iago convinces the distraught husband that Cassio's possession of the handkerchief is evidence that Desdemona has given it to this new lover: it is the "ocular proof" of her infidelity that Othello has demanded. Only at the end of the play, after Othello has been driven to murder his beloved wife, does he discover the truth about the accessory that has so often changed hands, and meanings, in the course of the play.

The significance of the symbolic object shifts with each character who possesses it. For Desdemona it is a precious token of her husband's love which, Emilia observes, she cherishes so much that she "reserves it evermore about her / To kiss and talk to." It is only a token, however. When Othello is suffering from a headache, it becomes merely a serviceable object that might bring him comfort. For him, the handkerchief is first the link between his exotic past and his new happiness, and then the source of his bitter disillusionment and agonizing jealousy. For Cassio, it is merely a pretty accessory, and he is willing to exploit his mistress to replicate it. For Iago, it is a device to ensnare the soul of the commanding general he envies and loathes and to destroy Desdemona, the lovely young woman whom he lusts after but could never corrupt. Finally, for Emilia, who emerges from her initial subservience to become Iago's nemesis, it begins as the instrument for trying to win some affection from her cold husband and then becomes the means of being an unwitting accessory to Desdemona's betrayal. Emilia's revelation of the truth about the handkerchief exposes Iago's treachery, leading to both his downfall and Othello's remorse.

In addition to this trail of connections to the characters and the plot, the appearance and the history of the handkerchief suggest its symbolic significance. Angling to convince Othello that he has seen the handkerchief in Cassio's possession, Iago describes its design as "spotted with strawberries." The participle and the color could suggest the blood that will be shed over it. At the height of his jealousy, Othello terrifies the innocent Desdemona with an account of the handkerchief's supernatural origins and powers. It was sewn by an ancient "sybil" in "prophetic fury" and the dye made from mummified "maidens' hearts." Further, it carries a magical curse:

> That handkerchief
> Did an Egyptian to my mother give.
> She was a charmer,[1] and could almost read
> The thoughts of people. She told her, while she kept it
> 'Twould make her amiable,[2] and subdue my father
> Entirely to her love; but if she lost it,
> Or made a gift of it, my father's eye

---

1. Sorceress.
2. Desirable.

Should hold her loathed, and his spirits should hunt
After new fancies. She, dying, gave it me,
And bid me, when my fate would have me wived,
To give it her.[3] I did so, and take heed on't.
Make it a darling, like your precious eye.
To lose't or give't away were such perdition[4]
As nothing else could match.

The properties that Othello attributes to the handkerchief ominously reflect Desdemona's situation. She has lost it, and he, her husband, now "loathe[s]" her, ironically, with no recognition that it was her utter devotion to his welfare that caused her to mislay it. The "perdition" which he predicts will destroy not only her life and his, but also his soul. A symbol in a particular work, then, is often subtle and enigmatic, which makes for both its richness and the challenge of interpreting its possible meanings.

Atmosphere

Atmosphere, a term taken from meteorology, means the predominant mood or TONE in all or part of a literary work, which may, for example, be joyous, tranquil, melancholy, eerie, tense, or ominous. The atmosphere, which may be suggested by such factors as the SETTING, DIALOGUE, DICTION, and SELECTION OF DETAILS in the narrative, usually foreshadows expectations about the outcome of the events. For example, Shakespeare's *Macbeth* begins with the following stage direction: *Thunder and lightning. Enter three WITCHES.* Immediately, the atmosphere becomes ominous as the storm in the natural world is linked with evil supernatural forces. The witches speak in curt TROCHAIC TETRAMETER COUPLETS, more a chant than naturalistic DIALOGUE, and in disquieting PARADOXES, such as "Fair is foul, and foul is fair," which suggest their satanic origins and duplicitous purposes. The object of their conclave adds to the ominous tone, for even before Macbeth has appeared, the witches are planning to "meet with" him "when the battle's lost and won." The PARADOX signals the contradictory portrait of Macbeth that the play will develop: we soon discover that he is a brave and victorious soldier, whose daring exploits have won the military battle to which they ALLUDE. At the same time, he secretly harbors illicit ambitions for the throne,

---

3. My wife.
4. Damnation.

which he is tempted to pursue ruthlessly, thereby losing the moral "battle." The witches' intense focus on Macbeth foreshadows his incipient corruption and the disruption to the natural order that it will create. Fittingly, at the end of the brief scene, the hags summon their satanic familiars, a cat and a toad, and prepare to "hover through the fog and filthy air" to the barren "heath" where they will confront Macbeth. The SETTING, DIALOGUE, DICTION, and descriptive DETAILS establish the tense, eerie atmosphere that will prevail throughout the tragedy.

An example of eerie, ominous atmosphere from narrative FICTION is "The Fall of the House of Usher" by Edgar Allan Poe, an acknowledged master of atmospheric effects. This is the SHORT STORY's opening paragraph:

> During the whole of a dull, dark, and soundless day in the autumn of the year, when the clouds hung oppressively low in the heavens, I had been passing alone, on horseback, through a singularly dreary tract of country; and at length found myself, as the shades of the evening drew on, within view of the melancholy House of Usher. I know not how it was—but, with the first glimpse of the building, a sense of insufferable gloom pervaded my spirit. I say insufferable; for the feeling was unrelieved by any of that half-pleasurable, because poetic, sentiment, with which the mind usually receives even the sternest natural images of the desolate or terrible. I looked upon the scene before me—upon the mere house, and the simple landscape features of the domain, upon the bleak walls, upon the vacant eye-like windows, upon a few rank sedges, and upon a few white trunks of decayed trees—with an utter depression of soul which I can compare to no earthly sensation more properly than to the after-dream of the reveler upon opium: the bitter lapse into everyday life, the hideous dropping off of the veil. There was an iciness, a sinking, a sickening of the heart, an unredeemed dreariness of thought which no goading of the imagination could torture into aught of the sublime. What was it—I paused to think—what was it that so unnerved me in the contemplation of the House of Usher? It was a mystery all insoluble; nor could I grapple with the shadowy fancies that crowded upon me as I pondered. I was forced to fall back upon the unsatisfactory conclusion, that while, beyond doubt, there ARE combinations of very simple natural objects which have the power of thus affecting us, still the analysis of this power lies among considerations beyond our depth. It was possible, I reflected, that a mere different arrangement of the particu-

lars of the scene, of the details of the picture, would be sufficient to modify, or perhaps to annihilate its capacity for sorrowful impression; and, acting upon this idea, I reined my horse to the precipitous brink of a black and lurid tarn that lay in unruffled luster by the dwelling, and gazed down—but with a shudder even more thrilling than before—upon the remodeled and inverted images of the gray sedge, and the ghastly tree-stems, and the vacant and eye-like windows.

Virtually every feature of the passage contributes to the atmosphere. The setting is a "dull, dark" autumn day in a desolate place that contains only a dilapidated mansion beside a "black and lurid tarn," the gloomy adjectives and the old-fashioned term for "lake" suggesting antiquity and isolation. The long, COMPLEX sentences are full of CONCRETE details, such as "white trunks of decayed trees" and "bleak walls." The FIGURATIVE descriptions—the SIMILE of the "vacant eye-like windows" and the METAPHORICAL comparison of the "utter depression" that the scene evokes to the "bitter lapse into everyday life" of the after-effects of an opium dream—reinforce the oppressive tone. The FIRST-PERSON NARRATOR does not allow such visual IMAGERY to stand alone, however. He states outright the effects of arriving at the scene on horseback: the "sense of insufferable gloom" and "sickening of the heart" that "so unnerved [him] in the contemplation of the House of Usher." His final attempt to overcome such feelings and literally gain a different perspective on the place, by looking at its reflection in the tarn, instead produces "a shudder even more thrilling than before." This last statement adds undertones of threat and revulsion to the atmosphere of gloom and desolation.

Sometimes an author creates an ironic reversal of the expectations suggested by the atmosphere at a work's outset, and so increases the shock of the outcome. Katherine Mansfield's "Bliss" begins, as the title suggests, in a mood of high euphoria:

> Although Bertha Young was thirty she still had moments like this when she wanted to run instead of walk, to take dancing steps on and off the pavement, to bowl a hoop, to throw something up in the air and catch it again, or to stand still and laugh at—nothing—at nothing simply.
>
> What can you do if you are thirty and, turning the corner of your own street, you are overcome, suddenly, by a feeling of bliss—absolute bliss!—as though you'd suddenly swallowed a bright piece of that late afternoon sun and it burned in your bosom, sending out a little shower of sparks into every particle, into every finger and toe . . . ?

▼

Oh, is there no way you can express it without being "drunk and disorderly"? How idiotic civilization is! Why be given a body if you have to keep it shut up in a case like a rare, rare fiddle?

"No, that about the fiddle is not quite what I mean," she thought, running up the steps and feeling in her bag for the key—she'd forgotten it, as usual—and rattling the letter-box. "It's not what I mean because—Thank you, Mary"—she went into the hall. "Is nurse back?"

The long, breathless sentences and THIRD-PERSON LIMITED POINT OF VIEW reflect the utter "bliss" felt by the PROTAGONIST. The childish expressions of joy to which she is tempted to give way—dancing "on and off the pavement," "bowl[ing] a hoop," and "laughing at nothing"—and the PUNS in her name—Bertha is as "young" and fresh as a newborn—add to the blithe atmosphere. The opening also contains hints, however, of the shift in tone that will occur at the end of the story. Bertha's fanciful SIMILE of having "swallow[ed] a bright piece of the afternoon sun" so that it "burn[s] in [her] bosom" foreshadows the physical desire for her husband that she is feeling for the first time but is too naïve to recognize. Bertha rejects the second SIMILE that she devises, comparing her "body" to "a rare, rare fiddle" that has been uselessly "shut up in a case." In fact, however, that is an apt analogy for the sexual frigidity that she has convinced herself that her husband understands and accepts. At the end of the story she discovers the devastating truth: that he is having a passionate affair with a beautiful friend of hers. The irony of the title, "Bliss," is implied by the words that would be needed to complete the APHORISM and to qualify the euphoric tone: "Ignorance is Bliss."

EXERCISES: Imagery, Symbolism, and Atmosphere

I. For each of the following passages:
*   Describe the physical senses—sight, hearing, smell, touch, temperature, or movement—that the IMAGERY involves or evokes.
*   Identify not only LITERAL objects, actions, and scenes but also VEHICLES of METAPHORS and SIMILES that contribute to the IMAGERY.
*   Explain the effects of the IMAGERY on the tone and meaning of the passage.

 They eat beans mostly, this old yellow pair.
Dinner is a casual affair.
Plain chipware on a plain and creaking wood.
Tin flatware.

▼

Two who are Mostly Good.   5
Two who have lived their day,
But keep on putting on their clothes
And putting things away.

And remembering . . .
Remembering, with twinklings and twinges,   10
As they lean over the beans in their rented back room that is full of
    beads and receipts and dolls and clothes, tobacco crumbs, vases
    and fringes.   —GWENDOLYN BROOKS, "The Bean Eaters"

2. Glory be to God for dappled things—
    For skies of couple-colour as a brinded[1] cow
      For rose-moles all in stipple upon trout that swim;
  Fresh-firecoal chestnut-falls;[2] finches' wings.

             * * *

  He fathers-forth whose beauty is past change: 5
    Praise him.   —GERARD MANLEY HOPKINS, "Pied Beauty"

3. I have lived long enough. My way of life
  Is fall'n into the sere,[3] the yellow leaf,
  And that which should accompany old age,
  As honour, love, obedience, troops of friends,
  I must not look to have, but in their stead   5
  Curses, not loud but deep, mouth-honour,[4] breath
  Which the poor heart would fain deny and dare not.
                —WILLIAM SHAKESPEARE, *Macbeth*

4. "Is my team ploughing,
    That I used to drive
  And hear the harness jingle
    When I was a man alive?"

  Ay, the horses trample,   5
    The harness jingles now;
  No change though you lie under
    The land you used to plough.
           —A. E. HOUSMAN, "Is My Team Ploughing"

---

1. Brindled.
2. Chestnuts as bright as coals.
3. Withered.
4. Lip service.

▼

5. The following passage is a description by the Roman soldier Enobarbus of the oar-driven ship on which the legendary Egyptian queen Cleopatra sat when she first met her lover, the Roman leader Marc Antony:

The barge she sat in, like a burnished throne
Burned on the water. The poop[5] was beaten gold;
Purple the sails, and so perfumèd that
The winds were love-sick with them. The oars were silver,
Which to the tune of flutes kept stroke, and made   5
The water which they beat to follow faster,
As amorous of their strokes.

          —WILLIAM SHAKESPEARE, *Antony and Cleopatra*

II. a. Identify the SYMBOLIC objects, actions, and events in the following poem, and explain their possible interpretations.

extended metaphor
development
"wrath"

"wrath"
poison tree

I was angry with my friend:
I told my wrath, my wrath did end.
I was angry with my foe:
I told it not, my wrath did grow.

"*telling wrath*"

And I waterd it in fears,   5
Night and morning with my tears;
And I sunnèd it with smiles,
And with soft deceitful wiles.

smiles: sunny warm fake

And it grew both day and night,
Till it bore an apple bright.   10
And my foe beheld it shine,
And he knew that it was mine,

grew like apple

And into my garden stole,
When the night had veild the pole;
In the morning glad I see   15
My foe outstretched beneath the tree.

garden of edin?

revenge / death

        —WILLIAM BLAKE, "A Poison Tree"

b. Describe an important symbol in a SHORT STORY, NOVEL, or PLAY that you have studied. Explain how its use contributes to the meaning of the work as a whole.

wrath is lethal
must be nurtured

---

5. Upper deck.

III. For each of the following passages:

- Describe the ATMOSPHERE that it evokes.
- Explain the techniques by which that ATMOSPHERE is conveyed and the
  effects on the TONE and the meaning that it creates.

(1.) *The narrator of the following lines is Tithonus, who in Roman mythology was*
loved by the goddess of the dawn, Aurora. She asked Jupiter to grant
Tithonus eternal life, which he did, but she forgot to ask that the god grant
him eternal youth.

The woods decay, the woods decay and fall,
The vapors weep their burthen to the ground,
Man comes and tills the fields and lies beneath,
And after many a summer dies the swan.
Me only cruel immortality   5
Consumes: I wither slowly in thine arms,
Here at the quiet limit of the world,
A white-haired shadow roaming like a dream
The ever-silent spaces of the East,
Far-folded mists, and gleaming halls of morn.   10
                            —ALFRED, LORD TENNYSON, "Tithonus"

2. The Rue du Coq d'Or, Paris, seven in the morning. A succession of
    furious, choking yells from the street. Madame Monce, who kept
    the little hotel opposite mine, had come out on to the pavement to
    address a lodger on the third floor. Her bare feet were stuck into
    sabots[6] and her grey hair was streaming down.
        Madame Monce: "Salope![7] Salope! How many times
    Have I told you not to squash bugs on the wallpaper? Do you
    think you've bought the hotel, eh? Why can't you throw them out
    of the window like everyone else? Putain![8] Salope!"
        The woman on the third floor: "Vache!"[9]
        Thereupon a whole variegated chorus of yells, as windows were
    flung open on every side and half the street joined in the quarrel.
    They shut up abruptly ten minutes later, when a squadron of cav-
    alry rode past and people stopped shouting to look at them.
                            —GEORGE ORWELL, *Down and Out in Paris and London*

---

6. Wooden shoes.
7. Slattern.
8. Whore.
9. Cow, slang for "bitch."

▼

3. Turning and turning in the widening gyre
    The falcon cannot hear the falconer;
    Things fall apart; the centre cannot hold;
    Mere anarchy is loosed upon the world,
    The blood-dimmed tide is loosed, and everywhere   5
    The ceremony of innocence is drowned;
    The best lack all conviction, while the worst
    Are full of passionate intensity.

    —WILLIAM BUTLER YEATS, "The Second Coming"

4. None of them knew the color of the sky. Their eyes glanced level
    and were fastened upon the waves that swept toward them. These
    waves were of the hue of slate, save for the tops, which were of
    foaming white, and all of the men knew the colors of the sea. The
    horizon narrowed and widened, and dipped and rose, and at all
    times its edge was jagged with waves that seemed thrust up in
    points like rocks.

    Many a man ought to have a bathtub larger than the boat
    which here rode upon the sea. These waves were most wrongfully
    and barbarously abrupt and tall, and each froth-top was a problem
    in small-boat navigation.

    —STEPHEN CRANE, "The Open Boat"

5. *In Shakespeare's* Henry V, *the Chorus gives the following description of the
    French and English armies on the eve of the decisive Battle of Agincourt:*

    Now entertain conjecture[1] of a time
    When creeping murmur and the poring dark
    Fills the wide vessel of the universe.
    From camp to camp through the foul womb of night
    The hum of either army stilly[2] sounds,   5
    That the fixed sentinels almost receive
    The secret whispers of each others' watch.
    Fire answers fire, and through their paly[3] flames
    Each battle sees the other's umbered[4] face.
    Steed threatens steed, in high and boastful neighs   10
    Piercing the night's dull ear, and from the tents
    The armourers, accomplishing[5] the knights,
    With busy hammers closing rivets up,
    Give dreadful note of preparation.

    ---

    1. Imagine.
    2. Softly.
    3. Pale.
    4. Shadowed. "Battle": army.
    5. Equipping.

▼

IV. In the following poem by Richard Wilbur, the NARRATOR recounts an experience of listening as his daughter writes a story on her type-writer. In a brief essay, describe the poem's use of IMAGERY and the ATMOSPHERE that it evokes around the act of creative writing. Then explain the SYMBOLISM implied in the NARRATOR's recollection about the starling.

The Writer

In her room at the prow of the house
Where light breaks, and the windows are tossed with linden,
My daughter is writing a story.

I pause in the stairwell, hearing
From her shut door a commotion of typewriter-keys   5
Like a chain hauled over a gunwale.

Young as she is, the stuff
Of her life is a great cargo, and some of it heavy:
I wish her a lucky passage.

But now it is she who pauses,   10
As if to reject my thought and its easy figure.
A stillness greatens, in which

The whole house seems to be thinking,
And then she is at it again with a bunched clamor
Of strokes, and again is silent.   15

I remember the dazed starling
Which was trapped in that very room, two years ago;
How we stole in, lifted a sash

And retreated, not to affright it;
And how for a helpless hour, through the crack of the door,   20
We watched the sleek, wild, dark

And iridescent creature
Batter against the brilliance, drop like a glove
To the hard floor, or the desk-top.

And wait then, humped and bloody,   25
For the wits to try it again; and how our spirits
Rose when, suddenly sure,

It lifted off from a chair-back,
Beating a smooth course for the right window
And clearing the sill of the world.   30

It is always a matter, my darling,
Of life or death, as I had forgotten. I wish
What I wished you before, but harder.

Repetition

Intentional—as opposed to careless or inadvertent—**repetition** of sounds, words, phrasing, or concepts is used in literary works to create unity and emphasis. The effects of repetition on the work's TONE and meaning vary with the context and with the form of the repeated element. Special forms of the repetition of sound in POETRY include RHYME, METER, and such SOUND PATTERNS as ALLITERATION, ASSONANCE, and CONSONANCE; the repetition of complete words or phrases occurs in ANAPHORA and the REFRAIN. In POETRY and FICTION, as well as in DRAMA, patterns of the repetition of words or phrases are crucial to many forms of SYMBOLISM and IMAGERY.

In a less specialized sense, repetition of words can signal a speaker's preoccupations and feelings. For example, at the end of Shakespeare's *King Lear*, the old sovereign is attempting to comprehend the horrifying reality that his best-loved daughter is dead, and that he has been indirectly responsible for her loss. Addressing her lifeless body, he emphasizes his devastating realization that she will "come no more" in a BLANK VERSE line that consists of a single repeated word: "Never, never, never, never, never!" The repetition expresses Lear's shock, as well as his heartbreak.

A different sort of shock, the shock of outrage, is expressed by Shakespeare's Emilia, the beset wife of the villain Iago in *Othello*. She has just heard the PROTAGONIST say that he has murdered his wife, Desdemona—whom Emilia knows to be a paragon of innocence and fidelity—on the strength of Iago's accusation that she has committed adultery. Emilia is aware that Iago is cynical and coarse, but she cannot believe that he is guilty of perpetrating what she later condemns to his face as this "odious damnèd lie." To each detail that Othello provides of Iago's fabrications, Emilia can only demand, "My husband?" After her third repetition of the question, Othello responds impatiently:

> He, woman.
> I say thy husband. Dost understand the word?
> My friend, thy husband, honest, honest Iago.

In confirming the identity of the accuser, Othello's repetition of "honest" stresses with unwitting irony the façade of candor that Iago has used to convince Othello and everyone else of his integrity. All too soon Othello will discover that Emilia's outrage is justified and that he has murdered the love of his life on grounds that are entirely false.

Some authors use a repeated word or phrase as a means of CHARACTERIZATION, especially in depicting FLAT, as opposed to

THREE-DIMENSIONAL, CHARACTERS. That is a favorite device of the Victorian novelist Charles Dickens. For example, the devious Uriah Heep in Dickens's *David Copperfield* (1850) always describes himself as "umble"—the cockney pronunciation of "humble"—even as he schemes with ruthless ambition to take over the business of his gullible employer and to force Mr. Wickfield's innocent daughter Agnes into a loveless marriage. In addition, Dickens often gives a character a favorite tag line that sums up his or her outlook or values. For example, each of the Micawbers, the kindly but hopelessly improvident couple who provide the young David with shabby room and board, has a favorite catch phrase. Mr. Micawber's is the conviction that "something will turn up" to rescue him and his growing family from debtors' prison, and Mrs. Micawber's is the melodramatic assertion, "I never will desert Mr. Micawber," even as she pawns their few possessions and begs petty loans to keep the leaky Micawber barge afloat a while longer.

Selection and Order of Details ◀

The **selection** and the **order of the details** in a literary work are crucial to its meaning and TONE. Because the form of a POEM, a PLAY, or a work of FICTION may look so inevitable and move so smoothly on the page, it is easy to forget that the work is the product of a series of deliberate choices that the author makes in the course of drafting and revising it. Such choices include both the nature and relative specificity of the details and the order in which they appear. For example, John Cheever's SHORT STORY "Reunion" opens with the following paragraph:

> The last time I saw my father was in Grand Central Station. I was going from my grandmother's in the Adirondacks to a cottage on the Cape that my mother had rented, and I wrote my father that I would be in New York between trains for an hour and a half, and asked if we could have lunch together. His secretary wrote to say that he would meet me at the information booth at noon, and at twelve o'clock sharp I saw him coming through the crowd. He was a stranger to me—my mother divorced him three years ago and I hadn't seen him since—but as soon as I saw him I felt that he was my father, my flesh and blood, my future and my doom. I knew that when I was grown I would be something like him; I would have to plan my campaigns within his limitations. He was a big, good-looking man, and I was terribly happy to see him again. He struck me on the back and shook my hand. "Hi,

Charlie," he said. "Hi, boy. I'd like to take you up to my club, but it's in the Sixties, and if you have to catch an early train I guess we'd better get something to eat around here." He put his arm around me, and I smelled my father the way my mother sniffs a rose. It was a rich compound of whiskey, after-shave lotion, shoe polish, woolens, and the rankness of a mature male. I hoped that someone would see us together. I wished that we could be photographed. I wanted some record of our having been together.

The details imply that the FIRST-PERSON NARRATOR is a teenage boy: his points of reference are the parent-figures in his life, but he is old enough to travel alone and to initiate the contact with his father by writing a letter. The main impressions that the details create—the boy's pride in the moment and longing for male company—are conveyed by his eager response to the sight, movement, and smell of his long-absent father. He is proud of the man's good looks, and he instantly recognizes their bond: the heritage of "flesh and blood" and the sense that his father's appearance and character represent his own "future" and "doom." The father's first actions are aggressively friendly: he claps the boy on the back, shakes his hand, offers to buy him lunch, and "put[s] his arm around" him. That close contact evokes Charlie's humorous SIMILE comparing his relish of his father's admittedly "rank" blend of smells to his mother's pleasure in "sniff[ing] a rose." The self-deprecating humor acknowledges his realization that his reaction is excessive. At the same time, his wish, REPEATED three times, that he could have some means to enshrine the moment suggests the loneliness of the fatherless boy and his fervent need for the relationship to be sustained.

Other details, however, qualify the largely joyous TONE of the passage and provide ominous foreshadowing. It is not the father but "his secretary" who responds to the boy's letter, and then only with factual information about the time and place of the meeting, as if she were making a business appointment. The wording of the sentence about the parents' divorce shows that the mother initiated the action, and that Charlie has had no contact with his father in the intervening three years. That last fact is the more surprising, given the man's extroverted nature and his seeming eagerness to claim Charlie as his "boy" at their moment of meeting. Another troubling factor is the order in which the NARRATOR lists the various scents emanating from his father: the first is that of "whiskey." That detail seems especially ominous given the time of day—noon, which means that the drinking must have taken place in the morning—and the nature of the occasion—the first reunion of father and son after a three-year hiatus. Such selection and order of details foreshadow the disillusioning course that the encounter will take. As the first sentence of the story states, this will be "the last time" that Charlie sees his father—not, in the phrase's innocuous sense, "the previous time," but the final occasion on which son and father meet.

The selection and order of the details in Donald Hall's autobiographical poem "Independence Day Letter," which ALLUDES to the death from cancer of his wife, Jane Kenyon, create a bleak, melancholy TONE:

> Five A.M., the Fourth of July.
> I walk by Eagle Pond[1] with the dog,
> wearing my leather coat
> against the clear early chill,
> looking at water lilies that clutch
> cool yellow fists together,
> as I undertake another day
> twelve weeks after the Tuesday
> we learned that you would die.
>
> This afternoon I'll pay the bills
> and write a friend about her book
> and watch Red Sox baseball.
> I'll walk Gussie again.
> I'll microwave some Stouffer's.[2]
> A woman will drive from Bristol[3]
> to examine your mother's Ford
> parked beside your Saab
> in the dead women's used car lot.
>
> Tonight the Andover[4] fireworks
> will have to go on without me
> as I go to bed early, reading
> *The Man Without Qualities*[5]
> with insufficient attention
> because I keep watching you die.
> Tomorrow I will wake at five
> to the tenth Wednesday
> after the Wednesday we buried you.

---

1. Near his home in New Hampshire.
2. A brand name for frozen meals.
3. A nearby town.
4. Another nearby town.
5. A long, unfinished novel by Robert Musil.

▼

The rawness of the NARRATOR's grief is revealed through Hall's skill-ful selection of details that describe his self-imposed isolation, the plodding pace of his days, and his efforts to will himself to carry out the minimum of necessary tasks: walking the dog, paying the bills, appeasing hunger with a frozen meal, and mechanically turning the pages of a long novel whose title, *The Man Without Qualities*, ironi-cally suggests his own feeling of emptiness. Interspersed with the account of those tedious actions are the details that show the real focus of his attention: the recent death of his beloved. That revela-tion comes at the end of the first stanza, when the NARRATOR meas-ures time by the number of weeks it has been since they received the fatal prognosis. His anguish is confirmed by several details: his bitterly ironic description of her car as parked beside her late mother's in "the dead women's used car lot"; the obsessive memory of "watching [her] die" that disrupts his ability to read; and his con-clusion with still another detail that marks the passage of time from the date of her death: the next morning he will awake to "the tenth Wednesday / after the Wednesday we buried you." The REPETITION of "Wednesday" makes the days seem like a prison sentence, monoto-nous in their dreariness and isolation. By the end of the poem, the irony of the seemingly upbeat title, "Independence Day Letter," emerges: rather than a happy account of Fourth of July celebrations, the "letter" is a poignant APOSTROPHE, addressed to the NARRATOR's dead wife, that recounts his agonizing efforts to "undertake another day" of his enforced "independence."

See also: CONCRETE DICTION, IMAGERY, SYMBOLISM, and DIALOGUE.

▶ Epiphany

An **epiphany** (eh-PIH-fanee, from the Greek word for "to manifest," or "to show") means a sudden, overwhelming insight or revelation evoked by a commonplace object or a scene in a POEM or a work of FICTION. The term is derived from Christian theology, where it means a manifestation of God's presence in the world, specifically the revelation to the Magi of Christ's divinity, celebrated in the Feast of the Epiphany on January 6. The literary meaning of epiphany was introduced by James Joyce, who, after rejecting the Catholicism of his youth, secularized many of the religion's terms and symbols in his SHORT STORIES and NOVELS. In *Stephen Hero* (published posthu-mously in 1944), the early draft of his autobiographical novel *A Por-trait of the Artist as a Young Man* (1916), Joyce defined an epiphany as "a sudden spiritual manifestation" of the significance of a commonplace object or scene.

Joyce's own works are full of such epiphanies. For example, in *A Portrait of the Artist as a Young Man*, the PROTAGONIST, Stephen Dedalus, struggles with a conflict between conforming to the moral strictures of his Jesuit education and breaking free to devote himself to his writing and to the expression of his sexual passion. A turning point comes when he happens upon a lovely girl who is wading in a rivulet of the sea. He is struck with "the wonder of mortal beauty" and conveys on the girl "the worship of his eyes." She returns his gaze, and he experiences an epiphany:

> Her image had passed into his soul for ever and no word had broken the holy silence of his ecstasy. Her eyes had called him and his soul had leaped at the call. To live, to err, to fall, to triumph, to recreate life out of life! A wild angel had appeared to him, the angel of mortal youth and beauty, an envoy from the fair courts of life, to throw open before him in an instant of ecstasy the gates of all the ways of error and glory.

Only the IMAGERY of religion seems adequate to Stephen to convey the "holy silence of his ecstasy." The sight has altered his "soul" for eternity: he sees the girl as "a wild angel" who represents access to both the "ways of error"—the human path—and of "glory"—the divine transfiguration of such earthly beauty that he now feels empowered to celebrate in his work.

Joyce reserves epiphanies for major characters, whose sudden self-awareness or intuitive understanding makes them more ROUND, and enhances their central roles in the narrative. In other stories, he depicts the characters as too naïve or too shallow to achieve such insight. For example, for Farrington, the loutish PROTAGONIST of Joyce's short story "Counterparts," the extent of any understanding he achieves is the petty realization that he has wasted all his money on a night of carousing and not even managed to stay drunk. Incapable of either self-reflection or sympathy for the family that he neglects, Farrington goes home and vents his frustration by beating his little son. FICTION writers since Joyce, such as Katherine Mansfield, Virginia Woolf, William Faulkner, Flannery O'Connor, John Cheever, and Raymond Carver, have made effective use of the epiphany.

A concept similar to that of the epiphany had been introduced a century earlier by the Romantic poets William Wordsworth and Percy Bysshe Shelley, who called such sudden evocations of insight by means of ordinary objects and experiences "moments." For example, Shelley's "To a Skylark" concerns the profound revelations about the beauty of nature and the quintessential meaning of "joy" that are inspired by the "crystal stream" of the skylark's song. Wordsworth called more extensive examples of such moments "spots of time." In his long autobiographical poem, "The Prelude," he recounts several such experiences and also summarizes their effects on him:

> Thus oft amid those fits of vulgar[1] joy
> Which, through all seasons, on a child's pursuits
> Are prompt attendants, 'mid that giddy bliss
> Which, like a tempest, works along the blood
> And is forgotten; even then I felt
> Gleams like the flashing of a shield—the earth
> And common face of Nature spake to me
> Rememberable things . . .

Even as a supposedly heedless child, caught up in the "giddy bliss" of daily life, the incipient poet sensed the **epiphanic** significance of such spots of time. Here it is conveyed by the SIMILE of the sudden gleam of light on a shield and the PERSONIFICATION of Nature speaking directly to the intuitive boy. Other poets who describe such epiphanic moments include Gerard Manley Hopkins, William Butler Yeats, T. S. Eliot, Wallace Stevens, and Sylvia Plath.

EXERCISES: Repetition, Selection and Order of Details, and Epiphany

I. For each of the following passages:
- Identify any REPETITION and/or describe THE SELECTION AND ORDER OF DETAILS.
- Explain the effects of those techniques on the TONE and the meaning of the passage.

1.   I work all day, and get half drunk at night,
    Waking at four to soundless dark, I stare.
    In time, the curtain-edges will grow light.
    Till then I see what's really always there:
    Unresting death, a whole day nearer now,   5
    Making all thought impossible but how
    And where and when I myself shall die.

---

1. Ordinary.

▼

Arid interrogation: yet the dread
Of dying, and being dead,
Flashes afresh to hold and horrify.   10

                                    —PHILIP LARKIN, "Aubade"

2. *The following description is of the outcome of Dr. Victor Frankenstein's
    attempt to create human life in his laboratory:*

    It was a dreary night of November that I beheld the accom-
    plishment of my toils. With an anxiety that almost amounted to
    agony, I collected the instruments of life around me, that I might
    infuse a spark of being into the lifeless thing that lay at my feet. It
    was already one in the morning; the rain pattered dismally against
    the panes, and my candle was nearly burnt out, when, by the glim-
    mer of the half-extinguished light, I saw the dull yellow eye of the
    creature open; it breathed hard, and a convulsive motion agitated
    its limbs.

    How can I describe my emotions at this catastrophe, or how
    delineate the wretch whom with such infinite pains and care I had
    endeavoured to form? His limbs were in proportion, and I had
    selected his features as beautiful. Beautiful! Great God! His yellow
    skin scarcely covered the work of muscles and arteries beneath; his
    hair was of a lustrous black, and flowing; his teeth of a pearly
    whiteness; but these luxuriances only formed a more horrid con-
    trast with his watery eyes, that seemed almost of the same colour as
    the dun-white sockets in which they were set, his shriveled com-
    plexion and straight black lips.   —MARY SHELLEY, *Frankenstein*

3. Still[1] to be neat, still to be dressed,
    As you were going to a feast;
    Still to be powdered, still perfumed;
    Lady, it is to be presumed,
    Though art's hid causes are not found,   5
    All is not sweet, all is not sound.

    Give me a look, give me a face
    That makes simplicity a grace;
    Robes loosely flowing, hair as free;
    Such sweet neglect more taketh me   10
    Than all the adulteries of art.
    They strike mine eyes, but not my heart.

                                    —BEN JONSON, "Still to Be Neat"

---

1. Always.

▼

4. All night at the ice plant he had fed
    the chute its silvery blocks, and then I
    stacked cases of orange soda for the children
    of Kentucky, one gray boxcar at a time

    with always two more waiting. We were twenty   5
    for such a short time and always in
    the wrong clothes, crusted with dirt
    and sweat. I think now we were never twenty.
                            –PHILIP LEVINE, "You Can Have It"

5. *The following passage, set in the 1920s, describes the visit of a "deputa-*
    tion" of political leaders in a Mississippi town who have gone to confront
    an elderly citizen about her failure to pay taxes:

    [They] knocked at the door through which no visitor had
    passed since she ceased giving china-painting lessons eight or ten
    years earlier. They were admitted by the old Negro[2] into a dim hall
    from which a stairway mounted into still more shadow. It smelled
    of dust and disuse—a close, dank smell. The Negro led them into
    the parlor. It was furnished with heavy, leather-covered furniture.
    When the Negro opened the blinds of one window, they could see
    that the leather was cracked; and when they sat down, a faint dust
    rose sluggishly about their thighs, spinning with slow motes in the
    single sun-ray. On a tarnished gilt easel before the fireplace stood a
    crayon portrait of Miss Emily's father.[3]
        They rose when she entered—a small, fat woman in black, with
    a thin gold chain descending to her waist and vanishing into her
    belt, leaning on an ebony cane with a tarnished gold head. Her
    skeleton was small and spare; perhaps that was why what would
    have been merely plumpness in another was obesity in her. She
    looked bloated, like a body submerged in motionless water, and of
    that pallid hue. Her eyes, lost in the fatty ridges of her face, looked
    like two small pieces of coal pressed into a lump of dough as they
    moved from one face to another while the visitors stated their
    errand.   –WILLIAM FAULKNER, "A Rose for Emily"

---

2. Her servant.
3. Now dead.

▼

6. *This is the conclusion to a description of an "oil-soaked" gas station that begins with the line: "Oh, but it is dirty!"*

Some comic books provide
the only note of color—
of certain color. They lie
upon a big dim doily
draping a taboret[4]   5
(part of the set), beside
a big hirsute begonia.

Why the extraneous plant?
Why the taboret?
Why, oh why, the doily?   10
(Embroidered in daisy stitch
with marguerites,[5] I think,
and heavy with gray crochet.)

Somebody embroidered the doily.
Somebody waters the plant,   15
or oils it, maybe. Somebody
arranges the rows of cans
so that they softly say:
ESSO—SO—SO—SO[6]
To high-strung automobiles.   20
Somebody loves us all.

—ELIZABETH BISHOP, "Filling Station"

7. *The following passage opens George Orwell's novel* 1984, *which is set in a future dystopia:*

It was a bright cold day in April, and the clocks were striking thirteen. Winston Smith, his chin nuzzled into his breast in an effort to escape the vile wind, slipped quickly through the glass doors of Victory Mansions, though not quickly enough to prevent a swirl of gritty dust from entering along with him.

The hallway smelt of boiled cabbage and old rag mats. At one end of it a colored poster, too large for indoor display, had been tacked to the wall. It depicted simply an enormous face, more than a meter wide: the face of a man of about forty-five, with a heavy black mustache and ruggedly handsome features. Winston made for

---

4. A drum-shaped table.
5. Small daisies.
6. Brand name, later changed to "Exxon."

▼

the stairs. It was no use trying the lift.[7] Even at the best of times it was seldom working, and at present the electric current was cut off during daylight hours. It was part of the economy drive in preparation for Hate Week. The flat was seven flights up, and Winston, who was thirty-nine, and had a varicose ulcer above his right ankle, went slowly, resting several times on the way. On each landing, opposite the lift shaft, the poster with the enormous face gazed from the wall. It was one of those pictures which are so contrived that the eyes follow you about when you move. BIG BROTHER IS WATCHING YOU, the caption beneath it ran.

II. For each of the following passages, describe the nature of the EPIPHANY and its effects on the TONE and meaning of the passage.

1. *The NARRATOR of James Joyce's "Araby," a young teenage boy, fails in an effort to buy a gift from a local bazaar, meant as a tribute to a young woman he is infatuated with, the older sister of a friend. Through no fault of his own, he arrives as the bazaar is closing, spends most of his money on an entrance ticket, and realizes that he cannot afford any of the wares on display at one of the few stalls still open. He then overhears a flirtatious conversation between the female stall keeper and two young Englishmen. The story ends as the lights in the hall are being turned off.*

      Gazing up into the darkness I saw myself as a creature driven and derided by vanity; and my eyes burned with anguish and anger.

2. Only this evening I saw again low in the sky
   The evening star, at the beginning of winter, the star
   That in spring will crown every western horizon,
   Again . . . as if it came back, as if life came back,
   Not in a later son, a different daughter, another place,   5
   But as if evening found us young, still young,
   Still walking in a present of our own.

   It was like sudden time in a world without time,
   This world, this place, the street in which I was,
   Without time . . .   10
                              —WALLACE STEVENS, "Martial Cadenza"

3. *In E. M. Forster's* A Passage to India, *as an elderly British woman is touring some Indian caves the noises of the crowd create what for her is "a terrifying echo." The NARRATOR describes the sound effect created by the cave:*

---

7. Elevator.

▼

"The echo in a Marabar cave is . . . utterly devoid of distinction. Whatever is said, the same monotonous noise replies, and quivers up and down the walls until it is absorbed into the roof. 'Boum' is the sound as far as the human alphabet can express it, or 'bou-oum,' 'ou-boum'—utterly dull. Hope, politeness, the blowing of a nose, the squeak of a boot, all produce 'boum.'" Mrs. Moore's reaction to the echo grows immediately after she emerges from the cave.

The more she thought over it, the more disagreeable and frightening it became . . . The crush and the smells she could forget, but the echo began in some indescribable way to undermine her hold on life. Coming at a moment when she chanced to be fatigued, it had managed to murmur, "Pathos, piety, courage—they exist, but are identical, and so is filth. Everything exists, nothing has value." If one had spoken vileness in that place, or quoted lofty poetry, the comment would have been the same—"ou-boum." If one had spoken with the tongues of angels and pleaded for all the unhappiness and misunderstanding in the world, past, present, and to come, for all the misery men must undergo whatever their opinion and position, and however much they dodge or bluff—it would amount to the same, the serpent would descend and return to the ceiling. Devils are of the North, and poems can be written about them, but no one could romanticize the Marabar because it robbed infinity and eternity of their vastness, the only quality that accommodates them to mankind.

She tried to . . . remind herself that she was only an elderly woman who had got up too early in the morning and journeyed too far, that the despair creeping over her was merely her despair, her personal weakness, and that even if she got a sunstroke and went mad the rest of the world would go on. But suddenly, at the edge of her mind, Religion appeared, poor little talkative Christianity, and she knew that its divine words from "Let there be Light" to "It is finished" only amounted to "boum." Then she was terrified over a larger area than usual; the universe, never comprehensible to her intellect, offered no response to her soul. . . .

III. Analysis of a long passage

1. *The following passage from Jack London's "To Build a Fire" occurs after the* PROTAGONIST, *a prospector in the Klondike, has fallen through the ice of a stream and wet his feet. With the temperature at seventy-five below zero, he realizes that his one chance of survival is to build a fire that will let him dry his moccasins and prevent his feet from freezing. He has taken off his mittens to light a match, but that exposure causes his fingers to freeze. As the passage opens, he is beating his hands against his sides to try to revive the feeling in his fingers. Explain how the* SELECTION *and* ORDER OF DETAILS *and the* REPETITION *of words and ideas reveal the narrator's* TONE *and suggest the emotional impact of the event that he describes.*

After a while he was aware of the first faraway signals of sensation in his beaten fingers. The faint tingling grew stronger till it evolved into a stinging ache that was excruciating, but which the man hailed with satisfaction. He stripped the mitten from his right hand and fetched forth the birchbark. The exposed fingers were quickly going numb again. Next he brought out his bunch of sulphur matches. But the tremendous cold had already driven the life out of his fingers. In his effort to separate one match from the others, the whole bunch fell in the snow. He tried to pick it up out of the snow, but failed. The dead fingers could neither touch nor clutch. He was very careful. He drove the thought of his freezing feet, and nose, and cheeks, out of his mind, devoting his whole soul to the matches. He watched, using the sense of vision in place of that of touch, and when he saw his fingers on each side of the bunch, he closed them—that is, he willed to close them, for the wires were down, and the fingers did not obey. He pulled the mitten on the right hand, and beat it fiercely against his knee. Then with both mittened hands, he scooped the bunch of matches, along with much snow, into his lap. Yet he was no better off.

After some manipulation, he managed to get the bunch between his mittened hands. In this fashion he carried it to his mouth. The ice crackled and snapped when by a violent effort he opened his mouth. He drew the lower jaw in, curled the upper lip out of the way, and scraped the bunch with his upper teeth in order to separate a match. He succeeded in getting one, which he dropped on his lap. He was no better off. He could not pick it up. Then he devised a way. He picked it up in his teeth and scratched it on his leg. Twenty times he scratched before he succeeded in lighting it. As it flamed he held it with his teeth to the birchbark. But the burning brimstone went up his nostrils and into his lungs, causing him to cough spasmodically. The match fell into the snow and went out.

2. *The following poem, by Shakespeare's contemporary Christopher Marlowe, purports to be a* DRAMATIC MONOLOGUE *spoken by a young shepherd. What* IMAGE *of the lifestyle proposed is created by the* SELECTION AND ORDER OF DETAILS *and the* REPETITION? *How might those aspects of the poem suggest that the* NARRATOR *is not an authentic shepherd, and that his intentions toward the "nymph" addressed might be less than honorable?*

The Passionate Shepherd to His Love

Come live with me and be my love,
And we will all the pleasures prove[8]
That valleys, groves, hills, and fields,
Woods, or steepy mountain yields.

And we will sit upon the rocks,   5
Seeing the shepherds feed their flocks,
By shallow rivers to whose falls
Melodious birds sing madrigals.

And I will make thee beds of roses
And a thousand fragrant posies,   10
A cap of flowers and a kirtle[9]
Embroidered all with leaves of myrtle;

A gown made of the finest wool
Which from our pretty lambs we pull;
Fair linèd slippers for the cold,   15
With buckles of the purest gold;

A belt of straw and ivy buds,
With coral clasps and amber studs;[1]
And if these pleasures may thee move,
Come live with me and be my love.   20

The shepherd swains[2] shall dance and sing
For thy delight each May morning:
If these delights thy mind may move,
Then live with me and be my love.

---

8. Try.
9. Skirt.
1. Buttons.
2. Country lovers.

Narration

Narration refers to the act of telling a story, whether in prose or in verse, and the means by which that telling is accomplished. The main **narrative** forms in prose are the NOVEL, the NOVELLA, and the SHORT STORY; narrative forms in verse are the EPIC, and other poems that contain an explicit or implicit PLOT and individualized CHARACTERS. The DRAMA is also narrative in the sense that it tells a story, but it does so directly, with characters who act out the plot on a stage and who speak for themselves, usually without the intermediary of a NARRATOR. In its broad sense, narration includes all of the aspects of a story and all of the techniques available to the author: the nature of the NARRATOR, the choice of POINT OF VIEW, the ROLES that the characters play in the PLOT, the PACE at which the narrative proceeds, the SETTING in which the story takes place, the means of conveying the CHARACTERIZATION, the use of DIALOGUE, the STRUCTURE, the THEMES that emerge, the TONE that the work conveys, and, standing behind the fictional NARRATIVE, the authorial VOICE implied by these various choices.

Voice

The **narrator** of a literary work, of FICTION or POETRY, is the one who tells the story. His or her identity differs from that of the author, because the narrator is always in some sense the author's invention, one of the devices that he or she is using to shape the narrative. The narrator often differs notably from the author in age, gender, outlook, or circumstances. For example, Mark Twain's NOVEL *Adventures of Huckleberry Finn* is narrated by a barely literate teenage boy; Langston Hughes's DRAMATIC MONOLOGUE "Mother to Son" by a poor, aging woman; and Edgar Allan Poe's SHORT STORY "The Cask of Amontillado" by a psychopathic murderer. In such works, it is easy not to confuse the narrator with the author. In other cases, though, such as the matter-of-fact husband reminiscing about an increasingly contentious party in Raymond Carver's SHORT STORY "What We Talk About When We Talk About Love," Edith Wharton's sympathetic newcomer in the NOVELLA *Ethan Frome*, F. Scott Fitzgerald's earnest moralist Nick Carraway in the NOVEL *The Great Gatsby*, and the urbane narrator of Lord Byron's comic epic *Don Juan*, the reader may have to guard against the temptation to equate the writer with his or her invented speaker. In fact, however, even when there is no clear distinction between the narrator and the character, the narrator remains a quasi-fictional speaker, contrived for the purposes of the particular story. The **voice** of the author, in the form of various convictions and values by which he or she judges characters and events as well as evokes judgments in the reader, stands behind every fictional narrative. That voice may be implied by various aspects of the NARRATION, listed above, which emerge in the telling and which may be discerned by the attentive reader.

POINT OF VIEW

Point of view can be identified by the pronoun that the NARRATOR uses to recount events: "I" (or, occasionally, "we" for the plural form) for the FIRST-PERSON; "he," "she," or "they" for the THIRD-PERSON; and "you" for the rarely used SECOND-PERSON.

First-Person ◀

The **first-person** POINT OF VIEW has the advantages of immediacy and directness. It invites the reader to engage with a speaker who seems to be relating first-hand experience. In the following passage, Huck Finn, who has been living the hardscrabble but unconfined life of a homeless orphan, describes the trials of undergoing the kindly widow Douglas's attempts to "sivilize" him:

> The widow she cried over me, and called me a poor lost lamb, and she called me a lot of other names, too, but she never meant no harm by it. She put me in them new clothes again, and I couldn't do nothing but sweat and sweat, and feel all cramped up. Well, then the old thing commenced again. The widow rung a bell for supper, and you had to come to time. When you got to the table you couldn't go right to eating, but you had to wait for the widow to tuck down her head and grumble a little over the victuals, though there warn't really anything the matter with them. That is, nothing only everything was cooked by itself. In a barrel of odds and ends it is different; things get mixed up, and the juice kind of swaps around, and the things go better.

The narration has a freshness and authenticity, from Huck's homely idioms to his restlessness under the regimen imposed by the social graces to his mistaking of the widow's saying of grace at the table for "grumbl[ing]."

The first-person also imposes limitations on the teller, however: the NARRATOR can relate only what he or she might have witnessed, and then only with the degree of understanding and objectivity appropriate to his or her circumstances and character. For example, a first-person narrator who is a child, such as Huck Finn, or whose mind is afflicted, such as Poe's paranoid speaker, cannot convincingly present a situation with the depth or subtlety of a more sophisticated or better balanced speaker. Nor can a first-person narrator logically describe the process of his or her own death, although such works as Emily Dickinson's "I heard a Fly buzz—when I died" and William Faulkner's *As I Lay Dying*, create enormous shock value by defying that logical impossibility. A special type of FIRST-PERSON NARRATION is the EPISTOLARY NOVEL, in which the narrative is written as a series of letters. See also: UNRELIABLE NARRATOR, STRUCTURAL IRONY.

Third-Person

The **third-person** point of view, in contrast, presents a NARRATOR that has a much broader view and, usually, an objective perspective on characters and events. Third-person narration falls into two major subtypes. An **omniscient third-person** narrator can enter the consciousness of any character, evaluate motives and explain feelings, and recount the background and predict the outcome of situations. The other major type of third-person point of view is called the **third-person limited**, which means that the narrator describes events only from the perspective and with the understanding of one, or sometimes, a select few characters.

One example of a work narrated in the omniscient third-person is George Eliot's *Middlemarch* (1872), a study of "provincial life" in Victorian England, which takes us into the thoughts and motives of a wide variety of characters during courtship and marriage and covers such broad social issues as political activism, religion, the ethics of financial investment, women's rights, and the development of medical science. Other examples are Stephen Crane's short story "The Open Boat" (1897–98), which follows the fortunes of four shipwrecked men as they try to reach land safely in their small lifeboat; and E. M. Forster's *A Passage to India* (1924), which recounts the complex tensions and bonds among various English officials and tourists and the native Indian population during the British Raj. Here is a passage from Forster's novel in which the all-knowing narrator reveals the chance circumstances and misunderstandings that lead to the disastrous Anglo-Indian excursion at the heart of the book:

> These hills look romantic in certain lights and at suitable distances, and seen of an evening from the upper verandah of the club they caused Miss Quested to say conversationally to Miss Derek that she should like to have gone, and that Dr. Aziz at Mr. Fielding's had said he would arrange something, and that Indians seem rather forgetful. She was overheard by the servant who offered them vermouths. This servant understood English. And he was not exactly a spy, but he kept his ears open, and Mahmoud Ali did not exactly bribe him, but did encourage him to come and squat with his own servants, and would happen to stroll their way when he was there. As the story traveled, it accreted emotion and Aziz learnt with horror that the ladies were deeply offended with him, and expected an invitation daily. He thought his facile remark had been forgotten. Endowed with two memories, a temporary and a permanent, he had hitherto relegated the caves to the former. Now he transferred them once and for all, and pushed the matter through. They were to be a splendid replica of the tea party.

The narrator is omniscient because it is assumed that he knows and can reveal everything about these characters and their situations, from the off-handed nature of the Englishwoman's remark to the means by which it is overheard by an eavesdropping servant to the grapevine of gossip by which it reaches, in greatly exaggerated form, the original source of the invitation. He also takes us into the consciousness of Dr. Aziz, to disclose both the well-meaning casualness with which he had offered to show the English ladies the hills and his eager resolve to set things right. The advantages of the omniscient point of view are the aura of wisdom and authority that it suggests and the unlimited range of material that it can cover. It can, though, create a feeling of distance, and so reduce the degree of connection between readers and characters.

An omniscient narrator who offers philosophical or moral commentary on the characters and the events he depicts is called an **intrusive narrator**. That technique was especially popular in nineteenth-century fiction, in such novels as William Makepeace Thackeray's *Vanity Fair* (1848), in which the account is punctuated by sly, often ironic judgments on the motives and actions of the characters as well as on contemporary mores. Here, for example, after quoting a long, obsequious speech to a wealthy heiress by a man eager to gain her friendship for himself and his daughters, the narrator of *Vanity Fair* interrupts the story to comment:

> There is little doubt that old Osborne believed all he said, and that the girls were quite earnest in their protestations of affection for Miss Swartz. People in Vanity Fair fasten on to rich folks quite naturally. If the simplest people are disposed to look not a little kindly on great Prosperity, (for I defy any member of the British public to say that the notion of Wealth has not something awful and pleasing to him; and you, if you are told that the man next to you at dinner has got half a million, not to look at him with a certain interest;)—if the simple look benevolently on money, how much more do your old worldlings regard it! Their affections rush out to meet and welcome money.

The narrator's IRONY is signaled by his exposure of the real motive for Osborne's sudden "affection" in Miss Swartz's "Wealth," capitalized along with "Prosperity" for extra emphasis. Also, he extends the target of his satire to involve not only the "people in Vanity Fair," the stereotype of society that he is depicting, but "any member of the British public," including, in a sudden shift to the SECOND-PERSON POINT OF VIEW, the reader at a hypothetical dinner party. An entirely different kind of intrusive narrator is that in Leo Tolstoy's *War and Peace* (1869), which includes long digressions on theories of military strategy and on the forces that shaped the course of the Napoleonic campaigns that the novel depicts.

A third-person narrator whose presence is merely implied is called an **objective narrator**. That subtler technique, more favored in recent times, is exemplified in such works as Bernard Malamud's *The Assistant* (1957), a novel about a lonely young drifter who is inspired by his relationship with a warm Jewish family to change his religion and way of life, and in several of Ernest Hemingway's short stories. In Hemingway's "The End of Something," the protagonist, Nick Adams, has just admitted to his girlfriend that he no longer loves her. They have been fishing, and she responds only that she is going to take the rowboat back while he walks. He offers to push it off for her, and the story ends with the following section:

> "You don't need to," she said. She was afloat in the boat on the water with the moonlight on it. Nick went back and lay down with his face in the blanket by the fire. He could hear Marjorie rowing on the water.
>
> He lay there for a long time. He lay there while he heard Bill come into the clearing, walking around the woods. He felt Bill come up to the fire. Bill didn't touch him, either.
>
> "Did she go all right?" Bill said.
>
> "Oh, yes," Nick said, lying, his face in the blanket.

"Have a scene?"

"No, there wasn't any scene."

"How do you feel?"

"Oh, go away, Bill! Go away for a while." Bill selected a sandwich from the lunch basket and walked over to have a look at the rods.

We are left to infer the characters' feelings from the spare, matter-of-fact report of their DIALOGUE and their actions: Nick's depression and guilt over the breakup, signaled especially by his prone position, hiding his face in the blanket, and by his curt replies; Marjorie's hurt and determination not to react; and Bill's half well-meaning, half prying curiosity, which provokes Nick's irritation.

A special case of the OMNISCIENT NARRATOR occurs as an element in certain plays. In DRAMA, there is usually no intermediary between audience and characters; each of the characters speaks in an individual voice, which the author has created for him or her. The exception is a narrator in a PLAY, a character who stands outside the action and comments on the characters and events, addressing the audience directly. One example is Tennessee Williams's *The Glass Menagerie*, in which the narrator, Tom Wingfield, an older version of the character of Tom in the main plot, is depicted as recounting his memories of his dysfunctional family. He keeps pausing the action to foreshadow events and evaluate the feelings and motives of the characters, including his younger self.

An earlier example is the Chorus in Shakespeare's *Henry V*, which is not a group of commentators like the chorus in Greek drama, but a single person. His initial function is to urge the audience to use their imaginations in order to attain what the Romantic poet Samuel Taylor Coleridge would later term a "willing suspension of disbelief" and persuade themselves that they are seeing not actors performing in the lowly "wooden O" of the Globe Theatre but the "vasty fields of France" and the "two mighty monarchies" that the play will depict. As the action continues, the functions of the Chorus become more diverse. He appears before each of the five acts and at the end, in the Epilogue, to bridge distances in time and place, create suspense about upcoming conflicts, pass judgment on characters and events, and, above all, glorify the play's hero, "this Star of England." By Shakespeare's day, Henry V had been dead nearly two hundred years and, in his capacity as the last English king to rule both England and France, was lionized. The play itself presents a considerably more complex, less idealized depiction of Henry, but the Chorus continually speaks in the voice of the king's champion; he is perhaps Shakespeare's concession to both popular appeal and to the court censors.

The **third-person limited**, as stated above, restricts the point of view to the understanding and experience of one or, in some cases, of a few characters. A poignant example is James Joyce's "A Painful Case," which focuses on the perspective of a wizened intellectual who discovers too late that he has rejected the one person who has ever loved him. In the following scene, the protagonist, Mr. Duffy, is reacting to a newspaper account of the woman's death, which includes the information that in the four years since he ended their relationship, she has continued to be neglected by her husband and grown daughter, taken to drink, and died by walking in front of a train:

> As he sat there, living over his life with her and evoking alternately the two images in which he now conceived her, he realized that she was dead, that she had ceased to exist, that she had become a memory. He began to feel ill at ease. He asked himself what else could he have done. He could not have lived with her openly. He had done what seemed to him best. How was he to blame? Now that she was gone he understood how lonely her life must have been, sitting night after night alone in that room. His life would be lonely too until he, too, died, ceased to exist, became a memory—if anyone remembered him.

The limited perspective follows Duffy from growing discomfort with his former self-righteousness to a first realization of his own guilt to sudden empathy for the woman's situation to the realization that he has doomed himself to share her terrible loneliness. An example of the third person limited point of view used to represent the perspective of a sequence of characters is Henry James's *The Wings of the Dove*, which takes us into the minds of the three members of a love triangle: a beautiful, socially ambitious young woman determined to marry well; the sensitive, penniless young man who loves her and with whom she is in love; and the generous, mortally ill young heiress whom they pretend to befriend and who also falls in love with the man.

An extreme form of the third-person limited point of view is the **stream of consciousness** technique, which is used to replicate the thought processes of a character, with little or no intervention by the narrator. The running meditation may include sensory impressions, memories, opinions, and insights, organized by free association, in just the digressive form that it might follow in real life. William Faulkner made masterful use of the technique, for example in *The Sound and the Fury* (1929), in which he simulates the inner workings of the minds of three markedly different brothers: a largely mute, mentally challenged man; a sensitive idealist living through the day that he commits suicide; and an outraged sadist, bent on revenge and suffering from a debilitating migraine.

Probably the most influential practitioner of stream of consciousness is James Joyce, who used it extensively in his innovative novel *Ulysses* (1922). Joyce's modern Odysseus ("Ulysses" is the Latin version of his name) is not a classical Greek hero but a middle-class Irish Jew named Leopold Bloom, and he wanders not for ten years in the ancient Mediterranean but through Dublin during a single day, June 16, 1904. His wife is not a paragon of devotion, like Penelope, but the promiscuous Molly, whom he nevertheless loves passionately:

> . . . Rover cycleshop. Those races are on today. How long ago is that? Year Phil Gilligan died. We were in Lombard street west. Wait, was in Thom's. Got the job in Wisdom Hely's year we married. Six years. Ten years ago: ninety-four he died, yes that's right the big fire at Arnott's. Val Dillon was lord mayor. The Glencree dinner. Alderman Robert O'Reilly emptying the port into his soup before the flag fell, Bobbob lapping it for the inner alderman. Couldn't hear what the band played. For what we have already received may the Lord make us. Milly was a kiddy then. Molly had the elephantgrey dress with the braided frogs. Mantailored with selfcovered buttons. She didn't like it because I sprained my ankle first day she wore choir picnic at the Sugarloaf. As if that. Old Goodwin's tall hat done up with some sticky stuff. Flies' picnic too. Never put a dress on her back like it. Fitted her like a glove, shoulder and hips. Just beginning to plump it out well. Rabbitpie we had that day. People looking after her.
>
> Happy. Happier then. Snug little room that was with the red wallpaper, Dockrell's, one and ninepence a dozen. Milly's tubbing night. American soap I bought: elderflower. Cosy smell of her bathwater. Funny she looked soaped all over. Shapely too. Now photography. Poor papa's daguerreotype atelier he told me of. Hereditary taste.

The ALLUSIVE, highly subjective nature of the style leaves some points unclear, such as personal references, many of which are explained elsewhere in the book, and peculiarly Irish institutions. For example, "Milly" is the Blooms' daughter, now a teenager, and the "photography" reference is to her new job in a photographer's shop. The political offices mentioned—"lord mayor" and "alderman"—refer to the city government, and the businesses, such as "Wisdom Hely's," to local establishments. In keeping with the impressionistic content, the style is fragmentary and elliptical, ignoring traditional rules of syntax and grammar. For example, sentences like the grace said at the dinner and Bloom's dismissal of the basis for Molly's superstition about the bad luck she associated with her dress ("As if that") are left incomplete.

The CHARACTERIZATION of Bloom that emerges from this process is moving and believable: the way that he measures the passing of time by means of ordinary events in his life, relishes the memory of his young wife's budding voluptuousness and of a dress that was especially flattering to it, and cherishes a recollection of his child's bath night, when she was snug and secure and the couple united, "happier then" than they are in the troublesome present. We also experience first-hand Bloom's sense of humor—his amusement at the slapstick of "Bobbob" "lapping" the port with which he has spiked his soup for the sake of his "inner alderman"—as well as his responsiveness to physical sensations in the description of Molly's clinging "elephantgrey" dress and the "cosy smell" of Milly's soapy bath water. His humane sympathies also come out, in his tender recollection of the little Milly and of his "poor papa," the sadness tempered by the consolation that his father has bequeathed to his granddaughter his interest in photography. The freshness and scope allowed by such direct access to his thought process—in the next paragraph, Bloom himself calls it a "stream of life"—help make him a fully THREE-DIMENSIONAL and highly appealing character.

The third-person limited has the advantages of both the immediacy of the first person and the authority and range of the third person omniscient. Perhaps for those reasons, it is the most frequently used point of view in all three of the fictional genres—the NOVEL, the SHORT STORY, and the NOVELLA.

Second-Person

The third major point of view is the **second-person**, in which the narrator addresses the audience directly using the pronoun "you," and assumes that the audience is experiencing the events along with the narrator. That implied audience may be the reader, a character who appears later in the story, or a listener who is never identified, such as a therapist in whom the narrator is confiding. The second-person occurs most frequently as a temporary departure from one of the other points of view. For example, Holden Caufield, the troubled teenage FIRST-PERSON NARRATOR in J. D. Salinger's *The Catcher in the Rye* (1951), introduces the younger sister he adores and then says several times with uncharacteristic enthusiasm, "You'd like her. . . . I swear to God you'd like her." Whether Holden is speaking to a sympathetic reader or to one of the doctors at the "crumby place" where, he tells us on the first page, he has been sent to recover from "some madman stuff" he has suffered, the shift in both his perspective and his attitude are striking.

John Cheever's "The Swimmer" (1964) is a THIRD-PERSON LIMITED story about an apparently carefree suburbanite who decides to return home after an afternoon poolside party by swimming across the intervening pools owned by his neighbors. One of the first hints of the devastating truth about his situation comes in a sudden switch to the **second-person** point of view as he waits to cross a busy, littered highway:

> Had you gone for a Sunday afternoon ride that day you might have seen him, close to naked, standing on the shoulders of Route 424, waiting for a chance to cross. You might have wondered if he was the victim of foul play, had his car broken down, or was he merely a fool.

His vulnerability and isolation foreshadow the terrible emptiness that awaits him at his journey's end.

In a METAFICTIONAL story entitled "Happy Endings" (1983), Margaret Atwood's wry narrator poses a series of possible plots for stories about various couples, all told in the THIRD-PERSON OMNISCIENT POINT OF VIEW. In the last section, presumably speaking as a writing teacher to students, the narrator shifts to the second-person and challenges:

> If you think this is all too bourgeois, make John a revolutionary and Mary a counter-espionage agent and see how far that gets you. Remember, this is Canada. You'll still end up with an A. . . .

The second-person has also been used effectively in entire works, such as Jay McInerney's *Bright Lights, Big City* (1984), which follows the nameless PROTAGONIST in his frenetic attempts to immerse himself in the distractions and dissipations of New York City in order to escape the chaos into which his life is falling. By the end, he is barely functional but more humble and self-aware:

> You get down on your knees and tear open the bag. The smell of warm dough envelops you. The first bite sticks in your throat and

you almost gag. You will have to go slowly. You will have to learn everything all over again.

Not surprisingly, the use of the second-person point of view is relatively rare. While it has the immediacy of the FIRST-PERSON, it can have the off-putting effects of seeming highly self-conscious and of calling constant attention to the process of narration. It also limits the kinds of scenes that can effectively be related through such constant back-and-forth involvement between narrator and audience.

EXERCISE: Point of View

For each of the following passages:

- Identify the POINT OF VIEW: FIRST-PERSON, SECOND-PERSON, THIRD-PERSON LIMITED, or THIRD-PERSON OMNISCIENT.
- If the POINT OF VIEW is THIRD-PERSON OMNISCIENT, state whether the NARRATOR is INTRUSIVE or OBJECTIVE. If it is THIRD-PERSON LIMITED, note whether or not it is an example of STREAM OF CONSCIOUSNESS.
- Explain why the term or terms apply.
- Describe the effects of the POINT OF VIEW on the meaning and the TONE of the passage.

first person

1. In walks these three girls in nothing but bathing suits. I'm in the third checkout slot, with my back to the door, so I don't see them until they're over by the bread. The one that caught my eye first was the one in the plaid green two-piece. She was a chunky kid, with a good tan and a sweet broad soft-looking can with those two crescents of white just under it, where the sun never seems to hit, at the top of the backs of her legs. I stood there with my hand on a box of HiHo crackers trying to remember if I rang it up or not.

   –JOHN UPDIKE, "A & P"

2. [Miss Bates] enjoyed a most uncommon degree of popularity for a woman neither young, handsome, rich, nor married. [She] stood in the very worst predicament in the world for having much of the public favour; and she had no intellectual superiority to make atonement to herself, or frighten those who might hate her into outward respect. She had never boasted either beauty or cleverness. Her youth had passed without distinction, and her middle of life was devoted to the care of a failing mother, and the endeavour to make a small income go as far as possible. And yet she was a happy woman, and a woman whom no one named without good-will. It

▼

was her own universal good-will and contented temper which worked such wonders. She loved every body, was interested in every body's happiness, quick-sighted to every body's merits; thought herself a most fortunate creature, and surrounded with blessings. . . .   –JANE AUSTEN, *Emma*

3. The hunter will talk about spring in Hawaii, summer in Alaska. The man who says he was always better at math will form the sentences so carefully it will be impossible to tell if you are included in these plans. When he asks you if you would like to open a small guest ranch way out in the country, understand that this is a rhetorical question.

    . . . He'll ask you if you've ever shot anything, if you'd like to, if you ever thought about teaching your dog to retrieve. Your dog will like him too much, will drop the stick at his feet every time, will roll over and let the hunter scratch his belly.
                                    –PAM HOUSTON, "How to Talk to a Hunter"

4. *This stanza follows a description of soldiers caught in a poison gas attack during World War I:*

    If in some smothering dreams you too could pace
    Behind the wagon that we flung him in,
    And watch the white eyes writhing in his face,
    His hanging face, like a devil's sick of sin;
    If you could hear, at every jolt, the blood   5
    Come gargling from the froth-corrupted lungs,
    Obscene as cancer, bitter as the cud
    Of vile, incurable sores on innocent tongues—
    My friend, you would not tell with such high zest
    To children ardent for some desperate glory,   10
    The old Lie: Dulce et decorum est
    Pro patria mori.[1]   –WILFRED OWEN, "Dulce Et Decorum Est"

5. Resentment. It was poisoning her. (She looked at this emotion and thought it was absurd. Yet she felt it.) She was a prisoner. (She looked at this thought too, and it was no good telling herself it was a ridiculous one.) She must tell Matthew[2] but what? She was filled with emotions that were utterly ridiculous, that she despised, yet that nevertheless she was feeling so strongly she could not shake them off.

---

1. Horace, *Ode* 3.2.13: "It is sweet and decorous to die for one's country."
2. Her husband.

▼

The school holidays came round, and this time they were for nearly two months, and she behaved with a conscious controlled decency that nearly drove her crazy. She would lock herself in the bathroom, breathing deep, trying to let go into some kind of calm. Or she went up to the spare room, usually empty, where no one would expect her to be. She heard the children calling "Mother, Mother," and kept silent, feeling guilty. Or she went to the very end of the garden, by herself, and looked at the slow-moving brown river; she looked at the river and closed her eyes and breathed slow and deep, taking it into her being, into her veins.

–Doris Lessing, "To Room Nineteen"

6. The morning of June 27th was clear and sunny, with the fresh warmth of a full-summer day; the flowers were blossoming pro-fusely and the grass was richly green. The people of the village began to gather in the square, between the post office and the bank, around ten o'clock; in some towns there were so many people that the lottery took two days and had to be started on June 26th, but in this village, where there were only about three hundred people, the whole lottery took less than two hours, so it could begin at ten o' clock in the morning and still be through in time to allow the villagers to get home for noon dinner.

–Shirley Jackson, "The Lottery"

[handwritten: 3rd omniscient objective]

7. I had a test today. I think I faled it. and I think that maybe now they wont use me. What happind is a nice young man was in the room and he had some white cards with ink spilled all over them. He sed Charlie what do you see on this card. I was very skared even tho I had my rabits foot in my pockit because when I was a kid I always faled tests in school and I spilled ink to.

I told him I saw a inkblot. He said yes and it made me feel good. I thot that was all but when I got up to go he stopped me. He said now sit down Charlie we are not thru yet.

–Daniel Keyes, "Flowers for Algernon"

[handwritten: 1st person]

8. *This speech occurs at the start of Act II of Thornton Wilder's* Our Town:

STAGE MANAGER Three years have gone by. Yes, the sun's come up over a thousand times. Summers and winters have cracked the mountains a little bit more and the rains have brought down some of the dirt. . . . Nature's been pushing and contriving in other ways, too; a number of young people fell in love and got married. Yes, the mountains got bit away a few fractions of an inch; millions of gallons of water went by the mill; and here and there a new home was set up under a roof. Almost everybody in

▼

the world gets married—you know what I mean? In our town
there aren't hardly any exceptions. Most everybody in the world
climbs into their graves married. The first act was called Daily
Life. This act is called Love and Marriage. There's another act
coming after this: I reckon you can guess what that's about.

9. *In the following passage from William Faulkner's* The Sound and the Fury,
*the unopened "it" is the invitation that the speaker has received to the
wedding of his sister, with whom he is hopelessly in love. "Shreve" is his
roommate at Harvard. The Latin phrase means "I was not. I am. I was. I
am not."*

2nd ?

A quarter hour yet. And then I'll not be. The peacefullest words.
Peacefullest words. *Non fui. Sum. Fui. Non sum.* Somewhere I heard
bells once. Mississippi or Massachusetts. I was. I am not. Massachusetts or Mississippi. Shreve has a bottle in his trunk. *Aren't you even
going to open it* Mr and Mrs Jason Richmond Compson announce
the *Three times. Days. Aren't you even going to open it* marriage of
their daughter Candace *that liquor teaches you to confuse the means
with the end* I am. Drink. I was not.

10. Now the broad road was crossed. The lane began, smoky and dark.
Women in shawls and men's tweed caps hurried by. Men hung over
the palings; the children played in the doorways. A low hum came
from the mean little cottages. In some of them there was a flicker of
light, and a shadow, crab-like, moved across the window. Laura
bent her head and hurried on. She wished now that she had put on
a coat. How her frock shone! And the big hat with the velvet
streamer—if only it was another hat! Were the people looking at
her? They must be. It was a mistake to have come; she knew all
along it was a mistake. Should she go back even now?
                                        —KATHERINE MANSFIELD, "The Garden-Party"

3rd Intrusive

CHARACTERIZATION

Characterization means the techniques by which an author of a
work of FICTION, DRAMA, or NARRATIVE POETRY represents the moral,
intellectual, and emotional natures of the characters. In *Aspects of the
Novel* (1927), the critic and novelist E. M. Forster introduced the
terms FLAT and ROUND CHARACTERS to describe the extent to which
literary characters are developed. In analyzing the methods by which
authors depict characters, a useful distinction is between SHOWING
and TELLING.

▶   # Flat Characters vs. Round Characters

A **flat character**, also called a **two-dimensional character**, is more a type than an individual, and stays essentially the same throughout the work. In Charles Dickens's *Great Expectations*, for example, the good-hearted Joe Gargery and the misanthropic Miss Havisham are flat characters. The term "two-dimensional," which refers to a line such as is used in drawing a sketch, should not be mistakenly called "one-dimensional," which means a single point and therefore does not apply. A **round**, or **three-dimensional**, **character**, in contrast, is multifaceted and subject to change and growth; he or she is also capable of inconsistencies, and in those ways similar to an actual human being. Pip, the PROTAGONIST/NARRATOR of Dickens's novel, for example, changes enormously from the naïve, sweet-tempered child of the early chapters as he grows to manhood, discovers new sides of his nature, and confronts various crises.

Some characters may surprise readers with their three-dimensionality as a work goes on. In Shakespeare's *Othello*, Emilia, the oppressed wife of Iago, seems at first to be a simple and largely silent TYPE rather than a round character. As she comes to realize the extent of her husband's villainy, however, she finds her voice and emerges as clear-sighted, insightful, and courageous. The reader must encounter round characters in several different contexts in order to gauge their complexities and inconsistencies, while flat characters tend to reveal their essence from the outset and to change little. This is not to imply that characters must be round to be effective. Their relative level of development depends on their role in the action and on the conventions of the genre in which they appear. Usually, except in long, complex novels such as Tolstoy's *Anna Karenina* and Eliot's *Middlemarch*, there is space for only a few ROUND characters, and sometimes for the PROTAGONIST alone to be shown THREE-DIMENSIONALLY. Also, characters in an adventure story, such as *The Lord of the Rings*; a SATIRE such as Jonathan Swift's *Gulliver's Travels*; or a farce, such as Shakespeare's *The Comedy of Errors*, remain FLAT in order to keep the reader's attention on more essential aspects of the genre, such as PLOT and TONE.

Showing vs. Telling ◀

In depicting characters, authors use methods of either **showing** or **telling**. **Showing** means simply presenting characters' words and actions without commentary and allowing that dramatization to imply their motives, feelings, and values. That direct approach has been favored since the late nineteenth century; masters of the technique have included Henry James, Anton Chekhov, Ernest Hemingway, Nadine Gordimer, and Raymond Carver. **Telling**, in contrast, is the method by which the author describes, and comments on, characters' motives and values and often also passes judgment on characters and events, as a means of shaping the audience's response. That intermediary approach has been used by most of the great nineteenth-century novelists, for example, Jane Austen, George Eliot, Chares Dickens, and Leo Tolstoy, as well as by many of their modern successors, including E. M. Forster, Willa Cather, D. H. Lawrence, and Saul Bellow.

For a description of techniques that are crucial to characterizing the personages in a NOVEL, SHORT STORY, or DRAMA, see NARRATOR, POINT OF VIEW, and DIALOGUE.

EXERCISES: Characterization

I. Name a FLAT CHARACTER and a ROUND CHARACTER from two narratives—NOVELS, SHORT STORIES, or DRAMAS—that you have studied recently, and explain why that term applies.

II. Return to the exercises on POINT OF VIEW and on DIALOGUE, and choose one passage that uses SHOWING to depict the characters and one that uses TELLING. Then explain why each of those terms applies.

III. Multilevel analysis of a long passage. The following passage is the last part of a short story about an Englishwoman who goes to a Paris park each Sunday; she is wearing her best fur stole. Comment on how the POINT OF VIEW, the DIALOGUE, and the CHARACTERIZATION (does it depend on SHOWING or TELLING?) convey the NARRATOR's attitude toward Miss Brill.

Oh, how fascinating it was! How she enjoyed it! How she loved sitting here watching it all! It was like a play. It was exactly like a play. Who could believe the sky at the back wasn't painted? But it wasn't till a little brown dog trotted on solemn and then slowly trotted off, like a little "theater" dog . . . that Miss Brill discovered what it was that made it so exciting. They were all on the stage. They weren't only the audience, not only looking on; they were acting. Even she had a part and came every Sunday. No doubt somebody would have noticed if she hadn't been there; she was part of the performance after all. How strange she'd never thought of it like that before! And yet it explained why she made such a point of starting from home at just the same time each week—so as not to be late for the performance—and it also explained why she had quite a queer, shy feeling telling her English pupils how she spent her Sunday afternoons. No wonder! Miss Brill nearly laughed out loud. She was on the stage. She thought of the old invalid gentleman to whom she read the newspaper four afternoons a week while he slept in the garden. She had got quite used to the frail head on the cotton pillow, the hollowed eyes, the open mouth and the high pinched nose. If he'd been dead she mightn't have noticed for weeks; she wouldn't have minded. But suddenly he knew he was having the paper read to him by an actress! "An actress!" The old head lifted; two points of light quivered in the old eyes. "An actress—are ye?" And Miss Brill smoothed the newspaper as though it were the manuscript of her part and said gently: "Yes, I have been an actress for a long time."

The band had been having a rest. Now they started again. And what they played was warm, sunny, yet there was just a faint chill—a something, what was it?—not sadness, no, not sadness—a something that made you want to sing. The tune lifted, the light shone; and it seemed to Miss Brill that in another moment all of them, all the whole company, would begin singing. The young ones, the laughing ones who were moving together, they would begin, and the men's voices, very resolute and brave, would join them. And then she, too, she too, and the others on the benches—they would come in with a kind of accompaniment—something low, that scarcely rose or fell, something so beautiful and moving. . . . And Miss Brill's eyes filled with tears and she looked smiling at all the other members of the company. Yes, we understand, we understand, she thought—though what they understood she didn't know.

Just at that moment a boy and a girl came and sat down where the old couple had been. They were beautifully dressed; they were in love. The hero and heroine, of course, just arrived from his father's yacht. And still soundlessly singing, still with that trembling smile, Miss Brill prepared to listen.

"No, not now," said the girl. "Not here, I can't."

"But why? Because of that stupid old thing at the end there?" asked the boy. "Why does she come here at all—who wants her? Why doesn't she keep her silly old mug at home?"

"It's her fu-fur which is so funny," giggled the girl. "It's exactly like a fried whiting."

"Ah, be off with you!" said the boy in an angry whisper. Then: "Tell me, ma petite chérie."[1]

"No, not here," said the girl. "Not *yet*."

On her way home, she usually bought a slice of honey-cake at the baker's. It was her Sunday treat. Sometimes there was an almond in her slice, sometimes not. It made a great difference. If there was an almond it was like carrying home a tiny present—a surprise—something that might very well have not been there. She hurried on the almond Sundays and struck the match for the kettle in quite a dashing way.

But today she passed the baker's by, climbed the stairs, went into the dark little room—her room like a cupboard—and sat down on the red eiderdown. She sat there for a long time. The box that the fur came out of was on the bed. She unclasped the necklet quickly; quickly, without looking, laid it inside. But when she put the lid on she thought she heard something crying.

–KATHERINE MANSFIELD, "Miss Brill"

ROLES IN THE PLOT

Most literary works of FICTION, DRAMA, and NARRATIVE POETRY contain a **plot**, a sequence of events leading to some sort of resolution that is designed to reveal the feelings, motives, and values of the characters. The main roles that the characters assume fall into three types: the PROTAGONIST, the ANTAGONIST, and the FOIL.

Protagonist

The **protagonist** (proh-TAG-ahn-ihst, from the Greek word for "first actor" or "first contender") is the main character in a work of DRAMA, FICTION, or NARRATIVE POETRY. The events of the work center on him or her, as does the reader's interest. Some examples are Elizabeth Bennet in Jane Austen's *Pride and Prejudice*, King Lear in the Shakespearean tragedy of the same name, and Odysseus in Homer's epic *The Odyssey*. An alternative term for the protagonist is the **hero** or **heroine**. That term, however, has a connotation of nobility, dig-

---

1. My little darling.

nity, and elevated status, which, while it is fitting for the chief character in an epic or a classic tragedy, does not suit the petty flaws and lowly status of more ordinary protagonists, such as Holden Caulfield, the confused adolescent in J. D. Salinger's *The Catcher in the Rye*, or the downtrodden Willy Loman in Arthur Miller's *Death of a Salesman*. In other words, the broader term "protagonist" is preferable in most cases. Some complex works lack a single protagonist and instead shift the focus as different characters play a central role in various subplots and SETTINGS, as in Shakespeare's *Antony and Cleopatra* and E. M. Forster's *A Passage to India*.

Antagonist

In many works, the main character has an **antagonist** (an-TAG-ahn-ihst, from the Greek word for "against the contender"), a character that opposes the PROTAGONIST's goals and interests and so creates the major conflict in the work. Examples are Poseidon in Homer's *Odyssey*, the Olympian god of the sea who continually blocks Odysseus's attempts to reach his homeland, and Augustus Caesar in *Antony and Cleopatra*, who opposes Marc Antony's political ambitions as well as his passion for Cleopatra. If the antagonist has evil intentions, like Iago in *Othello*, he is called the **villain**. If the protagonist is himself evil, however, like Shakespeare's Macbeth, the antagonist—in *Macbeth*, Macduff serves that function—is portrayed as a sympathetic character.

In a broad sense, an antagonist need not be another character. It may be some larger force that challenges the protagonist, such as fate, which, in Sophocles' *Oedipus Rex*, defeats all of Oedipus's attempts to circumvent the dire prophecy made at his birth. In Jack London's "To Build a Fire," the antagonist is the paralyzing cold of the Klondike, while in Stephen Crane's *The Red Badge of Courage*, it is the traumatic effect of battle. The antagonist may also be internal, in the form of conflicting desires or values within the protagonist. In Charlotte Brontë's *Jane Eyre*, for example, the protagonist is torn between remaining with the man she loves in an adulterous relationship, or else obeying the dictates of her conscience by leaving him for a life of emptiness and poverty. A work may contain more than one sort of antagonist. Shakespeare's *Hamlet*, for example, has a human antagonist in his uncle Claudius, who has murdered Hamlet's father, seduced his mother, and seized the Danish throne. Hamlet, however, is also beset by the demands of fate, which has designated him the "scourge and minister" who must restore order to Denmark, even at the cost of his life. The third antagonist that Hamlet faces is internal, the conflict between his desire to take swift and violent action and a propensity to introspection and moral scrupulousness that keeps him from acting.

Foil

A third kind of role that occurs in many works is that of the **foil**, a character who contrasts with the PROTAGONIST in ways that bring out certain of his or her moral, emotional, or intellectual qualities. Hamlet calls attention to that function just before his fatal duel with Laertes, the impulsive man of action who is his main foil in the play. The men are about to engage in what Hamlet believes is not a serious combat but a friendly demonstration of their skill with "foils," that is, swords. He has quarreled with Laertes earlier, and to make amends, he gives a flattering speech:

> I'll be your foil, Laertes. In mine ignorance
> Your skill shall, like a star i'th' darkest night,
> Stick fiery off indeed.

Here the PUN—"foil" in Shakespeare's day meant not only a rapier but a piece of thin metal foil on which jewels were placed to show off their sparkle—suggests both aspects of Laertes' relationship to the HERO: to oppose him in the conflict with Claudius, with whom Laertes is in league, and to highlight Hamlet's honorable conduct and contemplative nature. In Shakespeare's *Romeo and Juliet*, the hero has several foils: the cynical Mercutio, who mocks the very concept of the romantic love that Romeo celebrates with Juliet; the hot-tempered Tybalt, who is obsessed with defending his family name in the feud that Romeo sees as senseless; and the sweet-tempered Benvolio, who strives only to be a good friend and a peacemaker in the midst of all the violence. In keeping with their minor roles in the plot, each of these foils is a FLAT CHARACTER, while Romeo—fittingly, for one of the pair of protagonists in the play—is three-dimensional in his capacities as ardent lover, reluctant defender of family honor, and loyal friend.

EXERCISES: Roles

I. Name the PROTAGONIST in *three* different NOVELS, SHORT STORIES, DRAMAS, or EPICS that you have studied recently. In each instance, give the *title* of the work, followed by the name of the character.

II. Choose *three* literary works—either those listed above or additional ones—that contain an ANTAGONIST. Identify the nature of the ANTAGONIST(s), which may be a character, a larger force, and/or a set of conflicting emotions or desires within the PROTAGONIST. For each example, explain the effects that the ANTAGONIST has on the meaning and TONE of the work.

III. Name *four* FOIL CHARACTERS in at least *two* literary works—either those cited in I or II above or different ones. Then explain how each character acts as a FOIL to the PROTAGONIST.

DIALOGUE

Dialogue is the presentation of what characters in a literary work say. It is a crucial element of DRAMA, in which, except for STAGE DIRECTIONS, dialogue makes up the entire text; it is also an important aspect of FICTION and of some NARRATIVE POETRY. Dialogue has several possible uses: to reveal characters' motives, feelings, values, and relationships; to advance the PLOT; and to suggest TONE—that is, the speaker's attitude toward the character that he or she is addressing and the NARRATOR's attitude toward the audience.

Dialogue is a primary means of depicting CHARACTER. Both the style and the content of characters' words can reveal such qualities as their relative levels of intelligence and refinement, as well as their values. The responses of other characters can suggest their relationship, including the level of power relative to each other.

In works of FICTION, the NARRATOR's commentary on the dialogue also helps shape the reader's response. In the following episode from F. Scott Fitzgerald's *The Great Gatsby*, the narrator, Nick Carraway, has just been taken by Tom Buchanan, his cousin's husband, to meet his "girl." Tom's mistress is married to the owner of a dilapidated garage, George Wilson, who has no inkling of the adultery. The scene that ensues is Nick's—and the reader's—introduction to Wilson:

> . . . the proprietor . . . appeared in the door of an office, wiping his hands on a piece of waste. He was a blond, spiritless man,

▼

anemic, and faintly handsome. When he saw us a damp gleam of hope sprang into his light blue eyes.

"Hello, Wilson, old man," said Tom, slapping him jovially on the shoulder. "How's business?"

"I can't complain," answered Wilson unconvincingly. "When are you going to sell me that car?"

"Next week; I've got my man working on it now."

"Works pretty slow, don't he?"

"No, he doesn't," said Tom coldly. "And if you feel that way about it, maybe I'd better sell it somewhere else after all."

"I don't mean that," explained Wilson quickly. "I just meant—"

His voice faded off and Tom glanced impatiently around the garage.

Everything about the scene implies Wilson's weakness and subjugation to Tom's will: his faded physical appearance, tentative gestures, and pathetic hope that Tom will bring a bit of lucrative business to the failing shop. Nick first describes him as "spiritless" and "anemic," and, fittingly, he is "wiping his hands on a bit of waste." Tom immediately takes control, speaking the first words, and "slapping" Wilson with false joviality. The one time that Wilson attempts to assert himself, Tom cuts him off "coldly," and Wilson retracts his complaint and fades into silence. The FIRST-PERSON witness leaves no doubt of the cuckolded husband's powerlessness or of his betrayer's contempt.

Another technique for using dialogue to depict character is to recount differences between a character's reported thoughts and his or her spoken words. In Jane Austen's *Emma* (1816), for example, the PROTAGONIST is often constrained by the manners required in her upper-class society from expressing her actual opinions or preferences. She is adept, though, at avoiding uncomfortable topics by maintaining a polite silence or by changing the subject. The OMNISCIENT NARRATOR reveals the contrast between Emma's thoughts and words in such comments as the following, which describes her reaction to an awkward dispute she is having with a close family friend and mentor: "It was most convenient to Emma not to make a direct reply to this assertion; she chose rather to take up her own line of the subject again."

In "The Red Convertible," a SHORT STORY by Louise Erdrich, the teenage NARRATOR/PROTAGONIST, Lyman Lamartine, speaks words that are markedly at odds with his thoughts. Lyman is a Chippewa Indian who is struggling with how to deal with his older brother Henry's emotional illness. Henry, a former marine and captive in a prisoner of war camp in Vietnam, is suffering from post-traumatic stress disorder. The crisis is complicated by the brothers' isolation and poverty. They live on a remote reservation, which contains no Indian therapists, and no one in the family trusts mainstream hospitals. Even if they could afford such treatment, the mother charges that "'[the doctors] just give them drugs,'" and in any case both the mother and Lyman know that Henry would refuse to be committed.

At this point in the story, Henry is virtually mute with depression, and Lyman is desperate to help him. Suddenly, he thinks of the red convertible that the two of them had bought and fixed up before Henry was drafted:

> One night Henry was off somewhere. I took myself a hammer. I went out to that car and I did a number on its underside. Whacked it up. Bent the tail pipe double. Ripped the muffler loose. By the time I was done with the car it looked worse than any typical Indian car that has been driven all its life on the reservation roads, which they always say are like government promises—full of holes. It just about hurt me, I'll tell you that! I threw dirt in the carburetor and I ripped all the electric tape off the seats. I made it look just as beat up as I could. Then I sat back and waited.
>
> Still, it took him over a month. That was all right, because it was just getting warm enough, not melting, but warm enough to work outside.
>
> "Lyman," he says, walking in one day, "that red car looks like shit."
>
> "Well it's old," I say. "You got to expect that."
>
> "No way!" says Henry. "That car's a classic! But you went and ran the piss right out of it, Lyman, and you know it don't deserve that. I kept that car in A-one shape. You don't remember. You're too young. But when I left, that car was running like a watch. Now I don't even know if I can get it to start again, let alone get it anywhere near its old condition."
>
> "Well you try," I said, like I was getting mad, "but I say it's a piece of junk."
>
> Then I walked out before he could realize I knew he'd strung together more than six words at once.

Lyman's actions make clear the strength of his love for his brother. He is willing to sacrifice the car, despite how much he treasures it, in the hope of helping Henry. After pounding and ripping the convertible on which he has lavished so much care, he admits of the wrecking, "It just about hurt me, I'll tell you that!" Lyman's easy colloquialism and

his candor make his voice fresh and appealing. He is confiding in the
reader what he must be careful to keep secret from everyone else.

The plan is also a tribute to Lyman's cleverness. He creates a way to
draw Henry out of his depression, inspire his self-esteem, and give him
a meaningful project. He also knows enough to lie low and let Henry
discover the car on his own. Then he denies that the convertible has
been damaged, replying offhandedly to Henry's accusation, "'Well, it's
old.'" That dismissal triggers a heated protest from Henry that the car is
"'a classic'" that he had "'kept [running] in A-one shape.'" With typical
older brother condescension, Henry claims that Lyman is "'too young'"
to remember the car's former glory. Then he takes the bait that Lyman
has offered: the challenge of at least "'get[ting] it to start again'" and
perhaps "'get[ting] it anywhere near its old condition.'"

Lyman keeps up his pretense of defensiveness: "'Well you try,'" I
said, like I was getting mad." Then he gives what seems to be one last
jeer at Henry: "'but I say it's a piece of junk.'" As the narrator, however,
Lyman confides his true feelings in the narrative description that follows. He is delighted that he has tricked Henry into breaking his grim
silence and taking a new interest in the world: "Then I walked out
before he could realize I knew he'd strung together more than six words
at once." The dialogue shows the contrast between Lyman's pose of
indifference and sullenness and his love for his brother, which he feels
compelled by the circumstances to express only by indirect means.

In PROSE FICTION the relative proportion of dialogue to narration
varies enormously, according to the purposes of the author. Some
SHORT STORIES are comprised almost entirely of dialogue—for example, Ernest Hemingway's "Hills Like White Elephants," a simmering
quarrel between a couple at a foreign train station, in which the subject of their bitter conflict emerges only from hints in their words.
Sections of NOVELS, too, are limited largely to conversation between
characters, so that passages read like a short play. One example
occurs in Charlotte Brontë's *Jane Eyre* (1847) during the heroine's
reunion with her beloved Mr. Rochester, who is jealous of the relationship that she has had with another man, her cousin St. John
Rivers, during her absence. Mr. Rochester, who has been blinded
and maimed, has been severely depressed, and Jane is delighted at
this chance to revive his fighting spirit and direct his energies at
someone who, as she knows, is no rival to him:

> "How long did you reside with him and his sisters after the
> cousinship was discovered?"
> "Five months."
> "Did Rivers spend much time with the ladies of his family?"

"Yes; the back parlour was both his study and ours: he sat near the window, and we by the table."

"Did he study much?"

"A good deal."

"What?"

"Hindostanee."

"And what did you do meantime?"

"I studied German at first."

"Did he teach you?"

"He did not understand German."

"Did he teach you nothing?"

"A little Hindostanee."

"Rivers taught you Hindostanee?"

"Yes, sir."

"And his sisters also?"

"No."

"Only you?"

"Only me."

"Did you ask to learn?"

"No."

"He wished to teach you?"

"Yes."

Mr. Rochester's jealousy is implied by the precise cross-examination to which he subjects Jane. Knowing her intelligence and love of learning, he focuses on the role that she has played of star pupil, seeing it, rightly, for the show of favor that it is. His jealousy is further suggested through his concentration on the nature of their study, an esoteric subject that suggests both Rivers's erudition and his respect for Jane's abilities; it is also suggested by his pointed inquiry into whether or not Rivers singled her out from his sisters. Jane's curt answers of course pique Rochester's curiosity and tease him with the implication that she has something to hide. For the reader, the DRAMATIC IRONY achieved by knowing Jane's actual feelings and motives—she is the NARRATOR as well as the PROTAGONIST of the novel and has confided her intentions beforehand—makes the scene a comic interlude.

Such passages of straight dialogue may give readers the impression that they are eavesdropping on a real-life conversation, which the author has just happened to record. In actuality, the shaping hand of the writer is very much at work in such scenes, choosing words and phrases that are characteristic of each speaker; eliminating the pauses, stammerings, and irrelevancies that litter everyday talk; and pacing the exchange for both efficiency and **verisimilitude** (veh-rih-sih-MIL-ih-tood), Latin for "similar to the truth": plausibility, the semblance of truth.

In addition, any contrasts between what a character says in various contexts can be both convincing and revealing. That technique is especially crucial in DRAMA, since the CHARACTERIZATION must come almost entirely through the dialogue. In Shakespeare's *Romeo and Juliet*, for example, Lord Capulet makes a series of strikingly different pronouncements about his daughter Juliet's freedom to choose a husband. He first tells her new suitor, the County Paris, that he must "woo her" and "get her heart," for his own permission depends on her "consent." When, a short while later, Juliet has become deeply depressed, supposedly over her cousin Tybalt's death, Capulet decides that marriage would be the ideal cure for her melancholy. He tells the count that he can vouch for his daughter's agreement to an immediate wedding: "I think she will be ruled / In all respects by me; nay more, I doubt it not." Juliet, however, is grieving over her forced separation from Romeo, the son of her family's mortal enemy, whom she has secretly married. Without revealing the reason, she refuses the match with Paris. Capulet, outraged, tells her: "An you be mine, I'll give you to my friend; / An you be not, hang, beg, starve, die in the streets." Capulet's initial permissiveness, it is suggested, depended on his complacent conviction that his daughter's will coincides with his own. His authority threatened, Capulet goes from being the indulgent parent to the ruthless tyrant. The inconsistencies in his attitude make him a more plausible, albeit not a more sympathetic, character.

In a NOVEL, a NOVELLA, and a SHORT STORY, the author may also shape the impact of dialogue by using **speech headings**, descriptions of characters' vocal tones or gestures as they speak a line; examples are the phrases "slapping him jovially on the shoulder" and "explained Wilson quickly" in the passage from *The Great Gatsby*. The authorial presence is also usually evident in descriptions of action and setting that are interspersed with the dialogue, as in the description of Holden feeling compelled to fetch the exam book in the scene from *The Catcher in the Rye*. In plays, such functions may be served by the **stage directions**, available to readers of the text but needing to be suggested in performance. Some playwrights are markedly spare in the stage direction that they use. Those of Shakespeare and other Renaissance dramatists, for example, are usually limited to entrances, exits, and sound effects. Any slightly more elaborate descriptions of settings and actions in the plays, implied by the dialogue, have usually been added by various editors and enclosed in square brackets. An example is the stage direction in *Hamlet* after the distraught Laertes demands that the burial of his sister pause until he has "caught her once more in [his] arms": [*Leaps into the grave*]. In Shakespeare's case the reason for this sparsity was probably that he was writing primarily for the purposes of performance, and for a repertory company of which he was a member. Most recent playwrights, such as Tennessee Williams, Arthur Miller, and August Wilson, tend to give much more elaborate descriptions of how they want lines to be delivered and how they intend characters to move on stage. The following set of stage directions, for example, appears in Williams's *The Glass Menagerie* in the aftermath of a quarrel between the adult son and his mother:

> *The music of "Ave Maria" is heard softly.*
> *Tom glances sheepishly but sullenly at her averted figure and slumps at the table.*
> *The coffee is scalding hot; he sips it and gasps and spits it back in the cup. At his gasp,* AMANDA *catches her breath and half turns. Then she catches herself and turns back to the window.* TOM *blows on his coffee, glancing sidewise at his mother. She clears her throat.* TOM *clears his. He starts to rise, sinks back down again, scratches his head, clears his throat again.* AMANDA *coughs.* TOM *raises his cup in both hands to blow on it, his eyes staring over the rim of it at his mother for several moments. Then he slowly sets the cup down and awkwardly and hesitantly rises from the chair.*

From the background music to the gasps and throat clearings to the awkward glances, it is clear that both parties to the quarrel care about one another and are preparing to make up.

The style of dialogue also varies considerably from work to work. Some authors of FICTION, such as Henry James and George Eliot, give characters long, elaborate speeches. Others, such as Hemingway and Salinger, are notable for the economy and naturalness with which characters speak. DRAMA, too, shows an enormous range in degrees of FORMALITY, depending both on the period in which it was written and on the requirements of a particular scene. Even a play such as *Hamlet*, for example, written over four hundred years ago and full of famously poetic oratory, such as the "To be or not to be" SOLILOQUY, also contains lines of startling conciseness and modernity. Examples include the opening line, "Who's there?" and Hamlet's impatient demand, "Now, mother, what's the matter?"

Some authors of FICTION also use a combination of **direct** and **indirect discourse**, in which a THIRD-PERSON NARRATOR summarizes the words of a character but replicates his or her characteristic idioms and patterns of thought. In James Joyce's "Eveline," the protagonist is contemplating the freedom that she hopes to have, after she elopes to Buenos Aires, from the oppression that she suffers at work and at home:

> She would not cry many tears at leaving the Stores.
>
> But in her new home, in a distant unknown country, it would not be like that. Then she would be married—she, Eveline. People would treat her with respect then. She would not be treated as her mother had been.

Both the young woman's wonder at the new status that marriage will convey and her resentment of the ill treatment that she has undergone are reflected in the colloquial word choice—"would not cry many tears"—and simple sentences—"People would treat her with respect then." The use of her own name—"she, Eveline"—stresses her need to confirm that it is really she who will attain the incredible rise in status. The indirect discourse, the fact that the narrator is reporting Eveline's words, however, suggests what the story goes on to show, that Eveline does not have the confidence or the self-knowledge to carry through with her one chance to escape.

Jane Austen uses such THIRD-PERSON NARRATION of a character's dialogue very differently in the scene from *Emma* in which the social-climbing Mr. Elton proposes to the heroine. Emma, who has been angling to match him with her friend Harriet, is shocked. The episode is narrated from Emma's perspective:

> To restrain him as much as might be, by her own manners, she was immediately preparing to speak with exquisite calmness and gravity of the weather and the night; but scarcely had she begun, scarcely had they passed the sweep-gate and joined the other carriage, than she found her subject cut up—her hand seized—her attention demanded, and Mr. Elton actually making violent love to her: availing himself of the precious opportunity, declaring sentiments which must be already well known, hoping—fearing—adoring—ready to die if she refused him; but flattering himself that his ardent attachment and unequalled love and unexampled passion could not fail of having some effect, and in short, very much resolved on being seriously accepted as soon as possible. It really was so.

The OMNISCIENT NARRATOR makes clear Emma's aversion to his first hints by describing her plans to ignore them. That ploy swiftly fails, the fervor of Mr. Elton's advances reflected in the verbs: "seized," "demanded," and "making violent love"—in the last case, it should be noted for modern readers, only in words, not in actions. Then follows the summary of his proposal. Had the narrator allowed the young man to speak for himself, there is a chance that he might have gained some undeserved sympathy from readers. As the offer is presented, however, in a series of participles and with all of the "sentiments" focused on his own feelings and desires, rather than on Emma's, the superficial and self-serving nature of his "ardent attachment" is made abundantly clear. Indirect discourse can be an effective means to signal either PATHOS—pity for weakness and suffering, as with Eveline—or IRONIC detachment, as with Mr. Elton. In either case, the narrator is implying the tone by speaking for the characters rather than allowing their voices to be heard.

A technique for creating lively dialogue, common to both DRAMA and prose FICTION, is **repartee** (reh-par-TEE), a rapid-fire exchange of witty remarks in which each speaker tries to score against an opponent in a verbal fencing match. Shakespeare uses repartee to depict both serious conflicts, such as Hamlet's bitter confrontation with his mother in III.4, and comic clashes between sparring couples, for example, in *The Taming of the Shrew* the first meeting between the rebellious Kate and Petruchio, the man who has vowed to "tame" her:

> PETRUCHIO Nay, come, Kate, come, you must not look so sour.
> KATE It is my fashion when I see a crab.[1]
> PETRUCHIO Why, here's no crab, and therefore look not sour.
> KATE There is, there is.
> PETRUCHIO Then show it me.
> KATE   Had I a glass[2] I would.

It is clear from the brevity of the parries and the candor of Kate's witticisms both that Petruchio will have no easy task and that the couple is well matched. Later masters of repartee include the Restoration playwright William Congreve, as well as Oscar Wilde in the nineteenth century, and Noel Coward, Martin McDonough, David Mamet, and Wendy Wasserstein in the twentieth.

Since DRAMA consists almost entirely of dialogue, the means of direct access to a character's thoughts are confined to speeches that are directed at the audience. These are of two types: the SOLILOQUY and the ASIDE.

---

1. Crabapple.
2. Mirror.

Soliloquy

A **soliloquy** (soh-LIL-oh-kwee, from the Latin word for "to speak alone") is a monologue delivered by a character who is alone on stage. He or she may address the audience as though they are confidantes or simply seem to be thinking aloud, expressing thoughts that are too private or too risky to share with other characters. Soliloquies represent a break in the ongoing action and are reserved for major characters, usually the PROTAGONIST, and for important revelations. The technique was a popular convention in English drama during the seventeenth and eighteenth centuries. Shakespeare, in particular, uses it to great effect to reveal characters' most earnest convictions and deepest feelings.

Often, Shakespeare's villains, who are too wily to reveal their malevolent intentions to characters they are plotting against, confide in the audience in order to parade their cleverness and ruthlessness. Iago, the scheming malcontent in *Othello*, gives several such soliloquies. The first occurs at the end of Act I, just after he has plotted with a gullible companion, Roderigo, to destroy the new marriage of his commanding general, the Moor, Othello. Iago's only stated motive for his malice is that Othello has promoted another man, Cassio, to the lieutenancy that Iago coveted. Roderigo is in love with Desdemona, Othello's wife, and Iago has been duping him out of large sums of money, lying that he has spent it on courtship gifts, presented to Desdemona in Roderigo's name. He has just made a long pitch to Roderigo about the new scheme to seduce her and cuckold Othello, speaking in colloquial prose to indicate his presumed position as ally and blunt crony, and punctuated with the refrain "Put money in thy purse"—supposedly for more gifts. Now, alone on stage, Iago turns to the audience:

> Thus do I ever make my fool my purse;
> For I mine own gained knowledge should profane
> If I would time expend with such a snipe[1]
> But for my sport and profit. I hate the Moor,
> And it is thought abroad[2] that 'twixt my sheets
> H'as done my office.[3] I know not if't be true,
> But I, for mere suspicion in that kind,
> Will do for surety. He holds me well;[4]
> The better shall my purpose work on him.

---

1. Fool.
2. Rumored.
3. Business (in bed).
4. In high esteem.

Cassio's a proper[5] man. Let me see now:
To get his place, and to plume up my will[6]
In double knavery—how, how?—Let's see:
After some time, to abuse Othello's ears
That he[7] is too familiar with his wife
He hath a person and a smooth dispose[8]
To be suspected—framed to make women false.
The Moor is of a free and open nature
That thinks men honest that but seem to be so;
And will as tenderly be led by th' nose
As asses are.
I have't! It is engendered! Hell and night
Must bring this monstrous birth to the world's light.

Several aspects of Iago's nature are revealed in the soliloquy: his deviousness, his lack of scruples, his twisted values, and his wily intelligence. He scorns the hapless Roderigo, whom he sees as a "fool" and a "snipe," valuable only for the "profit" and amusement ("sport") that he provides. Toward Othello, his commanding officer and thus the man to whom he owes absolute loyalty, he feels "hate" and a raging jealousy, based merely on the "suspicion" that Othello has had an adulterous affair with his wife Emilia—a charge that even he admits is based on implausible gossip. It is not only human faults that evoke Iago's contempt, however; he is even more scornful of virtues: Cassio's handsomeness and courtly manner and Othello's "free and open nature" become grist for his plot, strengths that he can turn against them. He also shows a zest for the evil that he is plotting, the "double knavery" that will allow him to attain revenge against both of the men whom his twisted imagination has cast as rivals, Othello in a sexual context and Cassio in a military one. He concludes by allying himself eagerly with the forces of evil—"Hell" and the "night" in which he plans to carry out his dark deeds. For the entire soliloquy, Iago has been speaking not in the colloquial prose that he used with Roderigo but in BLANK VERSE. Its greater formality both elevates his stature and makes clear the intelligence and sophistication that will make him such a formidable schemer. He ends the speech on a RHYMED COUPLET, concluding the scene and capping the impression of the pleasure that he takes in the exercise of his wicked wit.

---

5. Handsome.
6. Gratify my desire.
7. Cassio.
8. Manner.

The effects of a soliloquy on the audience are similar to those of FIRST-PERSON NARRATION in a SHORT STORY or a NOVEL. In both cases, the audience has to gauge the RELIABILITY—the relative credibility and worthiness—of the speaker. If he is a villain, such as Iago or Richard III, the audience may feel both flattered by being taken into the confidence of so clever a schemer and disconcerted or revolted by being made a sort of accessory to his crimes. When the motives of the **soliloquizer** are benevolent, however, as in Juliet's soliloquy expressing her conflicting ardor and shyness about consummating her secret marriage to Romeo, "Gallop apace, you fiery footed steeds," the effect is to create bonds of sympathy between speaker and audience. The equivalent of the soliloquy in modern films is the voiceover, in which the camera shows a close-up of a silent character, focusing on the changing facial expressions while the soundtrack presents his or her voice. In fact, that method is often used to stage filmed versions of Shakespearean soliloquies, for example in Laurence Olivier's performance of the "To be or not to be" soliloquy from *Hamlet*.

Aside ◄

An **aside** is a speech, usually brief, that, according to theatrical conventions, is heard only by the audience, or, sometimes, is addressed privately to another character on stage. If only the audience hears the aside, it may be a softly spoken remark on the scene taking place, so that it represents a thought said aloud. For example, in Shakespeare's *Hamlet*, King Claudius plots to kill his stepson/nephew by poisoning his wine at a fencing match attended by the whole court. When, instead, the queen drinks the wine, Claudius knows that expressing his anguish aloud would risk revealing his treasonous scheme to the court, so he confines his reaction to a horrified aside: "It is the poisoned cup; it is too late."

An example of an aside addressed to another character occurs in Shakespeare's comedy *The Taming of the Shrew*. As part of his "taming" process, Petruchio is trying to teach his tempestuous wife the ill effects of bad temper as well as to make her submit to his will. He has been throwing a tantrum over an elaborate gown that a tailor has just delivered and that Kate protests that she adores. Just before Petruchio orders the beset tailor to take the gown away, he says in an aside to a friend who has been watching the quarrel: "Hortensio, say thou wilt see the tailor paid." The aside lets Petruchio keep up the pretense to Kate of being an iron-willed tyrant while at the same time assuring the audience that he is carrying on an elaborate farce.

▼

EXERCISE: Dialogue

For each of the following passages:

- Indicate those instances in which the dialogue is an example of REPARTEE, a SOLILOQUY, or an ASIDE, and explain why that term applies.
- Indicate whether the dialogue is direct or summarized.
- Explain the functions and effects of any NARRATIVE description, SPEECH HEADINGS, and/or STAGE DIRECTIONS.
- Explain how the style and content of the passage help to characterize the speaker or speakers.

1. *The following conversation is between the young Jane Eyre and the Reverend Mr. Brocklehurst, the proprietor of the boarding school to which she is being sent:*

    I stepped across the rug; he placed me square and straight before him. What a face he had, now that it was almost on a level with mine! What a great nose! and what a mouth! and what large prominent teeth!

    "No sight so sad as that of a naughty child," he began, "especially a naughty little girl. Do you know where the wicked go after death?"

    "They go to hell," was my ready and orthodox answer.

    "And what is hell? Can you tell me that?"

    "A pit full of fire."

    "And should you like to fall into that pit, and to be burning there for ever?"

    "No, sir."

    "What must you do to avoid it?"

    I deliberated a moment; my answer, when it did come, was objectionable: "I must keep in good health and not die."

    "How can you keep in good health? Children younger than you die daily. I buried a little child of five years old only a day or two since—a good little child, whose soul is now in heaven. It is to be feared the same could not be said of you, were you to be called hence."   —CHARLOTTE BRONTË, *Jane Eyre*

2. *The following speakers from Shakespeare's* King Lear *are sisters who are competing for the same lover. In her previous speech, Regan has said, "Lady, I am not well."*

    REGAN Sick, O, sick!

    GONERIL [*aside*] If not, I'll ne'er trust medicine.[1]

    ---
    1. A euphemism for poison.

3. *In the following scene, set in London in the 1890s, Algernon and Jack are old friends, and Gwendolen is Jack's fiancée:*

    ALGERNON Have you told Gwendolen yet that you have an excessively pretty ward who is only just eighteen?

    JACK Oh! One doesn't blurt these things out to people. Cecily and Gwendolen are perfectly certain to be extremely great friends. I'll bet you anything you like that half an hour after they have met, they will be calling each other sister.

    ALGERNON Women only do that when they have called each other a lot of other things first. Now, my dear boy, if we want to get a good table at Willis's, we really must go and dress. Do you know it is nearly seven?

    JACK [*Irritably*] Oh! it always is nearly seven.

    ALGERNON Well, I'm hungry.

    JACK I never knew you when you weren't. . . .

    ALGERNON What shall we do after dinner? Go to the theatre?

    JACK Oh no! I loathe listening.

    ALGERNON Well, let us go to the club?

    JACK Oh, no! I hate talking.

    ALGERNON Well, we might trot round to the Empire² at ten?

    JACK Oh no! I can't bear looking at things. It is so silly.

    ALGERNON Well, what shall we do?

    JACK Nothing!

    ALGERNON It is awfully hard work doing nothing. However, I don't mind hard work where there is no definite object of any kind.

    —OSCAR WILDE, *The Importance of Being Earnest*

4. *An old woman is preparing the narrator, an Irish Catholic boy, for his first experience of the sacrament of confession:*

    She lit a candle, took out a new half crown, and offered it to the first boy who would hold one finger—only one finger!—in the flame for five minutes by the school clock. Being always very ambitious I was tempted to volunteer, but I thought it might look greedy. Then she asked were we afraid of holding one finger—only one finger!—in a little candle flame for five minutes and not afraid of burning all over in roasting hot furnaces for all eternity.

    —FRANK O'CONNOR, "First Confession"

---

2. A music hall.

5. *Just before this speech, Hamlet has been an unwilling guest at his step-father/uncle's first public audience as king of Denmark, which was also a celebration of his marriage to Hamlet's mother.*

O, that this too too solid flesh would melt,
Thaw, and resolve itself into a dew,
Or that the Everlasting had not fixed
His canon[3] 'gainst self-slaughter! O God, God,
How weary, stale, flat, and unprofitable   5
Seem to me all the uses of this world!
Fie[4] on't, ah fie, fie! 'Tis an unweeded garden
That grows to seed; things rank and gross in nature
Possess it merely.[5] That it should come to this—
But two months dead—nay, not so much, not two—   10
So excellent a king that was to this
Hyperion[6] to a satyr, so loving to my mother
That he might not beteem[7] the winds of heaven
Visit her face too roughly! Heaven and earth,
Must I remember? Why, she would hang on him   15
As if increase of appetite had grown
By what it fed on, and yet within a month—
Let me not think on't; frailty, thy name is woman—
A little month, or ere those shoes were old
With which she followed my poor father's body,   20
Like Niobe,[8] all tears, why she, even she—
O God, a beast that wants discourse of reason
Would have mourned longer!—married with mine uncle,
My father's brother, but no more like my father
Than I to Hercules; within a month,   25
Ere yet the salt of most unrighteous tears
Had left the flushing of her gallèd eyes,
She married. O, most wicked speed, to post
With such dexterity to incestuous[9] sheets!
It is not, nor it cannot come to good.   30
But break my heart, for I must hold my tongue.
                                    —WILLIAM SHAKESPEARE, *Hamlet*

---

3. Law.
4. Expression of disgust.
5. Entirely.
6. The sun god. "King" (line 11): his father.
7. Allow.
8. A grieving mother in Greek mythology.
9. By marriage to her brother-in-law. "Post" (line 28): rush.

6. *In the following passage, set in Paris during the 1920s, Brett is a beautiful Englishwoman engaged to a wealthy alcoholic, and Jake is an expatriate American who is in love with her but was wounded in World War I and rendered impotent. Robert Cohn is a hanger-on in their set. The group is about to go on a fishing trip to Spain.*

    > We walked up the Rue Delambre.
    > "I haven't seen you since I've been back," Brett said.
    > "No."
    > "How *are* you, Jake?"
    > "Fine."
    > Brett looked at me. "I say," she said, "is Robert Cohn going on this trip?"
    > "Yes. Why?"
    > "Don't you think it will be a bit rough on him?"
    > "Why should it?"
    > "Who did you think I went down to San Sebastian with?"
    > "Congratulations," I said.
    > We walked along.
    > "What did you say that for?"
    > "I don't know. What would you like me to say?"
    >
    > —ERNEST HEMINGWAY, *The Sun Also Rises*

7. The next day at school I inquired among the students about jobs and was given the name of a white family who wanted a boy to do chores. That afternoon, as soon as school had let out, I went to the address. A tall, dour white woman talked to me. Yes, she needed a boy, an honest boy. Two dollars a week. Mornings, evenings, and all day Saturdays. Washing dishes. Chopping wood. Scrubbing floors. Cleaning the yard. I would get my breakfast and dinner. As I asked timid questions, my eyes darted about. What kind of food would I get? Was the place as shabby as the kitchen indicated?

    "Do you want this job?" the woman asked.

    "Yes, m'am," I said, afraid to trust my own judgment.

    "Now, boy, I want to ask you one question and I want you to tell me the truth," she said.

    "Yes, m'am," I said, all attention.

    "Do you steal?" she asked me seriously.

    I burst into a laugh, then checked myself.

    "What's so damn funny about that?" she asked.

    "Lady, if I was a thief, I'd never tell anybody."

    "What do you mean?" she blazed with a red face.

    I had made a mistake during my first five minutes in the white world. I hung my head.

▼

"No, m'am," I mumbled. "I don't steal."
She stared at me, trying to make up her mind.

–RICHARD WRIGHT, *Black Boy*

8.   *The following episode from Arthur Miller's* Death of a Salesman *occurs when Biff pays a surprise visit to his father, Willy, who is a traveling sales-man staying at a hotel. Biff has gone to tell him that he has failed math and will not graduate from high school unless Willy can persuade his teacher to bend the rules. Willy, who has long been married to Biff's mother, the self-sacrificing Linda, is not alone and has ordered the other woman to hide:*

[THE WOMAN *laughs offstage*]
BIFF Somebody got in your bathroom!
WILLY No, it's the next room, there's a party—
THE WOMAN [*Enters laughing*] Can I come in? There's something in
    the bathtub, Willy, and it's moving!
    [WILLY *looks at* BIFF, *who is staring open-mouthed and horrified at*
    THE WOMAN]
WILLY Ah—you better go back to your room. They must be finished
    painting by now. They're painting her room so I let her take a
    shower here. Go back, go back . . . [*He pushes her*]
THE WOMAN [*Resisting*] But I've got to get dressed, Willy, I can't—
WILLY Get out of here! Go back, go back . . . [*Suddenly striving for
    the ordinary*] This is Miss Francis, Biff, she's a buyer. They're
    painting her room. Go back, Miss Francis, go back . . .
THE WOMAN But my clothes, I can't go out naked in the hall!
WILLY [*Pushing her offstage*] Get outa here! Go back, go back!
    [*Biff slowly sits down on his suitcase as the argument continues
    offstage*]

9.   *In the following story, a family of five and their grandmother have had a car accident on an isolated road in Tennessee. A "big battered hearse-like automobile" has slowly driven toward them, and the driver and two boys with him have gotten out, holding guns.*

"We've had an ACCIDENT!" the children screamed.
    The grandmother had the peculiar feeling that the bespectacled
man was someone she knew. His face was as familiar to her as if she
had known him all her life but she could not recall who he was. He
moved away from the car and began to come down the embank-
ment, placing his feet carefully so that he wouldn't slip. He had on
tan and white shoes and no socks, and his ankles were red and thin.
"Good afternoon," he said. "I see you all had a little spill."

▼

"We turned over twice!" said the grandmother.

"Oncet," he corrected. "We seen it happen. Try their car and see will it run, Hiram," he said quietly to the boy with the gray hat.

"What you got that gun for?" John Wesley asked. "Whatcha gonna do with that gun?"

"Lady," the man said to the children's mother, "would you mind calling them children to sit down by you? Children make me nervous. I want you all to sit down right together there where you're at."

"What are you telling us what to do for?" June Star asked.

Behind them the line of woods gaped like a dark open mouth. "Come here," said their mother.

—FLANNERY O'CONNOR, "A Good Man Is Hard to Find"

10. *In the following story, an American-born Chinese daughter is quarreling with her mother over whether the daughter will continue with the piano lessons that she hates in order to prove herself the "prodigy" that her mother believes she can be.*

"You want me to be someone that I'm not!" I sobbed. "I'll never be the kind of daughter you want me to be!"

"Only two kinds of daughters," she shouted in Chinese. "Those who are obedient and those who follow their own mind! Only one kind of daughter can live in this house. Obedient daughter!"

"Then I wish I wasn't your daughter. I wish you weren't my mother," I shouted. As I said these things I got scared. I felt like worms and toads and slimy things were crawling out of my chest, but it also felt good, as if this awful side of me had surfaced, at last.

"Too late change this," said my mother shrilly.

And I could sense her anger rising to its breaking point. I wanted to see it spill over. And that's when I remembered the babies she had lost in China, the ones we never talked about. "Then I wish I'd never been born!" I shouted. "I wish I were dead! Like them."

It was as if I had said the magic words, Alakazam!—and her face went blank, her mouth closed, her arms went slack, and she backed out of the room, stunned, as if she were blowing away like a small brown leaf, thin, brittle, lifeless.

—AMY TAN, "Two Kinds"

SETTING

The **setting** is the time and place in which the events in a work of
FICTION, DRAMA, or NARRATIVE POETRY occur. Individual episodes
within a work may have separate, specific settings. For example, the
general setting of Homer's *The Odyssey* is ancient Greece, but various episodes are set in such places as Odysseus's native island of
Ithaca, Helen and Menelaus's palace in Sparta, and the home of the
gods on Mount Olympus.

With regard to a work's setting, "time" may be a historical
period, time of year, and/or time of day or night. "Place" may refer
to a geographical location, to a kind of edifice, or to a part of a
larger structure, such as a cave or a particular room. For example,
the main setting of Joseph Conrad's *Heart of Darkness* is a boat navi-
gating the waters of the Belgian Congo toward the end of the nineteenth century; E. M. Forster's *Howards End* is partly *set* at a family
manor north of London during the Edwardian period; and Tennessee Williams's "memory play," *The Glass Menagerie*, takes place
in a claustrophobic apartment in St. Louis during the Depression.

In some works, the setting is purely imaginary. For example,
Jonathan Swift's fantasy travelogue, *Gulliver's Travels*, is set in a
series of fictional lands, such as Lilliput, a country of minuscule and
petty-minded inhabitants; J. R. R. Tolkien's Middle Earth in *The Lord
of the Rings* trilogy is a fairy tale land inhabited by such mythical
creatures as trolls and elves; and although Illyria, the setting of
Shakespeare's ROMANTIC COMEDY *Twelfth Night*, takes its name from
the Greeks' and Romans' designation for the eastern coast of the
Adriatic, in the play Illyria is an indeterminate locale whose name
suggests a compound of "illusion," "lyrical," and "Elysium." The setting in a work may also shift back and forth between two markedly
contrasting places, such as the idyllic raft on the Mississippi River
and the contentious land in Mark Twain's *Adventures of Huckleberry
Finn*; and, in Shakespeare's *Antony and Cleopatra*, between sensual,
decadent Egypt and coldly rational imperial Rome.

As the examples above suggest, in many works, the setting is an
essential element in establishing the ATMOSPHERE of the story. For
example, *Romeo and Juliet*, Shakespeare's TRAGEDY of doomed love
and bitter feuding, is set in Italy, reputed during the Renaissance to
be a land of passionate romance and sudden violence. The time setting in the play is also significant: mid-July, the hottest point in the
hottest season in that southern climate. The climactic duel that sets
events on their tragic course occurs in a Verona piazza at high noon.

Just before it breaks out, the mild-mannered Benvolio tries to persuade his temperamental friend Mercutio to go indoors, cautioning:

> The day is hot, the Capels[1] are abroad,
> And, if we meet, we shall not scape a brawl,
> For now, these hot days, is the mad blood stirring.

In Shakespeare's *Macbeth*, in contrast, where the precipitating event
to the tragedy is a brutal, carefully plotted assassination, the murder
takes place in an isolated chamber of a castle in the dead of night.

In the most extreme examples of this connection between setting and plot, the setting plays a more pointedly SYMBOLIC role, FIGU-
RATIVELY reflecting the feelings and experiences of the characters. In
Charlotte Brontë's *Jane Eyre*, for example, each of the locations in
the PROTAGONIST's fictional autobiography has a SYMBOLIC name:
Lowood, the charity school to which the young Jane is sent, is
located in a *low*-lying valley and run by a tyrannical clergyman who
"would" wish to keep the social status of the hapless orphans in his
charge "low" and their demeanor humble. Thornfield, the manor
house of Jane's beloved but morally compromised Mr. Rochester, is
surrounded by thorn trees and is also the site of the trials that she
must undergo—"thorns" in her life—to win happiness in the end.
Jane, who is also the NARRATOR, calls attention to that METAPHORICAL
connection when she first arrives at Thornfield, before she has met
Mr. Rochester: "Externals have a great effect on the young; I thought
that a fairer era of life was beginning for me, one that was to have
its flowers and pleasures, as well as its thorns and toils."

In E. M. Forster's *A Passage to India*, set during the waning years
of the British Raj, the local landscape becomes virtually a character
in the narrative, intruding at key points to influence the fortunes of
the main characters. For example, the turning point of the novel
takes place in the Marabar hills, which the OMNISCIENT NARRATOR
describes as having an ancient and mystical essence; and at the end
of the novel, when two of the main characters, an Englishman and
an Indian, wish to reconcile after a long period of estrangement
caused by nationalistic conflict and misunderstanding, it is the landscape that actively opposes that reunion. They are on horseback, and
the Indian has just said that they cannot be friends until his people
have driven the English out of the country. The Englishman asks in
reply, "Why can't we be friends now? . . . It's what I want. It's what
you want." The following paragraph concludes the novel:

---

1. Capulets, their enemies.

▼

But the horses didn't want it—they swerved apart; the earth didn't want it, sending up rocks through which the riders must pass single file; the temples, the tank, the jail, the palace, the birds, the carrion, the Guest House[2] . . . : they didn't want it, they said in their hundred voices, "No, not yet," and the sky said, "No, not there."

Although the connection between setting and story is not often so explicit, it is nonetheless significant. As with other aspects of NARRATION, an author's choices about time and place exert an important influence on a work's TONE and meaning, which the reader must infer. See also ATMOSPHERE and PATHETIC FALLACY.

EXERCISES: Setting

I. For each of the following descriptions of a literary work, answer the questions about the probable effects of the SETTING.

1. *The entire description of the SETTING for Samuel Beckett's ABSURDIST DRAMA* Waiting for Godot *is: "A country road. A tree. Evening." The action covers a single night and day, during which the main characters, two homeless mendicants, try to wile away the hours while they await the arrival of a mysterious being named Godot, whom they may or may not have encountered before. Godot never comes, and each of the two acts concludes the same way: one man asks, "Well, shall we go?" The other responds, "Yes, let's go." That bit of DIALOGUE is followed by the STAGE DIRECTION "They do not move." What might the setting suggest about the play's TONE? How does it anticipate the characters' experiences?*

2. *Jane Austen's COMIC NOVEL* Emma *is SET in an English country village in the early nineteenth century. The PROTAGONIST is a privileged young woman who lives with her widowed father in a large manor house. The owner of the other large estate in town, a bachelor, is a close family friend. Other significant places in the story are the vicarage, recently occupied by a new young minister, also a bachelor; the house of Emma's dear friend, and former governess, who has recently married a widower with a highly eligible son, who has been raised by wealthy relatives and, as the book opens, has never visited the village; and a small rented flat inhabited by a kindly, talkative woman, her aged mother, and their talented, elegant niece, who is visiting*

---

2. All significant locations in the story.

them after a sojourn in the resort city of Bath. The action takes place over nearly a year, beginning in the fall of one year and concluding in mid-summer of the next. What would the setting lead readers to expect about the events and the TONE of the novel?

3. Shakespeare's TRAGEDY King Lear is SET during the reign of a legendary ruler of Britain. It begins with the old king holding court in his luxurious castle and deciding to divide his kingdom among his three daughters so that he can be free from the responsibilities of rule. The two older daughters, however, are disloyal and hypocritical and flatter him in order to receive a more opulent share of the territory. The youngest daughter, who is true to her father, refuses to flatter him, and Lear banishes her from Britain. She goes off with her new husband, the King of France, who reveres her integrity and rescues her from her father's wrath. The test of the older daughters' sincerity comes when they conspire to refuse to provide their father's upkeep and he goes off into a storm that is brewing on the barren heath. There, deprived of even the bare necessities of food and shelter, and in anguish over his older daughters' betrayal and his injustice to the youngest, Lear goes mad. The youngest daughter, still loyal, leads an army to try to recapture the kingdom for her father and to heal his broken mind. How might the contrasting settings of castle and heath reflect the conflicts within and among the characters? How might they influence the play's TONE?

4. Stephen Crane's SHORT STORY "The Open Boat" is SET in a small lifeboat that has escaped the sinking ship that carried it. Its passengers are four men, the captain, two of the crew, and a newspaper correspondent who had been a passenger on the ship. During the long day and night that the story describes, the men's survival depends on continuously bailing out the leaky boat and, at the same time, trying to navigate the enormous waves that threaten every moment to capsize the fragile vessel. The captain has been injured, and the other three men are obliged to share the arduous rowing duties. They are also threatened by an attack from a circling shark, and they are dismayed when they get within sight of land but find the surf too strong to allow them to row ashore. The men achieve a "subtle brotherhood" as they strive to survive. How might the SETTING influence the CHARACTERIZATION of the men and the TONE of the story?

5. Henrik Ibsen's PLAY A Doll's House is set in a prosperous middle-class home in Oslo, Norway, near the end of the nineteenth century. In that period women's rights were severely restricted and a wife was expected to defer to her husband's authority. The PROTAGONIST, Nora Helmer, has largely played the subservient role prescribed by her society, and her husband has treated her with condescending indulgence. She has secretly rebelled against that

role, however, by taking out an illegal loan and forging her late father's signature to the document, since women were not allowed to borrow money on their own. The loan was to finance a trip to a warmer climate for her husband, then seriously ill, which his doctor had recommended as necessary for saving his life. The cure worked, and Nora is proud of her initiative and resolve. As the play opens, however, the holder of the loan is threatening to expose the forgery, and Nora fears that her husband loves her so much that he will take the blame for her action and ruin his own reputation. When she discovers, to her shock, that he is instead concerned only about the effect on his public image, she realizes that she has never really known him, and she makes the radical decision to leave him. How might the SETTING, in time of the historical period and in place of the Helmers' house, affect the meaning and TONE of the play?

II.

- Specify the SETTING in time and place of *three* works of FICTION, DRAMA, or NARRATIVE POETRY that you have read. *Note:* A work may have multiple settings within the larger one. Include those that are most significant.
- Describe the effects that the time and place in which the work is SET have on the work's meaning and TONE.

III.

- Describe *two* works of literature that each contain two markedly contrasting SETTINGS.
- Explain how that contrast in time and place affects the work's meaning and TONE.

Theme

The **theme** of a literary work is a central idea that it conveys, either directly or implicitly. In its broad sense, the term refers to an abstract concept that recurs in many works of literature—for example, courtship, the horrors of war, or conflict between parents and children. The narrower meaning of theme is a view or a value conveyed by a particular literary work, either by assertion or by implication. The theme differs from the subject of the work, a neutral summary of the characters and events, and instead expresses a stance toward the subject as a moral or philosophical principle inherent in the work. For example, the subject of Charlotte Brontë's *Jane Eyre* is an orphan girl's growth to womanhood in nineteenth-century England. The novel's themes include the importance of being true to one's values and the transforming power of romantic love.

Some authors' thematic intentions are asserted openly, especially in works whose major purpose is to instruct or persuade. For example, Alexander Pope's didactic poem "An Essay on Man" is meant to teach such principles as morality and piety. To cite a sample passage:

> Hope humbly, then; with trembling pinions soar;
> Wait the great teacher Death, and God adore!
> What future bliss, he gives thee not to know,
> But gives that hope to be thy blessing now.

Other examples of works that state their themes explicitly are plays by such dramatists as Henrik Ibsen and George Bernard Shaw, which focus on themes like the rights of women and the evils of military profiteering, and satires such as George Orwell's *Animal Farm*, which exposes the tyranny and hypocrisy of totalitarianism.

In most works, however, a theme emerges by implication and is conveyed by the choices that the author makes about the NARRATION and the TONE. For example, one of the themes of Mark Twain's *Adventures of Huckleberry Finn* is that true morality depends on sympathy for others' suffering rather than on rules of conduct imposed by society or organized religion. That idea is never stated outright. Instead, it is suggested by the characters, benevolent and reprehensible, that the naïve, good-hearted narrator encounters and by his decision to ignore the legal and societal pressures he is under to turn in the escaped slave he has taken into his protection. Recognizing a theme can help readers to compare and contrast works that treat the same central concept and to articulate the values and attitudes that underlie a given literary work. At the same time, it is important to keep in mind that simply summing up the themes of complex poems, plays, and novels cannot yield their full meaning and literary power.

TONE

Tone designates the attitude that a literary speaker expresses toward his or her subject matter and audience. The term is derived from spoken discourse, in which listeners attend to a speaker's tone of voice in order to assess his feelings about the topic at hand and about his relationship to his audience and his conception of their intelligence, sensitivity, and receptivity to his views. Tone is described in adjectives that express emotion or manner: it may be compassionate or judgmental, scornful or reverent, formal or casual, arrogant or obsequious, serious or ironic, irate or serene, confident or timid. It may remain consistent, or it may change markedly at some point. In conversation, we receive clues to tone from the speaker's facial expressions, gestures, and vocal inflections. In written discourse, tone must be inferred from such factors as the SYNTAX, DICTION, POINT OF VIEW, and SELECTION OF DETAILS.

If the passage in question is a DIALOGUE, in either a DRAMA, a work of PROSE FICTION, or a NARRATIVE POEM, the listener as well as the speaker is present, and therefore the reader is able to witness directly the effects and implications of speakers' words. In Shakespeare's *Twelfth Night*, the Countess Olivia has fallen in love with the young servant sent to court her for another, a duke who is of her own aristocratic class and therefore a more suitable match. Before she makes a full confession, she apologizes for her forwardness and "shameful cunning" in hinting at her passion and pays a compliment to the messenger's discernment: "To one of your receiving [understanding, perception] / Enough is shown." In a delicious instance of DRAMATIC IRONY, however, the audience knows what Olivia does not: that the messenger is not the attractive boy he looks to be but a young woman in disguise, Viola, who has, to further complicate the situation, fallen in love with the very duke whom Olivia so staunchly rejects. The dialogue continues:

> OLIVIA So let me hear you speak.
> VIOLA I pity you.
> OLIVIA   That's a degree to[1] love.
> VIOLA No, not a grece,[2] for 'tis a vulgar proof[3]
>   That very oft we pity enemies.

---

1. Toward.
2. Step.
3. Commonplace.

Olivia's initial tone is humble and hopeful, reflected in her brief lines and simple DICTION. She asks for the "boy's" reaction to her declaration and then eagerly tries to put the best face on his answer, completing his BLANK VERSE line with her response. Viola's tone begins as compassionate—her parallel situation of being in love with someone who does not requite her feelings makes her "pity" Olivia's plight. She too speaks in the simplest style. As soon as she hears Olivia's misguided interpretation of that sympathy as an indication of love, however, her SYNTAX turns complex and her tone imperious. As in this case, a speaker's tone may shift in the course of a scene, an important signal of changing feelings and motives.

If the speaker in question is the NARRATOR of a literary work, he or she has an implied audience, in either the reader or some invented listener. In that case, the reader must note the POINT OF VIEW—the pronoun that the narrator uses to recount events—and infer his or her conception of the audience's qualities and expectations about whether or not the reader shares the assumptions and values expressed. A FIRST-PERSON NARRATOR may be UNRELIABLE, that is, biased, devious, or naïve, so that the tone that he or she takes is meant to be seen as exaggerated or misleading. Charlotte Perkins Gilman's short story "The Yellow Wallpaper" opens with what seems at first to be a cheerful, even enraptured tone. The verb tense is present, and the reader is led to experience the events along with the protagonist/narrator:

> It is very seldom that mere ordinary people like John and myself secure ancestral halls for the summer.
>
> A colonial mansion, a hereditary estate, I would say a haunted house and reach the height of romantic felicity—but that would be asking too much of fate!
>
> Still I will proudly declare that there is something queer about it.
>
> Else, why should it be let so cheaply? And why have stood so long untenanted?
>
> John laughs at me, of course, but one expects that.
>
> John is practical in the extreme. He has no patience with faith, an intense horror of superstition, and he scoffs openly at any talk of things not to be felt and seen and put down in figures.
>
> John is a physician, and *perhaps*—(I would not say it to a living soul, of course, but this is dead paper and a great relief to my mind)—*perhaps* that is one reason I do not get well faster.
>
> You see he does not believe I am sick!
>
> And what can one do?

▼

If a physician of high standing, and one's own husband, assures friends and relatives that there is really nothing the matter with one but temporary nervous depression—a slight hysterical tendency—what is one to do?

My brother is also a physician, and also of high standing, and he says the same thing.

So I take phosphates or phosphites—whichever it is, and tonics, and journeys, and air, and exercise, and am absolutely forbidden to "work" until I am well again.

Personally I disagree with their ideas.

Personally, I believe that congenial work, with excitement and change, would do me good.

But what is one to do?

I did write for a while in spite of them; but it *does* exhaust me a good deal—having to be so sly about it, or else meet with heavy opposition.

I sometimes fancy that in my condition if I had less opposition and more society and stimulus—but John says the very worst thing I can do is to think about my condition, and I confess it always makes me feel bad.

So I will let it alone and talk about the house.

At first, the narrator focuses on the "colonial mansion" that she and her husband have rented, and their seemingly light disagreement about it. She is charmed by the possibility that the estate is a "haunted house," a situation she calls "the height of romantic felicity." She contrasts her attitude with that of her husband, John, who "laughs at" her fascination, though, she adds wryly, "one expects that in marriage." He is an adamant pragmatist, "practical in the extreme" and openly scornful of religious "faith," "superstition," and anything that cannot be "felt and seen and put down in figures." At this point, the narrator reveals two key points of information: John is "a physician" and she is ill, though she does not yet specify the nature of her sickness. She does, however, twice venture the opinion that "*perhaps*" his profession and his condescending skepticism are why she does not "get well faster." Her timidity about disagreeing with his supposed expertise is suggested by the fact that the "perhaps" is both italicized and repeated. She also offers a parenthetical observation in the midst of this hesitant admission, describing her relief at being able to express her feelings, at least on paper. That admission suggests her fear of her husband's censure and her unwillingness to subject him to public criticism: she "would not say [this] to a living soul." She adds further emphasis to that assertion with an "of course," as though that subservient role were the universally agreed-upon lot of wives.

At the same time that she seems to be supporting that stance, however, she shows underlying disagreement by admitting to the reader that writing down this accusation against John provides "a great relief to [her] mind." She assures herself that no harm will be done to him by her candor, since her audience is "dead paper"—a poignant indication of her self-defeating wish to protect the husband whose cold and judgmental nature may be at the root of her illness. He, a "physician," should be a source of comfort and healing, but his contemptuous rejection of the spiritual/imaginative aspects of human consciousness undermines his wife's emotional health.

In mid-passage, she states her dilemma more explicitly, again appealing to the reader for understanding: "You see he does not believe I am sick!" Then she asks the question that will become a refrain: "And what can one do?" She sums up the odds against her: John is "a physician of high standing" and her "own husband." She also reveals the psychological nature of her illness, which he labels a "temporary nervous depression," a "slight hysterical tendency." That diagnosis is confirmed by her brother, "also a physician of high standing." The male establishment has lined up against her, and it is strangely hard to oppose it because the intentions are blindly benevolent. She tries to follow the regime that John establishes: to take "phosphates or phosphites—whichever it is, and tonics, and journeys, and air, and exercise," but signals her skepticism by her humorous confusion about the name of the medication. She also tries to obey the dictate that she is "absolutely forbidden to work."

Then, the narrator again shows her intuitive understanding of the harmful effects of this enforced invalidism: "Personally, I disagree with their ideas. Personally, I believe that congenial work, with excitement and change, would do me good." The repetition of "personally" suggests how eccentric she is made to feel about this opposition, and she asks for the third time, "But what is one to do?" Obedience, she implies, is a woman's lot. Then she shows her ambivalence about that precept and her incipient self-assertiveness, admitting, "I did write for a while in spite of them." The effect, however, is to "exhaust" her, but for the reason that she has had to do it secretly if she is not to "meet with heavy opposition." In other words, her husband's prohibition becomes a self-fulfilling prophecy. In contrast, she wants and feels that she needs "more society and stimulation," to which John replies that "the very worst thing [she] can do is to think about [her] condition." This is an ironically irrational directive, since the isolation that he imposes on her virtually guarantees an inward focus. The narrator vows to try to be the docile wife/patient, by shifting her attention away from herself to "the house." But since she has begun by asserting that it reminds her of a "haunted house," that decision has an ominous tone.

The impression established by the story's opening is of a quietly desperate woman, oppressed by a husband whose male chauvinist convictions and benevolent dictatorship are exacerbating her nervous depression. She senses that he is giving her frustratingly contradictory messages: On the one hand, he denies the seriousness of her condition and implies that its cure is within her control. At the same time he treats her like an invalid and forbids her to act on her convictions of how to ameliorate her illness. She is unable or unwilling fully to admit the extent of the harm that he is doing her, but the refrains in her narrative—"John says" and "what is one to do?"—suggest both her emotional imprisonment and the anguished loneliness that make her only confidants the "dead paper" on which she writes and the reader to whom she appeals for understanding.

A THIRD-PERSON NARRATOR, whether INTRUSIVE or OBJECTIVE, may adopt a tone that seems authoritative and neutral. A surface attitude of objectivity, however, may imply an underlying meaning at odds with that tone, creating VERBAL IRONY. For example, Franz Kafka's "A Hunger Artist" opens with what purports to be a brief history of a popular entertainment:

> During these last decades the interest in professional fasting has markedly diminished. It used to pay very well to stage such great performances under one's own management, but today that is quite impossible. We live in a different world now. At one time the whole town took a lively interest in the hunger artist; from day to day of his fast the excitement mounted; everybody wanted to see him at least once a day; there were people who bought season tickets for the last few days and sat from morning till night in front of his small barred cage; even in the nighttime there were visiting hours, when the whole effect was heightened by torch flares; on fine days the cage was set out in the open air, and then it was the children's special treat to see the hunger artist; for their elders he was often just a joke that happened to be in fashion, but the children stood open-mouthed, holding each other's hands for greater security, marveling at how he sat there pallid in black tights, with his ribs sticking out so prominently, not even on a seat but down among the straw on the ground, sometimes giving a courteous nod, answering questions with a constrained smile, or perhaps stretching an arm through the bars so that one might feel how thin it was, and then again withdrawing deep into himself, paying no attention to anyone or anything, not even to the all-important striking of the

clock that was the only piece of furniture in his cage, but merely staring into vacancy with half shut eyes, now and then taking a sip from a tiny glass of water to moisten his lips.

The first line is on the surface a matter-of-fact assertion about the art's diminishing popularity. It is only when the reader reconsiders the phrase that describes the practice being alluded to—"professional fasting"—that the discrepancy between the narrator's straightforward tone and the bizarre subject matter hits home. The account goes on from the perspective of an entrepreneur of this so-called spectator sport, commenting on how lucrative it once was to stage a fast, and disparaging the change that has taken place in the public's interest: "We live in a different world now," the OMNISCIENT NARRATOR pronounces sententiously. He then goes on to reminisce fondly, in a much-subordinated sentence that takes up the rest of the paragraph, about the former conditions for practicing the "entertainment": the "artist" sitting on straw in a barred cage, the crowd's excitement mounting as he fasted day after day, the children especially enthralled, and the signs of his growing emaciation in his ever thinner ribs and arms. In the midst of this public martyrdom, the hunger artist remains calm, "courteous," and utterly withdrawn, not even aware of the clock that marks the hours of his fast. Several aspects of this passage signal the ironic tone: the grotesquely inappropriate enthusiasm for this painfully slow form of suffering, the masochism of the practitioner, and, most notably, the fact that nothing usually associated with "art" is in fact achieved by the performance—no beauty of movement or visible product. It simply has the same effect as a wasting disease, so that it should inspire revulsion and horror. Because the narrator's tone is devoid of those feelings, the shock for the reader, and therefore the irony, are redoubled.

A narrative may, in contrast, create **pathos** (PAY-thohss, from the Greek word for "suffering"), the evocation in the audience of pity, tenderness, compassion, or sorrow. In nineteenth-century fiction, pathos was a frequent feature of death scenes, particularly those describing children, such as Paul Dombey in Charles Dickens's *Dombey and Son* and Beth in Louisa May Alcott's *Little Women*. To modern sensibilities, such scenes may seem too sentimental. Pathos that depends instead on UNDERSTATEMENT is often seen as subtler and therefore more moving. The protagonist of James Joyce's "Clay" is the tiny, elderly Maria, who works as a scullery maid in a charitable institution for fallen women. Maria is cheerful and uncomplaining—her favorite word is "nice." The story is set on All Hallows Eve (Halloween), and she is looking forward to her annual visit with the family of a man she once worked for as a nanny. In keeping with the Irish holiday tradition, they play a fortune-telling game, which involves being blindfolded and choosing an object that predicts one's future: a ring means marriage, a prayer book entrance to a convent. In this passage, Maria is serving the women their tea, her last task before her evening out:

> There was a great deal of laughing and joking during the meal. Lizzie Fleming said Maria was sure to get the ring and though Fleming had said that for so many Hallow Eves, Maria had to laugh and say she didn't want any ring or man either; and when she laughed her grey-green eyes sparkled with disappointed shyness and the tip of her nose nearly met the tip of her chin.

The suggestion of how much Maria would have wished to follow the conventional path of marriage and family is suggested by the "disappointed shyness" that she covers with her exaggerated laugh. The description of her witch-like features, ironically at odds with her kindly nature, hint at why Maria has never found love.

The pathos is increased when, at the party, some girls play a cruel joke and add clay from the backyard to Maria's choices. In polite versions of the game, clay is omitted because it symbolizes imminent death, and the adults are furious at the girls and appalled by their insensitivity. Maria, however, still blindfolded, has no idea what has caused the commotion. The THIRD-PERSON LIMITED NARRATOR takes us into her childlike perspective: "Maria understood that it was wrong that time and so she had to do it over again: and this time she got the prayer-book." The next morning, a mass day for which the pious Maria has set her alarm clock an hour early, is All Saints' Day. Joyce has suggested Maria's fate, as well as her naïve obliviousness to the harshness of her lot, with touchingly understated pathos.

EXERCISES: Theme and Tone

I. For each of the following passages:
- Describe the TONE.
- Explain the aspects of the passage's DICTION, SYNTAX, POINT OF VIEW, and SELECTION OF DETAILS that help to convey that TONE.
- If the predominant TONE changes, explain how and why.

1. Her doctor had told Julian's mother that she must lose twenty pounds because of her blood pressure, so on Wednesday nights Julian had to take her downtown on the bus for a reducing class at the Y. The reducing class was designed for working girls over fifty,

who weighed from 165 to 200 pounds. His mother was one of the slimmer ones, but she said ladies did not tell their age or weight. She would not ride the buses by herself at night since they had been integrated, and because the reducing class was one of her few pleasures, necessary for her health, and *free*, she said Julian could at least put himself out to take her, considering all she did for him. Julian did not like to consider all she did for him, but every Wednesday night he braced himself and took her.

—FLANNERY O'CONNOR, "Everything That Rises Must Converge"

2. Gr-r-r—there go, my heart's abhorrence!
        Water your damned flower-pots, do!
    If hate killed men, Brother Lawrence,
        God's blood, would not mine kill you!
    What? Your myrtle-bush wants trimming?   5
        Oh, that rose has prior claims—
    Needs its leaden vase filled brimming?
        Hell dry you up with its flames!

—ROBERT BROWNING, "Soliloquy of the Spanish Cloister"

3. The man . . . banged his fist on the table and shouted:
        —What's for my dinner?
        —I'm going . . . to cook it, pa, said the little boy.
        —On that fire! You let the fire out! By God, I'll teach you to do that again!
    He took a step to the door and seized the walking-stick which was standing behind it.
        —I'll teach you to let the fire out! he said, rolling up his sleeve in order to give his arm free play.
    The little boy cried *O, pa!* and ran whimpering round the table, but the man followed and caught him by the coat. The little boy looked about him wildly but, seeing no way of escape, fell upon his knees.
        —Now, you'll let the fire out the next time! Take that, you little whelp!
    The boy uttered a squeal of pain as the stick cut his thigh. He clasped his hands together in the air and his voice shook with fright.
        —O, pa! he cried. Don't beat me, pa! And I'll . . . I'll say a *Hail Mary*[1] for you. . . . I'll say a *Hail Mary* for you, pa, if you don't beat me. . . . I'll say a *Hail Mary* . . .

—JAMES JOYCE, "Counterparts"

1. A Catholic prayer to the Virgin Mary.

▼

4. Lay your sleeping head, my love,
    Human on my faithless arm;
    Time and fevers burn away
    Individual beauty from
    Thoughtful children, and the grave   5
    Proves the child ephemeral:
    But in my arms till break of day
    Let the living creature lie,
    Mortal, guilty, but to me
    The entirely beautiful.   10

                                    —W. H. AUDEN, "Lullaby"

5. *In Shakespeare's* King Lear, *the old king speaks these words over the body
    of his daughter Cordelia, who has been hanged and lies dead in his arms:*

    And my poor fool[2] is hanged! No, no, no life!
    Why should a dog, a horse, a rat, have life,
    And thou no breath at all? Thou'lt come no more,
    Never, never, never, never, never!

6. Is this a holy thing to see,
    In a rich and fruitful land,
    Babes reduc'd to misery,
    Fed with cold and usurous hand?

    Is that trembling cry a song?   5
    Can it be a song of joy?
    And so many children poor?
    It is a land of poverty!

                            —WILLIAM BLAKE, "Holy Thursday [II]"

7. *In Shakespeare's* Romeo and Juliet, *the couple, whose families are engaged
    in a bitter feud, have just met by chance at a feast. Romeo has
    subsequently been hiding beneath Juliet's balcony, eavesdropping as she
    reminisces rapturously to herself about their encounter.*

    JULIET What man art thou that, thus bescreened in night,
        So stumblest on my counsel[3]?
    ROMEO   By a name
        I know not how to tell thee who I am.
        My name, dear saint, is hateful to myself
        Because it is an enemy to thee.
        Had I it written, I would tear the word.

    _____

    2. A term of endearment, used here of Cordelia.
    3. Private thoughts.

JULIET My ears have not yet drunk a hundred words
    Of thy tongue's uttering, yet I know the sound.
    Art thou not Romeo, and a Montague?
ROMEO Neither, fair maid, if either thee dislike.[4]
JULIET How cam'st thou hither, tell me, and wherefore?[5]
    The orchard walls are high and hard to climb,
    And the place death, considering who thou art,
    If any of my kinsmen find thee here.
ROMEO With love's light wings did I o'erperch[6] these walls,
    For stony limits cannot hold love out,
    And what love can do, that dares love attempt.
    Therefore thy kinsmen are no stop[7] to me.

8. *The following passage describes American soldiers during the Vietnam War:*

    They carried all the emotional baggage of men who might die.
Grief, terror, love, longing—these were intangibles, but the intangibles had their own mass and specific gravity, they had tangible
weight. They carried shameful memories. They carried the common
secret of cowardice barely restrained, the instinct to run or freeze or
hide, and in many respects this was the heaviest burden of all, for it
could never be put down, it required perfect balance and perfect
posture. They carried their reputations. They carried the soldier's
greatest fear, which was the fear of blushing. Men killed, and died,
because they were embarrassed not to. It was what had brought
them to the war in the first place, nothing positive, no dreams of
glory or honor, just to avoid the blush of dishonor. They died so as
not to die of embarrassment. They crawled into tunnels and walked
point and advanced under fire. Each morning, despite the
unknowns, they made their legs move. They endured. . . . They did
not submit to the obvious alternative, which was simply to close
the eyes and fall. So easy, really. Go limp and tumble to the ground
and let the muscles unwind and not speak and not budge until
your buddies picked you up and lifted you into the chopper that
would roar up and dip its nose and carry you off into the world. A
mere matter of falling, yet no one ever fell. It was not courage,
exactly; the object was not valor. Rather, they were too frightened
to be cowards.   –TIM O'BRIEN, *The Things They Carried*

---

4. Displease.
5. Why.
6. Fly over.
7. Barrier.

II.   Summarize a major THEME in two DRAMAS, SHORT STORIES, or NOVELS that
      you have recently studied.

III. Analysis of a long passage. Describe the predominant TONE of the fol-
      lowing complete SHORT STORY, or prose poem. Explain the aspects of
      the DICTION, SYNTAX, POINT OF VIEW, and SELECTION OF DETAILS that help to
      convey it, as well as any shifts in TONE that take place.

What you have heard is true. I was in his house. His wife carried
a tray of coffee and sugar. His daughter filed her nails, his son went
out for the night. There were daily papers, pet dogs, a pistol on the
cushion beside him. The moon swung bare on its black cord over the
house. On the television was a cop show. It was in English. Broken
bottles were embedded in the walls around the house to scoop the
kneecaps from a man's legs or cut his hands to lace. On the windows
were gratings like those in liquor stores. We had dinner, rack of lamb,
good wine, a gold bell was on the table for calling the maid. The maid
brought green mangoes, salt, a type of bread. I was asked how I
enjoyed the country. There was a brief commercial in Spanish. His
wife took everything away. There was some talk of how difficult it
had become to govern. The parrot said hello on the terrace. The
colonel told it to shut up, and pushed himself from the table. My
friend said to me with his eyes: say nothing. The colonel returned
with a sack used to bring groceries home. He spilled many human
ears on the table. They were like dried peach halves. There is no other
way to say this. He took one of them in his hands, shook it in our
faces, dropped it into a water glass. It came alive there. I am tired of
fooling around he said. As for the rights of anyone, tell your people
they can go fuck themselves. He swept the ears to the floor with his
arm and held the last of the wine in the air. Something for your poetry,
no? he said. Some of the ears on the floor caught this scrap of his
voice. Some of the ears on the floor were pressed to the ground.

                                        —CAROLYN FORCHÉ, "The Colonel"

Structure

The **structure** of a literary work is its basic framework, the principles and the patterns on which it is organized. The structure may derive from the conventions of a certain form—for example, the five-act format of an Elizabethan tragedy or the OCTAVE/SESTET division of an ITALIAN SONNET. Alternatively, the structure may evolve as an individual work takes shape, creating what the critic and poet Samuel Taylor Coleridge called "organic form." His meditative lyric "Frost at Midnight," for example, is ordered partly by its BLANK VERSE form, the steady beat of the UNRHYMED IAMBIC PENTAMETER lines. But the irregular length of the stanzas, the many exclamations, and the extensive ENJAMBMENTS also make it seem like a spontaneous pouring forth of the NARRATOR's feelings that is unique to this poem: memories of his constricted childhood, hopes for his newborn son, and responsiveness to the beauty and regenerative power of nature. Both influences on the poem serve the major purposes of structure: to make the parts interdependent and give the whole unity.

Readers need to be alert to both the patterns of organization conventional for a given genre and to the techniques that create the structure of an individual work. Those factors include the order in which the story is told—whether it begins at the chronological beginning or plunges into that narrative at some later point, IN MEDIAS RES. Another set of choices involves the NARRATIVE PACE, the amount of time that is represented as passing within and between each episode of the story and the degree of detail used in its telling. A third factor is the focus of the narrative—whether it concentrates on a single plot and set of characters or includes a SUBPLOT, a subsidiary story that parallels or contrasts with the main one. Finally, there is the relative uniformity of the work's style, whether it follows the pattern initially established throughout or changes it markedly at certain points. In other words, a good deal of the art of narration involves aspects of the structure.

In Medias Res ◀

One technique that has been both a convention of some genres and an innovation in many works is *in medias res* (in MAY-dee-ass rayss, Latin for "in the middle of things"), beginning a narration not in chronological order, with the first event in the plot, but at some later point. To take an example of the former technique, the first lines of Edgar Allan Poe's poem "The Raven" begin with the first event in the story:

▼

> Once upon a midnight dreary, while I pondered, weak and
>   weary,
> Over many a quaint and curious volume of forgotten lore—
> While I nodded, nearly napping, suddenly there came a tapping,
> As of some one gently rapping, rapping at my chamber door—

What follows, as these lines promise, is the narrator's step-by-step account of how the mysterious bird has affected his life. A poem that begins *in medias res*, in contrast, is John Donne's "The Canonization," which begins with the demand: "For God's sake hold your tongue, and let me love." That abrupt challenge creates immediacy and surprise, advantages of the *in medias res* technique, but it also imposes on the author the obligation to go back in the story and fill in the essential background information—the **exposition**—that will allow the reader to understand the characters and the events that have been introduced.

The *in medias res* beginning is a convention of the EPIC form. For example, Homer's *Odyssey* opens not when the hero sets out from the Greeks' triumph in the Trojan War to return to his native island but near the end of his almost ten-year journey, when he is marooned on the island of the nymph Calypso. It is not until a third of the way into the EPIC that the audience learns how Odysseus came to be denied the swift return to home and family for which he longs. Homer's EXPOSITION takes the form of the **flashback**, the dramatization of scenes set earlier in a story, when Odysseus relates his adventures to the hospitable Phaeacians, in books 7–12. During those books, the eloquent PROTAGONIST assumes the role of the minstrel, the epic narrator whose role is to glorify the hero by recounting his extraordinary feats. Since Homer's day, the flashback has been used in countless works of *fiction*, *drama*, and film. For example, in Arthur Miller's *Death of a Salesman*, it consists of staging the PROTAGONIST'S memories and delusions, which alternate with the realistic scenes set in the present.

Another means of providing EXPOSITION is to have either the NARRATOR or a character summarize necessary background information. For example, in a manner typical of the THIRD-PERSON OMNISCIENT POINT OF VIEW, the INTRUSIVE NARRATOR of Jane Austen's *Emma* introduces each new character with a summary of his or her family origins, relationships, and sometimes, as in the passage below, physical appearance:

> Harriet Smith was the natural[1] daughter of somebody. Somebody had placed her, several years back, at Mrs. Goddard's school,

---

1. Illegitimate.

and Somebody had lately raised her from the condition of scholar to that of parlour-boarder. This was all that was generally known of her history. She had no visible friends but what had been acquired at Highbury, and was now just returned from a long visit in the country to some young ladies who had been at school there with her.

She was a very pretty girl, and her beauty happened to be of a sort which Emma particularly admired. She was short, plump and fair, with a fine bloom, blue eyes, light hair, regular features, and a look of great sweetness; and before the end of the evening, Emma was as much pleased with her manners as her person, and quite determined to continue the acquaintance.

This description occurs on the occasion of the first meeting between Harriet and the aristocratic heroine, the matchmaking Emma, who is looking for a new project to occupy her idle hours. Both the difference in their social status and Harriet's sweet naïveté deftly foreshadow the uneven course that the young women's friendship will take.

The process of EXPOSITION can be awkward, however, if it holds up the action for too long and depends too much on the process of TELLING. In Shakespeare's *The Tempest*, for example, Prospero gives a long account to his adolescent daughter about how they came to be marooned on the island that they inhabit and on the revelation of her noble heritage. He keeps interrupting his narrative to demand to know whether she is listening: "Dost thou attend me?"; "Dost thou hear?" She responds with a series of reassurances, sympathetic exclamations, and questions asking for fuller detail. No doubt, the VOICE of the author behind the anxious character is seeking reassurance that he has not alienated the larger audience in the theater by so static a form of exposition. More typically, as in *Antony and Cleopatra*, Shakespeare is adept at using various means of SHOWING to introduce the EXPOSITION: making it an integral part of the action, skillfully interweaving facts about old political conflicts, family relationships, and former love interests. The means include gossip among onlookers, lovers' spats, messengers who are unwillingly drawn into the quarrels between the principals, and reminiscences about the hero and heroine's past glories.

As the last example suggests, *in medias res* has been used effectively in contexts that, unlike the EPIC, do not depend on it as a convention of the form. Writers of FICTION, as well as DRAMA, have made extensive use of the technique. For example, James Joyce's SHORT STORY "Eveline" begins:

> She sat at the window watching the evening invade the
> avenue. Her head was leaned against the window curtains and in
> her nostrils was the odour of dusty cretonne.[2] She was tired.

It is several paragraphs before we learn that the PROTAGONIST is trying to decide whether or not to leave her dreary home and elope to
Buenos Aires with a kindly sailor who has proposed to her. The passive voice of the sentences—not "she leaned her head" but "her
head was leaned"—suggests her weary, defeated attitude. She is not
exerting the energy even to breathe—the dusty odour was "in her
nostrils." The THIRD-PERSON LIMITED POINT OF VIEW, which reflects not
only Eveline's outlook but also her voice, SHOWS rather than TELLS
her timid, passive nature and foreshadows the story's sad outcome.

The beginning *in medias res* of Virginia Woolf's *Mrs. Dalloway*,
in contrast, suggests the energetic voice and fine sensibility of the
PROTAGONIST:

> Mrs. Dalloway said she would buy the flowers herself.
> For Lucy had her work cut out for her. The doors would be
> taken off their hinges; Rumpelmayer's men were coming. And
> then, thought Clarissa Dalloway, what a morning—fresh as if
> issued to children on a beach.

In this case, too, the THIRD-PERSON LIMITED perspective replicates the
character's thought process and outlook, as well as sets up some
small sources of suspense: What is the occasion for the flowers? Who
is Lucy? Why need the doors be removed from their hinges? What is
the basis for Mrs. Dalloway's enthusiasm about the morning? As with
"Eveline," we later discover that the seemingly casual *in medias res*
opening has deftly anticipated key aspects of the story. The simple
errand will set Mrs. Dalloway on a leisurely quest through London
that will reveal her love for the city, wide sympathies, cultivated
tastes, and conflicted feelings about her family and her past.

Narrative Pace

Narrators, and the authors behind them, also make choices about
the **pace** at which they tell a story, speeding up or slowing down
some parts, and omitting others altogether. In Charlotte Brontë's
Jane Eyre, the NARRATOR/PROTAGONIST devotes the first nine chapters

---

2. A heavy unglazed cotton fabric, colorfully printed.

to recounting her childhood—her emotional abuse at the hands of her cruel aunt and cousins and her entry into a repressive boarding school for charity children. There, despite the harsh conditions, Jane makes friends and enjoys the first encouragement of her keen intellect. Then the NOVEL leaps over her remaining years at the school, a lapse which the NARRATOR defends:

> Hitherto I have recorded in detail the events of my insignificant existence: to the first ten years of my life, I have given almost as many chapters. But this is not to be a regular autobiography: I am only bound to invoke memory where I know her responses will possess some degree of interest; therefore I now pass a space of eight years almost in silence: a few lines only are necessary to keep up the links of connection.

The authorial VOICE behind the NARRATOR is aware that that choice about the novel's structure is aesthetically sound. The book has already described the emotional and intellectual experiences that will shape the PROTAGONIST's character. It is time for the narrative to move on to its central focus, the adult Jane's relationship with Mr. Rochester, for which the early episodes have provided background.

Shakespeare makes a similar choice about **narrative pace** in his bittersweet romance, *The Winter's Tale*. Act III ends with the rescue of the newborn princess, whom her irrationally jealous father has declared illegitimate and ordered to be put to death. At the beginning of Act IV, a personification of Time acts as the chorus who conveys us over a lapse of sixteen years. When the action begins again, the child, raised by kindly shepherds, has miraculously grown into a paragon of beauty and refinement, and the king, lonely and distraught, has come to repent his rash cruelty. In keeping with the fairy tale conventions of the romance genre, the princess is poised to become the means of restoring some measure of her father's happiness.

In other works, the opposite means of dealing with time occurs: the author slows the narrative pace as the story continues. For example, Leo Tolstoy's "The Death of Ivan Ilych" begins IN MEDIAS RES with the funeral of the title character. The predominant TONE of the scene is satiric, with most of the mourners, from Ivan's closest friend at the law courts where he has been an important judge to his grasping wife, feigning their grief, playing the part that propriety requires, while privately intent on selfish and petty interests. The time then FLASHES BACK to an account of Ivan's childhood, education, marriage, and career, which proceeds at an efficient pace and takes up about a third of the story. Once Ivan has the accident that will lead to his death, however, the pace slows. At first, the reader, like the PROTAGONIST, sees the injury as a minor inconvenience—Ivan slips while hanging drapes in his fancy new house and bruises his side. As the unspecified illness—probably cancer, though it is never properly diagnosed—progresses, however, the passage of time slows down, so the reader experiences in great detail Ivan's increasing physical pain and emotional anguish. The final sections are devoted to descriptions of single days and then to hours passed in terrible agony and almost total loneliness. Only when Ivan is able to admit his faults, to let go of his materialistic values and egotistical concerns, does he find peace, and then only in the final minutes before his death. The change is internal. By that point he is too weak to speak, and his family hears only his screams. The reader is present, however, through the medium of the THIRD-PERSON LIMITED perspective, to witness the change of heart that lets Ivan find sympathy for his family's suffering and ask forgiveness for his shortcomings. Tolstoy's THEMES emerge in part from the techniques used to create the structure: the slowing of the NARRATIVE PACE to replicate the inescapable suffering and the opportunity for spiritual growth attendant on terminal illness. The dying man learns the value of compassion, sincerity, and piety, all of which are missing from the satiric funeral scene that opens the story.

Parenthetical Observation

Within a shorter space, too, for example, in a paragraph or a poem, an author may change the initial structure to move in a new direction. Sometimes that shift takes the temporary form of a **parenthetical observation**, a brief interruption during which the character or the narrator reflects on a minor point that seizes his attention. For example, in Shakespeare's *Hamlet*, the self-important old courtier Polonius interrupts himself several times in the course of explaining to the king and queen his theory about the cause of Hamlet's madness. Sometimes it is to critique his own oratorical style:

> That he is mad, 'tis true; 'tis true 'tis pity,
> And pity 'tis 'tis true—a foolish figure,[1]
> But farewell it, for I will use no art.

---

1. Figure of speech: *chiasmus.*

Sometimes it is to denigrate Hamlet's love letters to Ophelia, Polonius's daughter, which the officious father has confiscated as evidence that Hamlet is mad from unrequited love:

> 'To the celestial and my soul's idol, the most beautified Ophelia'— that's an ill phrase, a vile phrase, 'beautified' is a vile phrase. But you shall hear—

And sometimes it is simply to qualify a point to a nicety: "I have a daughter—have while she is mine—." The queen, eager for him to get to the point, demands impatiently, "More matter with less art." The effect of the parenthetical comments is to suggest that Polonius is relishing this chance to make the most of his moment in the spotlight.

Later in the play, during a SOLILOQUY, Hamlet himself makes a PARENTHETICAL OBSERVATION from a very different motive. He is berating himself because he has not yet acted on the command of his father's ghost to avenge his murder:

> Now whether it be
> Bestial oblivion, or some craven scruple
> Of thinking too precisely on th'event—
> A thought which, quartered, hath but one part wisdom
> And ever three parts coward—I do not know
> Why yet I live to say 'This things's to do.'

In typical fashion, Hamlet is looking at the issue from multiple angles: he reasons that only the "oblivion" of an unthinking beast or its polar opposite quality, excessive thought resulting in "scruple[s]" against the murder, can explain his delay. The PARENTHETICAL OBSERVATION about the second reason shows the depth of his self-loathing: although he acknowledges that his hesitation is based on some "wisdom," nevertheless he also condemns it as the rationalization of a "coward." The prince is working himself up for the slaughter that he feels compelled to undertake.

In Laurence Sterne's *Tristram Shandy*, the parenthetical observation abounds, to the extent that virtually every page is a quilt of disconnected thoughts and random associations, stitched together by dashes. The following passage occurs in the middle of the FIRST-PERSON NARRATOR'S meandering account of his own birth. While Tristram Shandy's mother is in labor in the next room, his eccentric Uncle Toby has distracted the doctor with a discussion of military fortifications, a subject with which he is obsessed. Toby's brother, the expectant father, has just berated him and cursed "the whole science of fortification." The narration continues:

> My uncle Toby was a man patient of injuries;—not from want of courage,—I have told you in the fifth chapter of this second book, "That he was a man of courage:"—And will add here, that where just occasions presented, or called it forth,—I know no man under whose arm I would sooner have taken shelter; nor did this arise from any insensibility or obtuseness of his intellectual parts;—for he felt this insult of my father's as feelingly as a man could do;—but he was of a peaceful, placid nature,—no jarring element in it,—all was mix'd up so kindly within him; my uncle Toby had scarce a heart to retaliate upon a fly.
>
> —Go—says he, one day at dinner, to an over-grown one which had buzz'd about his nose, and tormented him cruelly all dinner-time,—and which, after infinite attempts, he had caught at last, as it flew by him;—I'll not hurt thee, says my uncle Toby, rising from his chair, and going across the room, with the fly in his hand,—I'll not hurt a hair of thy head:—Go, says he, lifting up the sash, and opening his hand as he spoke, to let it escape;—go, poor Devil, get thee gone, why should I hurt thee?—This world is surely wide enough to hold both thee and me.

After these digressions, the narrator then goes on to reflect how this release of the fly, which he witnessed when he was ten years old, taught him "the lesson of universal good-will," and veers off into a comparison of the temperaments of the two brothers. It is several paragraphs before the narrative returns to the initial dispute and the drama of the pending birth. In Sterne's case, the PARENTHETICAL OBSERVATION is not a temporary interruption of the main narrative thread but an intrinsic quality of the eccentric, digressive voice of the FIRST-PERSON NARRATOR. Tristram Shandy's narration is a patch-work of qualifications, free associations (such as the cliché about not hurting a fly, which evokes the anecdote), veerings back and forth in chronology, and sudden shifts between the account of the imme-diate situation and the commentary that is the essence of Sterne's comic genius.

Subplot

In addition to decisions about where a narrative will begin and the PACE at which it will proceed, authors also make other key choices about its structure. A work may have only a single unified plot, or it may abruptly shift focus, to a different set of characters or a new location. The drama of the English Renaissance, for example, is full of **subplots**, secondary stories that parallel or contrast with the main action. The characters in a subplot may have a major impact on those in the main plot, or they may simply mirror some aspect of it, in either precise or distorted form. In Shakespeare's COMEDY *A Midsummer Night's Dream*, the main plot involving the romantic intrigues of the noble couples is entirely separate from the subplot of the crass workmen, the "rude mechanicals," who are rehearsing a play that they hope to perform at court. At the same time, the workmen's play, a crude rendition of the tragedy of "Pyramus and Thisbe," concerns the same theme of separated lovers as the main plot, though in ludicrous form. Only the supernatural characters in the second subplot, the fairy king and queen and their trains, are aware of those in the other plots. When the two sets of human beings enter the woods, the fairies' province, and the characters from the three plot strands intermix, comic mayhem results. The effects of the fairies' magical intervention are to mock the concepts of love at first sight and the lover's blindness to the beloved's faults: The maiden who has been the object of both swains' desires is made to change places with the young woman who had been rejected by both, and the delicate fairy queen is smitten with Bottom the weaver, who has been transformed into an ass. By the end, a combination of the fairy king's magic and the ruling duke's magnanimity restores order and brings all three plots to a happy resolution.

In Shakespeare's TRAGEDY *King Lear*, the subplot is much more closely intertwined with the main story. Two elderly noblemen, Lear himself and the Earl of Gloucester, have adult children. In each case, the father puts his trust in the treacherous child and rejects the loyal one, who has in the past been his favorite. Both fathers suffer the consequences of those misplaced affections. In other ways, however, the subplots diverge. Lear has three daughters, Gloucester two sons. Lear's loyal child is his youngest, Gloucester's his elder son. Lear's daughters are legitimate and born of the same mother. Gloucester's younger son is illegitimate, the product of an adulterous affair, and deeply resentful of his father's public mockery of his begetting and of his virtual banishment from the kingdom. The stories converge as the villainous offspring form a conspiracy against their fathers that drives Lear to madness and leaves Gloucester blind and, literally, heartbroken. Lear's treacherous daughters die by murder and suicide, and his youngest is killed by one of her sisters' henchmen. Her death causes Lear's heart, like Gloucester's, to break. The earl's treacherous son repents at the end, after losing a duel to his brother, and the last of Gloucester's line goes on to inherit the throne. It is he who makes the solemn pronouncement at the end that the "the oldest hath borne most," a claim reinforced by the fathers' movingly interwoven tragedies.

A NOVEL, too, may shift among various subplots. George Eliot's *Middlemarch* (1872), for example, traces the fortunes of several couples as they meet, court, and marry: the fervently idealistic young Dorothea Brooke and the desiccated scholar, Mr. Casaubon; Dorothea's light-hearted sister, Cecilia, and the stolid, earnest nobleman, Sir James Chettam; the ambitious medical researcher and doctor, Lydgate, and the self-centered beauty Rosamond Vincy; and Rosamond's impulsive and impecunious brother, Fred Vincy, and the practical, responsible Mary Garth. Many other long novels have had multiple subplots, for example, William Makepeace Thackeray's *Vanity Fair* (1847), Harriet Beecher Stowe's *Uncle Tom's Cabin* (1852), Charles Dickens's *Our Mutual Friend* (1864), Leo Tolstoy's *War and Peace* (1869), E. M. Forster's *A Passage to India* (1924), and Zadie Smith's *White Teeth* (2000).

► ## Shift in Style

A narrative may also shift structure by introducing a marked change in style, usually accompanied by a corresponding alteration in TONE. For example, "Lapis Lazuli," William Butler Yeats's poem about the consolations of art in the midst of tragedy, **shifts style** and TONE in each of its five stanzas. It begins with a mocking echo of "hysterical women" who denigrate the value of "the palette and fiddle-bow" and of "poets that are always gay"—that is, optimistic. The women vent their hysteria in childish terrors, demanding that something "drastic" be done to stop "aeroplane and Zeppelin" before the enemy can "Pitch like King Billy bomb-balls in." The NARRATOR'S IRONY emerges from the combination of their childish diction and their conflation of the weapons used in World War II and the seventeenth-century Battle of the Boyne. The second stanza shifts to a somber tone and a focus on the performance of Shakespearean tragedy, in which "Hamlet and Lear," like the poets of the first stanza, are described as "gay." The key for the narrator is that in the theater, no matter how dire the suffering depicted, it has a fixed limit: "It cannot grow by an inch or an ounce." The poem then shifts to a focus on all the ancient civilizations that have disappeared, taking with them the work of their artists, and yet, the narrator reiterates, the "gaiety" derived from the renewing power of the creative process remains: "All things fall and are built again, / And those that build them again are gay."

The final two stanzas allude at last to the poem's title; it refers to an ancient Chinese sculpture made from the blue stone, which the narrator is contemplating. It depicts three men climbing a mountain—"an ascetic and pupil," according to Yeats's own note—followed by a servant who "carries a musical instrument." The last stanza brings the figures to life in the narrator's imagination: they look down on "all the tragic scene," then ask to hear "mournful melodies," which "accomplished fingers begin to play." The final lines focus on "their eyes, / Their ancient, glittering eyes," which, fittingly, "are gay." The implication is that art, the ability to create beautiful music, has given the artist/philosophers the perspective and tranquility to remain above the fray. That point is given double impact by the fact that the sculpture itself is a work of art and that, in animating and describing it, the observer/narrator has himself created a piece of art that assures his own "gaiety." Such insight and perspective would be impossible for the "hysterical women" of the opening stanza.

Prose narratives may also shift from their established style and tone. In *Black Boy* (1945, 1991), Richard Wright's autobiographical novel, the narrative sometimes departs abruptly from the usual structure, a chronological account of Richard's troubled childhood and youth, depicted in dramatized episodes. In one such shift, Wright introduces a randomly ordered list of sense impressions that make an impact on the young boy's feelings:

> Each event spoke with a cryptic tongue. And the moments of living slowly revealed their coded meanings.
> . . . There was the tantalizing melancholy in the tingling scent of burning hickory wood.
> . . . There was the languor I felt when I heard green leaves rustling with a rainlike sound.
> . . . There was the experience of feeling death without dying that came from watching a chicken leap about blindly after its neck had been snapped by a quick twist of my father's wrist.
> . . . There was the thirst I had when I watched clear, sweet juice trickle from sugar cane being crushed.
> . . . And there was the quiet terror that suffused my senses when vast hazes of gold washed earthward from star-heavy skies on silent nights . . .

For the reader, the list is a sign of the curiosity, candor, and imagination that have miraculously survived the abuses to which Richard is subjected. These are the seeds of the consciousness that will grow up to produce the remarkable novel. At another point, Richard stops the narrative flow to list the superstitions that he believed in as a boy. A few are commonplace—for example, "If I broke a mirror, I would have seven years of bad luck." Most, however, are idiosyncratic pieces of folk wisdom designed to signal good fortune, ward off undesirable outcomes, or gain favor with the deity:

> If my right ear itched, then something good was being said about me by somebody.
> . . . If I covered a mirror when a storm was raging, the lightning would not strike me.
> . . . If I walked in my sleep, then God was trying to lead me somewhere to do a good deed for him.

The adult narrator, looking back, comments on the fervor of his childish belief:

> Anything seemed possible, likely, feasible, because I wanted everything to be possible . . . Because I had no power to make things happen outside of me in the objective world, I made things happen within. Because my environment was bare and bleak, I endowed it with unlimited potentialities, redeemed it for the sake of my own hungry and cloudy yearning.

Rather than ignore or dismiss such inconsistencies in style and shifts in structure, readers should attend to them closely, as potential keys to revelations about meaning and TONE.

EXERCISES: Structure

I. Each of the following passages opens a NOVEL, SHORT STORY, PLAY, or NARRATIVE POEM.

- Explain whether the work is STRUCTURED so as to begin in chronological order or *in medias res*.
- Describe how that way of beginning the work affects the meaning and the TONE.

1. True! Nervous—very, very dreadfully nervous I had been and am; but why *will* you say that I am mad? The disease had sharpened my senses—not destroyed—not dulled them. Above all things was the sense of hearing acute. I heard all things in the heaven and in the earth. I heard many things in hell. How, then, am I mad? Hearken! And observe how healthily—how calmly I can tell you the whole story.   —EDGAR ALLAN POE, "The Tell-Tale Heart"

▼

2. It is a truth universally acknowledged, that a single man in posses-
    sion of a good fortune, must be in want of a wife.

    However little known the feelings or views of such a man may
    be on his first entering a neighborhood, this truth is so well fixed
    in the minds of the surrounding families, that he is considered as
    the rightful property of some one or other of their daughters.

    –JANE AUSTEN, *Pride and Prejudice*

3. *Enter* BERNARDO *and* FRANCISCO, *two sentinels.*
    Location: A guard platform at Elsinore Castle, Denmark.

    BERNARDO Who's there?
    FRANCISCO Nay, answer me. Stand and unfold[1] yourself.
    BERNARDO Long live the king!
    FRANCISCO   Bernardo?
    BERNARDO   He.
    FRANCISCO You come most carefully upon your hour.
    BERNARDO 'Tis now struck twelve. Get thee to bed, Francisco.   5
    FRANCISCO For this relief much thanks. 'Tis bitter cold,
                And I am sick at heart.
    BERNARDO   Have you had quiet guard?
    FRANCISCO Not a mouse stirring.
    BERNARDO   Well, good night.
                If you do meet Horatio and Marcellus,
                The rivals[2] of my watch, bid them make haste.   10

    –WILLIAM SHAKESPEARE, *Hamlet*

4. My father's family name being Pirrip, and my Christian name Phillip,
    my infant tongue could make of both names nothing longer or more
    explicit than Pip. So, I called myself Pip, and came to be called Pip.

    I give Pirrip as my father's family name, on the authority of his
    tombstone and my sister—Mrs. Joe Gargery, who married the
    blacksmith. As I never saw my father or my mother, and never saw
    any likeness of them (for their days were long before the days of
    photographs), my first fancies regarding what they were like, were
    unreasonably derived from their tombstones. The shape of the let-
    ters on my father's, gave me an odd idea that he was a square,
    stout, dark man, with curly black hair. From the character and turn
    of the inscription, 'Also Georgiana Wife of the Above,' I drew a child-
    ish conclusion that my mother was freckled and sickly. To five little
    stone lozenges,[3] each about a foot and a half long, which were

---

1. Identify.
2. Partners.
3. Slabs.

arranged in a neat row beside their grave, and were sacred to the
memory of five little brothers of mine—who gave up trying to get a
living, exceedingly early in that universal struggle—I am indebted
for a belief I religiously entertained that they had all been born on
their backs with their hands in their trousers-pockets, and had
never taken them out in this state of existence.

—CHARLES DICKENS, *Great Expectations*

5. It is an ancient Mariner
And he stoppeth one of three,
—"By thy long gray beard and glittering eye,
Now wherefore stopp'st thou me?

The Bridegroom's doors are opened wide,   5
And I am next of kin;
The guests are met, the feast is set:
May'st hear the merry din."

He holds him with his skinny hand,
"There was a ship," quoth he.   10
"Hold off! unhand me, graybeard loon!"
Eftsoons[4] his hand dropped he.

He holds him with his glittering eye—
The wedding guest stood still,
And listens like a three years' child: 15
The Mariner hath his will.

—SAMUEL TAYLOR COLERIDGE,
"The Rime of the Ancient Mariner"

6. I am a rather elderly man. The nature of my avocations, for the last
thirty years, has brought me into more than ordinary contact with
what would seem an interesting and somewhat singular set of men,
of whom, as yet, nothing, that I know of, has ever been written—I
mean, the law-copyists, or scriveners. I have known very many of
them, professionally and privately, and, if I pleased, could relate
divers histories, at which good-natured gentlemen might smile, and
sentimental souls might weep. But I waive the biographies of all
other scriveners, for a few passages in the life of Bartleby, who was
a scrivener, the strangest I ever saw, or heard of. While of other
law-copyists I might write the complete life, of Bartleby nothing of

---

4. Immediately.

the sort can be done. I believe that no materials exist, for a full and satisfactory biography of this man. It is an irreparable loss to literature. Bartleby was one of those beings of whom nothing is ascertainable, except from the original sources, and, in his case, those are very small. What my own astonished eyes saw of Bartleby, *that* is all I know of him, except, indeed, one vague report, which will appear in the sequel.

–HERMAN MELVILLE, "Bartleby the Scrivener"

For each of the following passages:

- Explain whether the technique for providing EXPOSITION is a FLASHBACK or a narrative summary.
- Describe how that technique affects the meaning and the TONE of the passage.

1. The last time I talked to my mother, I remember I was restless. I wanted to get out and see Isabel. We weren't married then and we had a lot to straighten out between us.

   There Mama sat, in black, by the window. She was humming an old tune, *Lord, you brought me from a long ways off.* Sonny was out somewhere. Mama kept watching the streets.

   "I don't know," she said, "if I'll ever see you again, after you go off from here. But I hope you'll remember the things I tried to teach you."

   "Don't talk like that," I said, and smiled. "You'll be here a long time yet."

   She smiled, too, but she said nothing. She was quiet for a long time. And I said, "Mama, don't worry about nothing. I'll be writing all the time, and you'll be getting the checks. . . . "

   "I want to talk to you about your brother," she said, suddenly. "If anything happens to me he ain't going to have nobody to look out for him."

   "Mama," I said, "ain't nothing going to happen to you *or* Sonny. Sonny's all right. He's a good boy and he's got good sense."

   "It ain't a question of his being a good boy," Mama said, "nor of his having good sense. It ain't only the bad ones, nor yet the dumb ones that gets sucked under." She stopped, looking at me. "Your Daddy once had a brother," she said, and she smiled in a way that made me feel she was in pain. "You didn't never know that, did you?"

   "No," I said, "I never knew that," and I watched her face.

–JAMES BALDWIN, "Sonny's Blues"

2. There was a good deal of fussing to be done before Mr. Summers declared the lottery open. There were the lists to make up—of heads of families, heads of households in each family, members of each household in each family. There was the proper swearing-in of Mr. Summers by the postmaster, as the official of the lottery; at one time, some people remembered, there had been a recital of some sort, performed by the official of the lottery, a perfunctory, tuneless chant that had been rattled off duly each year; some people believed that the official of the lottery used to stand just so when he said or sang it, others believed that he was supposed to walk among the people, but years and years ago this part of the ritual had been allowed to lapse. There had been, also, a ritual salute, which the official of the lottery had had to use in addressing each person who came up to draw from the box, but this also had changed with time, until now it was felt necessary only for the official to speak to each person approaching. Mr. Summers was very good at all this; in his clean white shirt and blue jeans, with one hand resting care-lessly on the black box, he seemed very proper and important as he talked interminably to Mr. Graves and the Martins.

    —Shirley Jackson, "The Lottery"

III. For each of the following passages:

*   Identify the PARENTHETICAL OBSERVATION.
*   Explain its effect on the meaning and the TONE of the passage.

1. In the following passage, a mother is speculating on the sources of her older daughter's "corroding resentment" toward her younger sister:

    Susan, the second child, Susan, golden- and curly-haired and chubby, quick and articulate and assured, everything in appearance and manner Emily was not; . . . Susan telling jokes and riddles to company for applause while Emily sat silent (to say to me later: that was *my* riddle, Mother, I told it to Susan). . . .

    —Tillie Olsen, "I Stand Here Ironing"

2. And indeed there will be time
    To wonder, "Do I dare?" and, "Do I dare?"
    Time to turn back and descend the stair,
    With a bald spot in the middle of my hair—
    [They will say: "How his hair is growing thin!"]   5
    My morning coat, my collar mounting firmly to the chin,
    My necktie rich and modest, but asserted by a simple pin—
    [They will say: "But how his arms and legs are thin!"]

Do I dare
Disturb the universe?   10
In a minute there is time
For decisions and revisions which a minute will reverse.
               –T. S. ELIOT, "The Love Song of J. Alfred Prufrock"

IV.

- Name two NOVELS, SHORT STORIES, or DRAMAS that you have read in which the NARRATIVE PACE is markedly sped up or slowed down at some point.
- Explain the effects of that shift in PACE on the work's meaning and TONE.

V.

- Name two NOVELS or DRAMAS that you have read that contain a SUBPLOT.
- Explain how the SUBPLOT parallels or contrasts with the main PLOT and how it contributes to the meaning of the work as a whole.

Syntax

Syntax is sentence structure: the sequence and connection of the words, phrases, and clauses that constitute the sentences in a work. A **sentence** in English contains a **subject** and a **predicate** and can stand alone as a grammatical unit, or **independent clause**. A **dependent clause** is a group of words that contains a subject and a predicate but cannot stand alone as a grammatical unit. In order to form a sentence; it must be combined with an INDEPENDENT CLAUSE. A **phrase** is a group of words that lacks a subject, a predicate, or both, and that functions as a part of speech, such as a noun, an adverb, or an adjective. The subject designates who or what the sentence is about. The **simple subject** is a noun or a pronoun; the **complete subject** consists of the simple subject and all of its modifiers. In the following sentences, the simple subject is underlined, and the complete subject is italicized:

> _<u>Polonius</u> loves to talk._
>
> _The <u>intensity</u> of Romeo's love for Juliet_ never flags.
>
> _The main <u>goal</u> that drives Odysseus_ is to reach his homeland of Ithaca.

The **predicate** is the part of the sentence that acts upon, describes, or is performed by the subject. The **simple predicate** is the **verb**—the word that signifies an action or a state of being. The **complete predicate** consists of the verb and all of its modifiers, objects, and complements. In the following sentences, the simple predicate is underlined, and the complete predicate is italicized:

> The rain _<u>fell</u>._
>
> Jane Eyre _<u>flees</u> from Thornfield in a state of panic._
>
> Horatio _<u>is</u> loyal to Hamlet throughout the play._

In addition to the subject and the predicate, a sentence may contain one or more additional elements.

- A **direct object**, which completes the predicate by indicating who or what receives the action expressed by the verb:

> Emma paints _a portrait_ of Harriet.
>
> Gatsby loves _Daisy Buchanan._

- An **indirect object**, which is a noun or a pronoun that indicates to whom or for whom an action is done:

Olivia gives a ring *to Viola*.

Orlando writes *Rosalind* several verses.

- An **appositive**, a noun or a noun phrase that describes or equates with a nearby noun or pronoun:

Darcy, *a supremely proud aristocrat*, at first snubs Elizabeth Bennet.

An unscrupulous thief, he exploits young Oliver Twist.

Sentence Fragments

In English, sentences are indicated by beginning the first word with a capital letter and placing a period after the last word. A sentence that is so punctuated but that lacks either a subject, a predicate, or both is called a **sentence fragment**. For example, the fragment "*Did, too*" lacks a subject. The fragment "*A huge wave*" lacks a predicate. The fragment "*On the corner of the street*"—a prepositional phrase because it begins with a preposition—lacks both a subject and a predicate. An unintentional sentence fragment disrupts the sense of a sentence and, in formal prose, is a grammatical error. Writers sometimes use fragments deliberately, however. One reason is to create naturalistic, casual dialogue. The following passage from Tillie Olsen's SHORT STORY "Tell Me a Riddle" uses three sentence fragments in a row to capture the impatient voice of a sick old woman:

"A babbler. All my life around babblers. Enough!"

An intentional sentence fragment can also create emphasis. In the following passage, the NARRATOR of Alice Walker's "Everyday Use," a concerned mother, is making an effort to understand her overbearing daughter. She makes a brief statement, and then uses two long sentence fragments to specify past examples of her daughter's ambition and enterprise:

Dee wanted nice things. A yellow organdy dress to wear to her graduation from high school; black pumps to match a green suit she'd made from an old suit somebody gave me.

Kinds of Sentences

Sentences may be classified in several ways.

* The **simple sentence** consists of a single INDEPENDENT CLAUSE:

  Jane rebels.

  Jay Gatsby gives lavish parties.

  The Earl of Gloucester, misled by Edmund's lies, puts his trust in the wrong son.

* The **compound sentence** contains more than one INDEPENDENT CLAUSE, with no SUBORDINATE CLAUSES. Those clauses may be linked either by a semicolon or by a **coordinating conjunction**, such as *for, and, nor, or, but, yet,* or *so*:

  Huck Finn outsmarts his ne'er-do-well father; he has to do that in order to survive.

  Odysseus never gives up hope, *and* eventually he triumphs.

* The **complex sentence** contains not only an INDEPENDENT CLAUSE but also one or more **subordinate clauses**—that is, a clause that lacks either a SUBJECT or a PREDICATE and so cannot stand alone as a grammatical unit. A SUBORDINATE CLAUSE may either precede or follow the INDEPENDENT clause in a sentence. In the following examples, the SUBORDINATE clause is in italics:

  When Romeo first sees Juliet, he falls instantly in love with her.

  Elizabeth rejects Mr. Collins's proposal, *which shocks and frustrates him.*

  Although Macbeth acknowledges that murder is evil, he goes through with the assassination of King Duncan.

Means of Linkage: Coordination, Subordination, and Parallelism

The clauses in COMPOUND SENTENCES are linked by what is called **coordination**, a reference to the equivalent importance of the two clauses. Writers sometimes intentionally use excessive coordination, especially in successive sentences linked by the neutral "and." One reason is to suggest the childish or simplistic nature of a character's way of speaking or thinking. For example, Daniel Keyes's "Flowers for Algernon" is a science fiction story told in the form of a diary kept by a mentally challenged man who becomes the subject of an intelligence-enhancing operation. The following is an entry by the PROTAGONIST before the surgery, describing the aftermath of an intelligence test that the researchers have just given him. The COORDINATING CONJUNCTIONS are italicized.

> I dint get all the words *and* they were talking to fast *but* it sounded like Dr Strauss was on my side *and* like the other one wasn't.
> Then Dr Nemur nodded he said all right maybe your right. We will use Charlie. When he said that I got so exited I jumped up *and* shook his hand for being so good to me. I told him thank you doc you wont be sorry for giving me a second chance. *And* I mean it like I told him.

Charlie's mental limitations are suggested not only by his simple vocabulary and misspelling but also by his use of excessive coordination to link clauses and sentences.

Excessive COORDINATION may also be used to create a flat, UNDERSTATED TONE. Here, for example, is the opening paragraph of William Faulkner's SHORT STORY "That Evening Sun." Again, the COORDINATING CONJUNCTIONS are italicized.

> Monday is no different from any other weekday in Jefferson now. The streets are paved now, *and* the telephone and electric companies are cutting down more and more of the shade trees—the water oaks, the maples and locusts and elms—to make room for iron poles bearing clusters of bloated and ghostly and bloodless grapes, *and* we have a city laundry which makes the rounds on Monday morning, gathering the bundles of clothes into bright-colored, specially-made motor cars: the soiled wearing of a whole week now flees apparitionlike behind alert and irritable electric horns, with a long diminishing noise of rubber and asphalt like tearing silk, *and* even the Negro women who still take in white people's washing after the old custom, fetch and deliver it in automobiles.

The LOOSE structure of the long second sentence and the ugliness of the innovations listed, along with the string of **coordinated clauses** suggest the NARRATOR'S IRONIC reservations about the so-called progress that has come to the town.

COMPLEX SENTENCES, in contrast, use a kind of linkage called **subordination**, because it reflects the lesser, or subordinate, importance of the dependent clause. The following passage from Charles

▼

Dickens's *Great Expectations* describes the reaction of the NARRATOR, Pip, to the "desolation" of Miss Havisham, the bitter old recluse who raised her ward, Estella, to take revenge upon the entire male sex. Now that her machinations have deprived Pip of the woman he loves, Miss Havisham is remorseful at last. Just before this passage occurs, she has cried, "What have I done!" The **subordinate clauses** are italicized.

> I knew not how to answer, or *how to comfort her. That she had done a grievous thing in taking an impressionable child to mould into the form that her wild resentment, spurned affection, and wounded pride, found vengeance in,* I knew full well. *But that, in shutting out the light of day,* she had shut out infinitely more; *that, in seclusion, she had secluded herself from a thousand natural and healing influences; that her mind, brooding solitary, had grown diseased, as all minds do and must and will that reverse the appointed order of their Maker;* I knew equally well. And could I look upon her without compassion, *seeing her punishment in the ruin she was, in her profound unfitness for this earth on which she was placed, in the vanity of sorrow which had become a master mania, like the vanity of penitence, the vanity of remorse, the vanity of unworthiness, and other monstrous vanities that have been curses in the world?*

The opening COMPLEX SENTENCE contains an INDEPENDENT CLAUSE linked by a COORDINATING CONJUNCTION to a SUBORDINATE CLAUSE that parallels it. The syntax reflects Pip's perplexity about how to react to Miss Havisham's pain. The sentences that follow, all COMPLEX, analyze the aspects of her guilt and of the irreparable damage that her vindictiveness has done to her own emotional health and well-being. The second sentence begins with a long SUBORDINATE CLAUSE (italicized above) that sums up Miss Havisham's offense and, in a series of PARALLEL PHRASES, her petty motives. That long list, contrasted as it is with the simple statement of Pip's conviction that he understands her culpability—"I knew full well"—gives that INDEPENDENT CLAUSE more force. The second sentence includes multiple CLAUSES, SUBORDINATE and INDEPENDENT, that summarize the dire personal effects of her self-imposed isolation. The final sentence begins with a simple question, expressing the sensitive Pip's compassion even for someone who has ruined his own hopes, elaborated on in a series of PARALLEL clauses and phrases that build to a ringing crescendo about the nature of human vanity.

Another means of signaling the relationships among the parts of a sentence is through **parallelism**: making the elements in a series or in pairs of words, phrases, or clauses analogous in part of speech, grammatical structure, and concept. For instance, in "The Fall of the House of Usher," Edgar Allan Poe modifies the noun "day" with three successive adjectives:

> During the whole of a *dull, dark* and *soundless* day in the autumn of the year . . . I . . . found myself . . . within view of the melancholy House of Usher.

The three parallel adjectives all help to establish the SHORT STORY'S SETTING and ATMOSPHERE. In the following example from one of Julius Caesar's speeches, the three INDEPENDENT CLAUSES consist of the same pronoun, followed by a VERB in the past tense:

> I came, I saw, I conquered.

Here, the parallelism serves to build toward a climax: the action expressed in each **parallel clause** is more significant than the last.

A FORMAL style will be scrupulously attentive to the principle of parallelism, while an INFORMAL style may intentionally break that guideline to create an especially emphatic effect. For example, in Cormac McCarthy's NOVEL *The Crossing,* the NARRATOR describes a wolf that has been killed accidentally and that he then envisions undergoing an apotheosis into a transcendent, supernatural being. To emphasize the extraordinary quality of this vision, he intentionally departs from the conventional rules governing grammar and syntax by using a SENTENCE FRAGMENT, eliminating most punctuation, and breaking the parallelism of the subject complements:

> But which cannot be held never be held and is no flower [*noun*] but is swift [*adjective*] and a huntress [*article and noun*] and the wind itself is in terror of it and the world cannot lose it.

Syntactical Order

The **loose** or the **cumulative sentence** presents ideas in the order of subject-verb-object. Sentences written in English typically follow that order. For example, in the following sentence from "A Good Man Is Hard to Find," Flannery O'Connor begins with the main clause (italicized here) and adds modifiers to amplify it:

> *She pointed out interesting details of the scenery:* Stone Mountain; the blue granite that in some places came up to both sides of the highway; the brilliant red clay banks slightly streaked with purple; and the various crops that made rows of green lace-work on the ground.

Although the elements of the cumulative sentence are connected, they do not have a climactic order, and the sentence would be grammatically complete if it ended earlier. The effect is to create a casual, associative TONE. Here is another example, from Shirley Jackson's SHORT STORY "The Lottery":

> *The rest of the year, the box was put away,* sometimes one place, sometimes another; it had spent one year in Mr. Graves's barn and another year underfoot in the post office, and sometimes it was set on a shelf in the Martin grocery and left there.

The **periodic sentence**, in contrast, is not complete in either syntax or sense until its end, as in the following example from Doris Lessing's SHORT STORY "To Room Nineteen":

> It was a long time later that Susan understood that that night, when she had wept and Matthew had driven the misery out of her with his big solid body, was the last time, ever in their married life, that they had been—to use their mutual language—with each other.

By saving its essential phrase, "with each other," for the last and building to a climax, the periodic sentence creates emphasis and suspense. It also tends to sound more formal and declamatory than the loose sentence. A famous example is the periodic sentence that opens Franz Kafka's nightmarish tale, "The Metamorphosis":

> As Gregor Samsa awoke one morning from uneasy dreams he found himself transformed in his bed into a gigantic insect.

Writers also sometimes reverse the subject-verb-object order of the usual English sentence, to create what is called **inversion**. In the following examples, the inverted word or phrase is italicized, and the conventional order given in brackets:

> *Rarely had* she felt so awkward. [She had rarely felt so awkward.]
> *Lying beside the road was* the injured collie. [The injured collie was lying beside the road.]

The technique of inversion is used frequently in poetry, as, for example, in the following COUPLET from Andrew Marvell's "To His Coy Mistress":

> *Had we* but world enough, and time,   [This coyness would not be a crime if we
> *This coyness,* lady, were no crime.   had enough time and worldly life]

Used in prose, inversion calls attention to the sentence element that is out of conventional order and so creates a special kind of emphasis. It also makes the TONE sound more formal and self-conscious. In his inaugural address, for example, President John F. Kennedy employed inversion to memorable effect:

> "*Ask not* [Do not ask . . .]what your country can do for you; ask what you can do for your country."

Sentence Variety

Most writers strive for variety in their use of SYNTAX; for example, striking effects can be created from varying long, COMPLEX SENTENCES with short, SIMPLE ones. The following passage from Tim O'Brien's fictionalized memoir of his army service in Vietnam, *The Things They Carried*, describes the lot of the ordinary infantryman (in military jargon the "grunt"), who must carry, literally and metaphorically, the weight of his duty:

> They carried the land itself—Vietnam, the place, the soil—a powdery orange-red dust that covered their boots and fatigues and faces. They carried the sky. The whole atmosphere, they carried it, the humidity, the monsoons, the stink of fungus and decay, all of it, they carried gravity. They moved like mules. By daylight they took sniper fire, at night they were mortared, but it was not battle, it was just the endless march, village to village, without purpose, nothing won or lost. They marched for the sake of the march. They plodded along slowly, dumbly, leaning forward against the heat, unthinking, all blood and bone, simple grunts, soldiering with their legs, toiling up the hills and down into the paddies and across the rivers and up again and down, just humping, one step and then the next and then another, but no volition, no will, because it was automatic, it was anatomy, and the war was entirely a matter of posture and carriage, the hump was everything, a kind of inertia, a kind of emptiness, a dullness of desire and intellect and conscience and hope and human sensibility. Their principles were in their feet. Their calculations were biological. They had no sense of strategy or mission. They searched the villages without knowing what to look for, not caring, kicking over jars of rice, frisking children and old men, blowing tunnels, sometimes setting fires and sometimes not, then forming up and moving on to the next village, then other villages,

where it would always be the same. They carried their own lives. The pressures were enormous.

The NARRATOR suggests the mind-numbing monotony of the march—the "hump" in military parlance—in the LOOSE COMPOUND SENTENCE that describes the men "plod[ing] along slowly, dumbly," a syntax that reflects their step-by-step robotic pace and their "dullness" to all human feeling. In contrast, he uses short, SIMPLE SENTENCES to give stark expression to their lack of purpose and understanding: "Their principles were in their feet." Once arrived at an arbitrary village, they commit random violence—described in another long LOOSE SENTENCE—and then "mov[e] on to the next village," dangerous and themselves endangered. Lest we think that the automatons are truly without sense of their situation, the last curt sentence reminds us of the terrible stress they are under.

A style in which too many of the sentences fall into the same syntactical pattern can sound monotonous. At times, however, an author will intentionally repeat a syntactical pattern to create a particular effect, as Tim O'Brien does in the passage above. Another master of that technique is Ernest Hemingway, who was renowned for his use of SIMPLE and COMPOUND SENTENCES to create a TONE of understated tension and stoicism. The following description from his novel *The Sun Also Rises* occurs just after the NARRATOR, Jake Barnes, has had a fistfight with a rival in which he was knocked unconscious:

> Walking across the square to the hotel everything looked new and changed. I had never seen the trees before. I had never seen the flagpoles before, nor the front of the theatre. It was all different. I felt as I felt once coming home from an out-of-town football game. I was carrying a suitcase with my football things in it, and I walked up the street from the station in the town I had lived in all my life and it was all new. They were raking the lawns and burning leaves in the road, and I stopped for a long time and watched. It was all strange. Then I went on, and my feet seemed to be a long way off, and everything seemed to come from a long way off, and I could hear my feet a great distance away. I had been kicked in the head early in the game. It was like that crossing the square. It was like that going up the stairs in the hotel. Going up the stairs took a long time, and I had the feeling that I was carrying my suitcase.

The short, mostly SIMPLE SENTENCES or COMPOUND SENTENCES linked by neutral "and's," the repetition of words and phrases (for exam-

▼

ple, "I had never," "I felt," and "It was like that") recreate Jake's
dazed state of consciousness. Both light-headed and weighed down
by the imaginary suitcase, he seems convincingly the victim of a
concussion, an effect wrought by Hemingway's masterful use of
syntax.

Samuel Johnson, in contrast, often wrote in an ornate style that
made ample use of COMPLEX SENTENCES, PARALLELISM, INVERSION,
ANTITHESIS, and the PERIODIC SENTENCE that built to a resounding climax. Here, for example, is the opening of his philosophical fable *The
History of Rasselas, Prince of Abyssinia* (1759). Johnson wrote it in
the style of an Oriental tale, a genre that was popularized during the
eighteenth century by the first translation into English of *The Arabian Nights*.

> Ye who listen with credulity to the whispers of fancy, and
> pursue with eagerness the phantoms of hope; who expect that age
> will perform the promises of youth, and that the deficiencies of
> the present day will be supplied by the morrow—attend to the
> history of Rasselas, prince of Abyssinia.
>
> Rasselas was the fourth son of the mighty emperor in whose
> dominions the Father of Waters[1] begins his course; whose bounty
> pours down the streams of plenty, and scatters over half the world
> the harvests of Egypt.
>
> According to the custom which has descended from age to
> age among the monarchs of the torrid zone, Rasselas was confined
> in a private place, with the other sons and daughters of Abyssin-
> ian royalty, till the order of succession should call him to the
> throne.

The PERIODIC SENTENCE that opens the work uses a series of PARALLEL
CLAUSES to create a picture of an eager but naïve hypothetical reader,
susceptible to the influences of "fancy" (fantasy) and the delusions
of "hope," and confident that the future will bring the fulfillment of
his or her potential and the resolution of any "deficiencies" in his or
her situation. It builds up to a warning, urging such naïve individu-
als to "attend" to what promises to be a cautionary tale about a
young Oriental potentate. The implication is that if such a royal per-
sonage can fall, the ordinary reader should be doubly wary. The
next sentence recounts Rasselas's heritage: he is the son of a "mighty
emperor." The impression of the monarch's high status is enhanced
by the PERSONIFICATION of the powerful river that runs through his
"dominions" and by the HYPERBOLIC description of his country's har-

---

1. The Nile.

vests as distributed "over half the world." The INVERSION of the prepositional phrase and the SUBJECT—the normal sentence order would be "scatters the harvests of Egypt over half the world"—puts special emphasis on the "bounty" of the Abyssian kingdom. The third sentence, which like the first is PERIODIC and COMPLEX, concludes with the suspenseful description of the young prince, kept in isolated splendor until fate "should call him to the throne." Johnson's elaborate SYNTAX and FORMAL, LATINATE DICTION give the style an authority and a dignity that are in keeping with the work's lofty purpose. That stately manner, which contrasts totally with Hemingway's spare, understated style, exactly suits Johnson's role as moral philosopher.

As the examples above suggest, a writer's choices about syntax have important effects on the meaning and TONE of a work and are also key to establishing his or her individual style. See also DICTION.

EXERCISES: Syntax

I. For each of the following passages:
- Identify the kind(s) of sentence that it contains: SIMPLE, COMPOUND, or COMPLEX.
- State whether each is LOOSE or PERIODIC, and explain the basis for that choice.
- If the passage contains an intentional SENTENCE FRAGMENT, explain its effect.

1. I am getting angry enough to do something desperate. To jump out of the window would be admirable exercise, but the bars are too strong even to try.
    Besides I wouldn't do it. Of course not.
    —CHARLOTTE PERKINS GILMAN, "The Yellow Wall-paper"

2. It is a truth universally acknowledged, that a single man in possession of a good fortune, must be in want of a wife.
    —JANE AUSTEN, *Pride and Prejudice*

3. After a night behind the scenes, Paul found the schoolroom more than ever repulsive; the bare floors and naked walls; the prosy men who never wore frock coats, or violets in their buttonholes; the women with their dull gowns, shrill voices, and pitiful seriousness about prepositions that govern the dative.
    —WILLA CATHER, "Paul's Case"

4. Knowing that Mrs. Mallard was afflicted with a heart trouble, great care was taken to break to her as gently as possible the news of her husband's death.   –KATE CHOPIN, "The Story of an Hour"

5. Wednesdays after school, at four; Saturday mornings at ten. Mother drives me to Dr. Coronet. Ferns in the office, plastic or real, they look the same. Dr. Coronet is a queenly, an elegant nicotine-stained lady who would have studied with Freud had circumstances not prevented it. . . . Highly recommended by Father! Forty dollars an hour, Father's forty dollars! Progress! Looking up! Looking better!
    –JOYCE CAROL OATES, "How I Contemplated the World from the Detroit House of Correction and Began My Life Over Again"

II. For each of the following passages, specify the means of linkage that it exemplifies—COORDINATION, SUBORDINATION, PARALLELISM, or INVERSION— and explain the basis for that choice. Note that some examples may use more than one kind of linkage.

1. While of other law-copyists I might write the complete life, of Bartleby nothing of the sort can be done.
    –HERMAN MELVILLE, "Bartleby the Scrivener"

2. It is to be observed, that these ambassadors spoke to me by an interpreter; the languages of both empires differing as much from each other as any two in Europe, and each nation priding itself upon the antiquity, beauty, and energy of their own tongues, with an avowed contempt for that of their neighbor; yet our Emperor, standing upon the advantage he had got by the seizure of their fleet, obliged them to deliver their credentials, and make their speech, in the Lilliputian tongue.
    –JONATHAN SWIFT, *Gulliver's Travels*

3. *After speculating that a woman who had tried to become a playwright in Shakespeare's day would have been under enormous stress, Virginia Woolf continues:*

    And undoubtedly, I thought, looking at the shelf where there are no plays by women, her work would have gone unsigned. That refuge she would have sought certainly.
    –VIRGINIA WOOLF, *A Room of One's Own*

4. But the thing did not then leave the vicinity of the boat. Ahead or astern, on one side or the other, at intervals long or short, fled the long sparkling streak, and there was to be heard the *whirroo* of the dark fin.   —STEPHEN CRANE, "The Open Boat"

5. Thus relieved of a grievous load, I from that hour set to work afresh, resolved to pioneer my way through every difficulty: I toiled hard, and my success was proportionate to my efforts; my memory, not naturally tenacious, improved with practice: exercise sharpened my wits; in a few weeks I was promoted to a higher class; in less than two months I was allowed to commence French and drawing.
                                —CHARLOTTE BRONTË, *Jane Eyre*

III. Analysis of syntax. For each of the following passages:
   • Describe the kinds of sentences that it contains, and list the means that are used to link the clauses.
   • Describe the effects of those aspects of the syntax on the meaning and the TONE of the passage.

1. *The following passage describes the aftermath of a quarrel between Mona, a rebellious Chinese American girl, and her mother over Mona's decision to buy a down jacket. The next morning Mona discovers that her mother, who thinks that the purchase is another sign of her daughter's excessive Americanization, has put the jacket out with the garbage.*

   Mona must look really forlorn, because Helen softens. "Oh, not that big a deal, you don't have to cry," she says, and taking the jacket from her daughter, she drapes it on top of the space heater to warm. "There." She says this in a leave-it-to-mommy voice she seems to have learned from TV, even though the Changs don't have a TV. (*The idiot box*, Ralph calls it.)
   "Ma," Mona says, "I don't think that's such a good idea."
   But Helen is the mother, and Mona is the daughter, which means that Helen knows what is a good idea and what isn't. And so it is that they take the jacket off the heater really at the first whiff of trouble, before too large a hole has been burnt. Still, down goes exploding through the kitchen. Who could believe a couple of jacket baffles could produce such a veritable snowstorm? But it just goes to show what a good value Mona got on her jacket, that so much went into it. There are goose feathers flying everywhere. Mona and Helen have to wave their hands in front of their faces to keep from breathing them; Helen very sensibly closes the door to the dining room while Mona opens the regular window, and the

storm window too. Cold air rushes in as she tries to shoo the feathers out. "A broom!" Helen cries, and so they try that. Sweeping at the air with long swings, short swings—they could be the sorcerer's apprentice, it's that effective.

Still they keep on, so that this is what they're doing when Mickey the milkman appears on the other side of the sill.

"Having a problem?" Mickey is a trim man with an ever-moist mustache they have ascribed to nasal drip; Mona stops shooing feathers in his face, for fear one might stick.

"Oh, no," Helen says, nonchalant. "Just helping my daughter with her homework."

"It's a science project," Mona says. "There's a contest at school."

—GISH JEN, *Mona in the Promised Land*

2. *The following description of the* PROTAGONIST *opens Jane Austen's novel* Emma:

Emma Woodhouse, handsome, clever, and rich, with a comfortable home and happy disposition, seemed to unite some of the best blessings of existence; and had lived nearly twenty-one years in the world with very little to distress or vex her.

She was the youngest of two daughters of a most affectionate, indulgent father, and had, in consequence of her sister's marriage, been mistress of his house from a very early period. Her mother had died too long ago for her to have more than an indistinct remembrance of her caresses, and her place had been supplied by an excellent woman as governess, who had fallen little short of a mother in affection.

Sixteen years had Miss Taylor been in Mr. Woodhouse's family, less as a governess than a friend, very fond of both daughters, but particularly of Emma. Between *them* it was more the intimacy of sisters. Even before Miss Taylor had ceased to hold the nominal office of governess, the mildness of her temper had hardly allowed her to impose any restraint; and the shadow of authority being now long passed away, they had been living together as friend and friend very mutually attached, and Emma doing just what she liked; highly esteeming Miss Taylor's judgment, but directed chiefly by her own.

The real evils indeed of Emma's situation were the power of having rather too much her own way, and a disposition to think a little too well of herself; these were the disadvantages which threatened to alloy her many enjoyments. The danger, however, was at present so unperceived, that they did not by any means rank as misfortunes with her.

Prosody

Prosody is a collective term that describes the technical aspects of verse relating to rhythm, stress, and meter.

METER

Meter (from the Greek word for "measure") is the recurring pattern of sounds that give poems written in VERSE their distinctive rhythms. (Many POEMS, especially those written since the nineteenth century, do not use regular meter or consistent RHYME. The term for that open form is FREE VERSE.) The recurrence of rhythms is basic to human life: tied to our breathing, our heartbeats, and such natural cycles as the ebb and flow of the tides and the processes of birth and death. In fact, the random rhythms of ordinary speech may sometimes fall into the regularity of recurrent units that are called "meter." The distinguishing feature of poetic meter, however, is that such units recur in sustained and regular patterns. Meter, like other aspects of sound in POETRY, is a crucial aspect of meaning. The system for indicating metrical patterns and analyzing their effects, called SCANSION, will be described at the end of this section.

There are four basic systems for describing meter in POETRY, which depend on what serves as the distinguishing feature of the pattern of sound and on the particular pattern that recurs in a given line. In **quantitative meter**, used most prominently in Greek and Latin poetry, the distinctive feature is the relative length of the utterance (long or short) of the syllables that constitute a poetic line. **Syllabic meter** depends on the number of syllables in a line, without regard to their **stress**—that is, the special emphasis given in pronouncing some syllables. It is used in poetry written in such relatively evenly stressed languages as French, Spanish, and Japanese. In **accentual meter**, used primarily in Germanic languages, including Old English, the key feature is the number of stressed syllables in each line, without regard to the unstressed syllables.[1]

Far and away the most common metrical system in English verse, from the fourteenth century on, is **accentual-syllabic meter**.

---

1. For a more extensive description of these metrical systems, see the essay on "Versification" by Jon Stallworthy in *The Norton Anthology of Poetry*, Fifth Edition, pp. 2029–30, 2035–36.

As the name indicates, it is based both on the number of syllables in a line and on the pattern of stresses in each metrical unit, or **foot**.

Several factors determine where the stresses fall in a line of verse. The first is the normal pattern of stresses in the pronunciation of individual words and phrases, for example: óthĕr, prŏvíde, dángĕrŏus, ŏn thĕ tóp, ĭndĭvídŭăl. Note that the unstressed syllable is indicated by a crescent, the stressed by an acute accent. Another factor is the relative importance of the words in the line. For example, in the sentence "Look at me," either the first or the last word could be stressed, depending on how the speaker wanted to direct the listener's attention: "Lóok at me" or "Look at mé." Finally, the words' grammatical functions influence their stress. For example, nouns, verbs, and adjectives, the major parts of speech, tend to be accented more strongly to show their importance, while articles and prepositions are usually stressed lightly. There are exceptions to those general guidelines, however, as when a preposition or article is emphasized because it is important to the meaning or TONE: "Gĕt óut!"; Thĕ Mr̆. Smĭth." We naturally "hear" such stresses as we read and listen, especially when they recur, as they do in lines of poetry. Readers must be taught, however, to go beyond such instinctive perceptions by learning the terms for various metrical units and the system for recording them. That process is analogous to learning to read music. For example, the following lines of William Blake's "Song" have clear and regular metrical feet:

Hŏw swéet / I rŏam'd / frŏm fiéld / tŏ fiéld
Ănd tást / ĕd áll / thĕ súm / mĕr's príde.

Note that a foot may contain more than a single word, and that a word may be divided between different feet, as with "tasted" and "summer" above. In marking a line of verse, a slash is used to separate the individual feet.

METRICAL FEET

Iambic (eye-AM-bick); the noun is **iamb** (EYE-amb), an unstressed followed by a stressed syllable:

Hĕ thoúght / hĕ képt / thĕ ú / nĭvérse / ălóne.
                                    —ROBERT FROST, "The Most of It"

The example from Blake's "Song" is also iambic. The iamb comes naturally to speakers of English—it has been said to imitate the soft/loud sound of a heartbeat—and is the most frequently used meter in poetry written in English.

▼

Anapestic (an-uh-PES-tick; the noun is **anapest**: AN-uh-pest), two unstressed syllables followed by a stressed one; for example:

> Aňd thĕ eýes / ŏf thĕ sléep / ĕrs wăxed déad / lÿ ănd chíll,
> Aňd thĕir heárts / bŭt oňce heáved, / aňd fŏré / vĕr grĕw stíll!
> –GEORGE GORDON, LORD BYRON, "The Destruction of Sennacherib"

Trochaic (troh-KAY-ick; the noun is **trochee**: TROH-key), a stressed syllable followed by an unstressed syllable:

> Dóu blĕ, / dóublĕ, / tóil aňd / tróublĕ,
> Fíře / búrn aňd / caúldrŏn / búbblĕ.
> –WILLIAM SHAKESPEARE, *Macbeth*

Dactylic (dak-TILL-ic, or the **dactyl**: DAK-till), a stressed syllable followed by two that are unstressed:

> Cánnŏn ĭn / frónt ŏf thĕm
>   Vóllĕyed aňd / thúndĕred.
> –ALFRED, LORD TENNYSON, "The Charge of the Light Brigade"

Here, the first line and the first foot of the second line are regular dactyls; the last foot lacks the final unstressed syllable. See SUBSTITUTION.

▶ # Number of Feet in a Line

In describing a poem's meter, one needs to name the prevailing metrical foot and to specify the number of feet in each line. This number is indicated by terms derived from the Greek. The most common are the following:

Monometer (mon-OM-eh-ter), one foot. Such a line usually occurs only as a variant in poems comprised largely of longer lines. In the following example, only the third and fourth lines are **monometric**:

> Though she / were true / when you / met her,
> And last / till you / write your / letter,
>   Yet she
>   Will be
> False, ere / I come, / to two, / or three.
> –JOHN DONNE, "Song"

Dimeter (DIM-eh-ter), two feet:

> Wild nights— / Wild nights!
> Were I / with thee
> Wild nights / should be
> Our lux / ury!
> –EMILY DICKINSON, "Wild nights"

Trimeter (TRIM-eh-ter), three feet:

> We romped / until / the pans
> Slid from / the kit / chen shelf;
> My mo / ther's coun / tenance
> Could not / unfrown / itself.
>
> —THEODORE ROETHKE, "My Papa's Waltz"

Tetrameter (te-TRAM-eh-ter), four feet:

> She walks / in beau / ty, like / the night
>   Of cloud / less climes / and star / ry skies.
>
> —GEORGE GORDON, Lord Byron, "She Walks in Beauty"

Pentameter (pen-TAM-eh-ter), five feet:

> When I / have fears / that I / may cease / to be
>   Before / my pen / has gleaned / my teem / ing brain.
>
> —JOHN KEATS, "When I Have Fears"

Hexameter (hex-AM-eh-ter), six feet:

> I cried / for mad / der mu / sic and / for strong / er wine,
> But when / the feast / is fin / ished and / the lamps / expire,
> Then falls / thy sha / dow, Cy / nara! / The night / is thine.
>
> —ERNEST DOWSON, "Cynara"

Heptameter (hep-TAM-eh-ter), seven feet:

> 'Twas on / a ho / ly Thurs / day, their / inno / cent fa / ces clean.
> The chil / dren walk / ing two / & two, / in red / & blue / &
>   green.   —WILLIAM BLAKE, "Holy Thursday (I)"

Naming the Meter ◀

The meter is designated by combining the adjectival form of the
term for the foot with the term that specifies the number of feet in a
line. For example, a line comprised of five iambs would be labeled
iambic pentameter:

> When you / are old / and grey / and full / of sleep,
> And nod / ding by / the fire, / take down / this book.
>
> —WILLIAM BUTLER YEATS, "When You Are Old"

Iambic pentameter is the meter closest to the rhythm of ordinary
English speech. To take a prose example: "I think / that you / can
hear / this rhy / thm now." For that reason, it is the most common
meter in English poetry of every age. See also BLANK VERSE.

To cite a few more examples of names for meter, the following lines, made up of three feet of trochees, are in **trochaic trimeter**:

Higher / still and / higher
    From the / earth thou / springest
Like a / cloud of / fire
    The deep / blue thou / wingest
                          —PERCY BYSSHE SHELLEY, "To a Skylark"

This line, comprised of four dactyls, is in **dactylic tetrameter**:

Woman much / missed, how you / call to me, / call to me
                          —THOMAS HARDY, "The Voice"

An important consideration is that few poems fall into a regular, unvarying meter. In fact, rigidly regular meter tends to be monotonous and simplistic, more doggerel than poetry. It is often the variations in a poem's basic meter that give a line special resonance or power.

► ## Common Substitutions

Any variant foot within a line that consists predominantly of another metrical pattern is called a **substitution**. The most common substitutions are the following:

A **spondaic** (spahn-DAY-ick) **foot**, or **spondee** (SPAHN-dee), two stressed syllables in a row:

Roúgh wińds / dó sháke / the dar / ling buds / of May,
And sum / mer's lease / hath all / tóo shórt / a date.
                          —WILLIAM SHAKESPEARE, Sonnet 18

Here, the first foot of the iambic pentameter first line and the fourth foot of the next are spondees. The second foot in the first line ("do shake") might also be considered a spondee, as it is here. Some readers, though, might hear it as a regular IAMB, in keeping with the rest of the line: "dŏ sháke." There is room for such variation in marking individual feet; expert readers would not disagree, however, on the predominant METER or on the strong spondees cited.

A TROCHEE at the start of an IAMBIC line:

Géttĭng / and spend / ing, we / lay waste / our powers;
Líttlĕ / we see / in Na / ture that / is ours.
                          —WILLIAM WORDSWORTH, "The World Is Too Much with Us"

An ANAPESTIC foot within an IAMBIC line: in the following example, both the fourth foot of the first line and the third foot of the second are anapests.

> There mid / night's all / a glim / mĕr, ănd nóon / a pur / ple glow,
> And eve / ning's full / ŏf thĕ lín / net's wings.
>
> —WILLIAM BUTLER YEATS, "The Lake Isle of Innisfree"

A missing unstressed syllable at the end of a TROCHAIC or DACTYLIC line; such a line is called **catalectic** (cat-uh-LEK-tick; the noun is **catalexis**: cat-uh-LEX-iss). Both of these TROCHAIC lines are catalectic:

> Gó ănd / cátch ă / fállĭng / stár,
> Gét wĭth / chíld ă / mándrăke / róot
>
> —JOHN DONNE, "Song"

The first and third of the following DACTYLIC lines are catalectic·

> Ríght thrŏugh thĕ / líne thĕy brŏke;
> Cóssack ănd / Rússĭan
> Reéled frŏm thĕ / sábĕr-stróke
> Sháttĕred ănd / súndĕred.
>
> —ALFRED, LORD TENNYSON, "The Charge of the Light Brigade"

Lines that end with a strong stress, such as those in the catalectic examples above or in regular lines, are said to have a **masculine ending**. The following is a regular IAMBIC PENTAMETER line with a masculine ending:

> Ĭ wáke / tŏ sléep / ănd táke / my̆ wák / ĭng slów.
>
> —THEODORE ROETHKE, "The Waking"

Lines that end in an unstressed syllable, as do regular TROCHAIC and DACTYLIC lines, are said to have a **feminine ending**. Another common substitution is an added unstressed syllable at the end of an IAMBIC line:

> Tŏ bé / ŏr nót / tŏ bé, / thát ĭs / thĕ qués / tiŏn.
>
> —WILLIAM SHAKESPEARE, Hamlet

> Thĕ whís / kĕy ón / yŏur bréath
> Cŏuld máke / ă smáll / bŏy díz /zy̆.
>
> —THEODORE ROETHKE, "My Papa's Waltz"

Often, as in these cases, the final unstressed syllable can be a subtle sign that the speaker is off balance or uncertain.

▶ Pauses Within and Between Lines of Verse

The other key aspect of noting poetic rhythms is discerning the pauses that occur, both between and within lines of verse:

End-stopped lines contain a complete sentence or independent clause and so have a distinct pause at the end, usually indicated by a mark of punctuation:

> The sea is calm tonight.
>
> —MATTHEW ARNOLD, "Dover Beach"

> Little Lamb, who made thee?
> Dost thou know who made thee?
>
> —WILLIAM BLAKE, "The Lamb"

End-stopped lines call attention to the complete thought expressed in the single line.

Enjambed lines (en-JAMMED, from the French word for "stride over" or "straddle": the noun is **enjambment**), also called **run-on lines**, are those in which the sentence or clause continues for two or more lines of verse; no punctuation appears at the end of the enjambed lines:

> She is as in a field a silken tent
> At midday when a sunny summer breeze
> Has dried the dew and all its ropes relent,
>
> —ROBERT FROST, "The Silken Tent"

The first two lines are enjambed, the third end-stopped. Here the effect of the enjambment is to give a more leisurely pace to the lines, so that the luxurious billowing of the "silken tent," and therefore the voluptuousness of the woman being compared to it, is suggested by the clause stretching out over three lines. Another effect can be to call attention to the words that appear at the end and the beginning of the enjambed lines:

> The glamour
> Of childish days is upon me, my manhood is cast
> Down in the flood of remembrance, I weep like a child for the
>   past.
>
> —D. H. LAWRENCE, "Piano"

Here, the enjambment gives special emphasis to "cast" and "down," so that the narrator's giving way to helpless weeping is reflected in the structure of the lines.

A **caesura** (say-ZYOOR-a, from the Latin word for "a cutting off") is a pause in the midst of a verse line; the pause is indicated by a mark of punctuation, such as a comma, a question mark, a period, or a dash. The effect of a caesura is to create a shift in the rhythmic pattern of a line, which parallels a shift in its focus. In scanning a poem, **caesuras** (or **caesurae**, the Latin plural) are marked with a double slash:

> St. Agnes' Eve—// Ah, // bitter chill it was!
> The owl, // for all his feathers, // was a-cold.
>
> —JOHN KEATS, "The Eve of St. Agnes"

Scansion

The process of analyzing and marking the type and the number of feet in each line of verse is called **scansion**. A reader **scans** several lines to determine the basic metrical foot that the poet is using and then counts the number of feet that a typical line or, in some poems, a varying pattern of lines contain. (For example, in **ballad meter**, IAMBIC TETRAMETER alternates with IAMBIC TRIMETER.) It is important to note that scansion is not an exact art. Ambiguities exist about the degrees of stress and the predominant meter of some lines, and expert readers may vary in the ways that they apportion stresses in a line. What they would agree on is the predominant meter of a poem.

Scanning a poem should not be confused with performing it. A scanned poem is roughly analogous to a musical score: it marks the stresses and pauses and provides a guide to the rhythms, but it takes a performance with the instrument of the human voice to bring out the variations in intonations, lengths of syllables, and emphases that give the work full meaning. The value of scansion is not in mechanically showing the understructure that it exposes but in the access that it can provide to the poem's TONE. Noting the choices that poets make in creating the rhythm and pace of a poem can be an important guide to understanding its sense.

Here is the scansion of John Keats's sonnet, "Bright Star," with the stressed and unstressed syllables and the caesuras marked:

Bright Star

Bríght stár, // woúld Í / wĕre stéad / fást ăs / thóu árt—
   Nót ĭn / lóne splén / dŏr húng / ăloft / thĕ níght
Aňd wátch / ĭng, // wĭth / ĕtér / năl líds / ăpárt,
   Líke ná / tŭre's pá / tiĕnt, // sléep / lĕss Ér / ĕmíte,[2]
Thĕ móv / ĭng wá / tĕrs at / thĕir príest / lĭke tásk
   Ŏf púre / ăblú / tĭon[3] róund / eărth's hú / măn shóres,
Ŏr gáz / ĭng ón / thĕ néw / sŏft fál / lĕn másk
   Ŏf snów / ŭpón / thĕ móun / tăins ănd / thĕ móors—
Nó—// yét / stíll stéad / fást, // stíll / ŭn chánge / ăblé,
   Píllŏwed / ŭpón / my fáir / lóve's rípe / nĭng bréast,
Tŏ féel / fŏr é / ĕr ĭts / sŏft fáll / ănd swéll,
   Ăwáke / fŏr é / vĕr ĭn / ă swéet / unrést,
Stíll, // stíll / tŏ héar / hĕr tén / dĕr ták / ĕn bréath,
Ănd só / líve é / vĕr—// ŏr / ĕlse swóon / tŏ déath.

As noted above, even expert readers vary in scanning complex meters, and some might scan some of these lines a bit differently, to mark various ways of emphasizing certain words in performance. All would agree, though, that the dominant meter is IAMBIC PENTAMETER. The SUBSTITUTIONS of other poetic feet, and the various pauses within and between lines are crucial to the meaning. The SPONDEES suggest the narrator's fervor: he longs to be as "steadfast" as the "bright star" that he APOSTROPHIZES. Yet he distinguishes between the star's isolation—its "lone splendor"—and his own desire to be joined with his beloved: "pillowed upon my fair love's ripening breast." Again, the spondee at "fair love" suggests the strength of his longing. The enjambments are reserved for lines that describe the star, "hung aloft the night / And watching" and "gazing on the new soft fallen mask / Of snow upon the mountains and the moors," the flowing rhythms suggesting its chaste self-possession and aloofness. The caesura at "No" marks the SONNET'S turn from OCTAVE to SESTET and the speaker's rejection of the star as a complete model. The lover, in contrast, imagines his bliss in a series of end-stopped lines that imply his ecstasy. The spondee at "still, still" emphasizes his fervent will to sustain that communion "for ever." The meditation concludes with the strong caesura that contrasts the hyperbolic options that he envisions: to "live ever" in this suspended moment of sensual anticipation, or to "swoon to death," carried out of his bodily senses at the height of sensual pleasure.

---

2. Hermit.
3. Cleansing.

Poets tend to choose a given meter and its variations not for mechanical reasons but, rather like verbal musicians, they use this aspect of sound to express feelings, create TONE, and enhance certain meanings. The effects of meter are often subtle. Highly regular meter can signal a positive TONE, a narrator who feels in tune with the world and content, as in Christina Rossetti's "Up-Hill." In contrast, a highly irregular meter can imply distress or uncertainty, as in Byron's "When We Two Parted." This distinction is not absolute, however. Regular meter can be used to create a strident tone, so that the narrator's voice is outraged or condemnatory, as in William Blake's "London." Regular meter can also be used for ironic contrast. For example, a poem's surface may be rhythmic and melodic but its underlying meaning may be pessimistic or eerie, as in Emily Dickinson's "Because I could not stop for Death."

In some poems, the tone undergoes an important shift, especially near the end, as in the eventual tranquility and acceptance of George Herbert's rebellious speaker in "The Collar," or the final desperation of Blake's initially carefree lover in "How Sweet I Roam'd from Field to Field." SUBSTITUTIONS tend to occur most often at the start of poems, and in the first lines of a stanza. The surest way to determine the predominant meter is to scan some lines in the middle of the poem. Once both the prevalent pattern and the variations in it have been noted, the reader can be more alert to the effects of such choices on the poem's TONE and meaning.

EXERCISES: Meter

I. Scan the meter of the following passages of poetry.

- Mark the STRESSED and UNSTRESSED SYLLABLES.
- Separate the FEET with slashes.
- Name the METER. *Note:* Some examples may contain more than one kind of METER.

1. A Chapel was built in the midst,
   Where I used to play on the green.
   —WILLIAM BLAKE, "The Garden of Love"

2. The woods decay, the woods decay and fall,
   The vapors weep their burthen to the ground,
   Man comes and tills the field and lies beneath,
   And after many a summer dies the swan.
   —ALFRED, LORD TENNYSON, "Tithonus"

3. Jewels in joy designed
        To ravish the sensuous mind
    Lie lightless, all their sparkles bleared and black and blind.
                    —THOMAS HARDY, "The Convergence of the Twain"

4. Earth, receive an honoured guest:
    William Yeats is laid to rest.
    Let the Irish vessel lie
    Emptied of its poetry.
                    —W. H. AUDEN, "In Memory of W. B. Yeats"

5. When a man hath no freedom to fight for at home,
        Let him combat for that of his neighbors;
    Let him think of the glories of Greece and of Rome,
        And get knocked on the head for his labors.
                    —GEORGE GORDON, LORD BYRON, "When a Man Hath no
                                            Freedom to Fight for at Home"

II. Substitutions. For each of the following passages:
*   Scan the lines, marking the STRESSED and UNSTRESSED SYLLABLES and
    separating the FEET with slashes.
*   Name the predominant METER.
*   List any SUBSTITUTIONS that occur. *Note:* Some examples may contain
    more than one.
*   Describe the effects of the SUBSTITUTIONS on the TONE and meaning.

1. Ah! well-a-day! what evil looks
    Had I from old and young!
    Instead of the cross, the Albatross
    About my neck was hung.
                    —SAMUEL TAYLOR COLERIDGE, "The Rime of the Ancient Mariner"

2. The hand that held my wrist
    Was battered on one knuckle;
    At every step you missed
    My right ear scraped a buckle.
                    —THEODORE ROETHKE, "My Papa's Waltz"

3. I will arise and go now, for always night and day
    I hear lake water lapping with low sounds by the shore.
                    —WILLIAM BUTLER YEATS, "The Lake Isle of Innisfree"

4. The dew of the morning
        Sunk chill on my brow—
   It felt like the warning
        Of what I feel now.
                        —GEORGE GORDON, LORD BYRON, "When We Two Parted"

5. Woman much missed, how you call to me, call to me,
   Saying that now you are not as you were
   When you had changed from the one who was all to me,
   But as at first, when our day was fair.
                        —Thomas Hardy, "The Voice"

III. **Pauses.** For each of the following passages:

- Say whether each line is END-STOPPED or ENJAMBED.
- Mark any CAESURAS.
- Explain the effects of those choices on the TONE and meaning.

1. How do I love thee? Let me count the ways.
   I love thee to the depth and breadth and height
   My soul can reach, when feeling out of sight
   For the ends of being and ideal grace.
                        —ELIZABETH BARRETT BROWNING, from *Sonnets from the Portuguese* (43)

2. I wandered lonely as a cloud
   That floats on high o'er vales and hills,
   When all at once I saw a crowd,
   A host, of golden daffodils.
                        —WILLIAM WORDSWORTH, "I Wandered Lonely as a Cloud"

3. What the hammer? what the chain?
   In what furnace was thy brain?
   What the anvil? what dread grasp
   Dare its deadly terrors clasp?
                        —WILLIAM BLAKE, "The Tyger"

4. No longer mourn for me when I am dead
   Than you shall hear the surly sullen bell
   Give warning to the world that I am fled
   From this vile world, with vilest worms to dwell.
                        —WILLIAM SHAKESPEARE, Sonnet 71

---

1. Carelessly cultivated.

5. The flowers do fade, and wanton[1] fields
    To wayward winter reckoning yields;
    A honey tongue, a heart of gall,
    Is fancy's spring, but sorrow's fall.

                    —SIR WALTER RALEGH, "The Nymph's Reply to the Shepherd"

IV. Scan the following poem by Robert Hayden to determine the pre-
     dominant METER, the SUBSTITUTIONS, the ENJAMBED or END-STOPPED LINES, and
     the CAESURAS. Then write a brief essay in which you discuss the specific
     effects of the poet's METRICAL choices.

                        Those Winter Sundays

     Sundays too my father got up early
     and put his clothes on in the blueblack cold,
     then with cracked hands that ached
     from labor in the weekday weather made
     banked fires blaze. No one ever thanked him.   5

     I'd wake and hear the cold splintering, breaking.
     When the rooms were warm, he'd call,
     and slowly I would rise and dress,
     fearing the chronic angers of that house,

     Speaking indifferently to him,   10
     who had driven out the cold
     and polished my good shoes as well.
     What did I know, what did I know
     of love's austere and lonely offices?

RHYME

Rhyme is the repetition in two or more nearby words of the last
stressed vowel and all the syllables that follow it. Although rhyme
does not have to be an element of poetry, as the many works written
in BLANK VERSE and FREE VERSE attest, poetry is the LITERARY FORM that
uses rhyme systematically and pervasively. Something about rhyme
is pleasing to the human ear, as is clear from the delight with which
small children attend to nursery rhymes. It recalls poetry's earliest
origins in song and, like METER, can be an important element in a
work's verbal music. This is not to suggest, however, that rhyme
need be merely decorative. It can serve several important functions.
Perhaps most important, rhyme may be used to create unity, by setting up and confirming a pattern in which sound and meaning con-
cur. It can link or contrast ideas and put STRESS on particular words.

Rhyme may also be used to lighten the TONE, especially if the rhymes are exaggerated or ingenious, as in this passage from Lord Byron's mock epic, *Don Juan*:

> Brave men were living before Agamemnon
>   And since, exceeding valorous and sage,
> A good deal like him too, though quite the same none;
>   But then they shone not on the poet's page,
> And so have been forgotten:—I condemn none,
>   But can't find any in the present age
> Fit for my poem (that is, my new one);
> So, as I said, I'll take my friend Don Juan.

Here such rhymes as "Agamemnon / same none / and Juan" (pronounced JOO-uhn) both link and contrast the Greek military hero with the notorious rake, creating a humorously ironic deflation.

Rhyme may also signal a surprising departure if it does not occur in the expected place. Shakespeare includes rhymed passages in the BLANK VERSE form of his plays for variety and emphasis, as do modern poets writing in FREE VERSE.

End Rhyme ◄

Most rhymes occur at the end of the poetic line, the term for which is **end rhyme**. The rhyme may consist of only one syllable, as in "fónd" and "pónd," or it may be multisyllabic: "hásty / tásty." If two of the syllables rhyme, as in the second example, the rhyme is called **double**; if three syllables do, as in "atténtion / diménsion," the rhyme is called **triple**. Rhymes that end on a STRESSED syllable, such as "fond / pond" and "on the spot / in the pot," are called **masculine**; rhymes that end on an UNSTRESSED syllable, as do "hasty / tasty" and "attention / dimension," are called **feminine**. See also POETIC FORMS.

Internal Rhyme ◄

Rhymes may also occur within a line of poetry rather than at the end, as in this example from William Blake's "The Garden of Love":

> And binding with *briars* my joys & *desires*.

In this case, the device is called **internal rhyme**. Edgar Allan Poe used that technique extensively in "The Raven":

Ah, distinctly I *remember* it was in the bleak *December*,
And each separate dying *ember* wrought its ghost upon the floor.
Eagerly I wished the *morrow*;—vainly I had sought to *borrow*
From my books surcease of *sorrow*—sorrow for the lost
    Lenore—
For the rare and radiant maiden whom the angels name
    Lenore—
                    Nameless here for evermore.

Here, the combination of internal rhymes and repetitive END RHYMES helps create the poem's incantatory tone and claustrophobic atmosphere.

Rhyme Scheme

In SCANNING a poem, rhymes are marked with letters of the alphabet, with the first rhyme designated as *a*, the second as *b*, etc. The pattern of recurrences is called a **rhyme scheme**. For example, the following stanza from William Wordsworth's "Three Years She Grew" has a rhyme scheme of *aabccb*. No letters are used to mark INTERNAL RHYME.

Three years she grew in sun and shower	*a*
Then Nature said, "A lovelier flower	*a*
On earth was never sown;	*b*
This Child I to myself will take;	*c*
She shall be mine, and I will make	*c*
A Lady of my own."	*b*

Unlike the Wordsworth example, some stanzaic patterns are identified by particular rhyme schemes, for example, the SONNET, the COUPLET, and BALLAD METER.

In "Dover Beach," Matthew Arnold uses a highly irregular RHYME SCHEME to moving effect. To take a sample STANZA:

The Sea of Faith	*a*
Was once, too, at the full, and round earth's shore	*b*
Lay like the folds of a bright girdle furled.	*c*
But now I only hear	*d*
Its melancholy, long withdrawing roar,	*b*
Retreating, to the breath	*a*
Of the night-wind, down the vast edges drear	*d*
And naked shingles[1] of the world.	*c*

---

1. Beaches covered with small stones.

The lack of recurrent pattern in either the rhyme or the METER reflects the breakdown of order that the narrator laments and suggests the signs of the incipient chaos.

Perfect and Imperfect Rhyme ◀

When the rhyming sounds match exactly, as in the Wordsworth poem above, the rhyme is called **perfect**. An alternative form is **eye rhyme**, in which words look on the page like perfect rhymes but over time have come to be pronounced differently: "cover / over," "bough / tough."

Rhymes may also be partial rather than perfect, varying the corresponding vowel sounds and/or the consonant sounds, as in the following pairs from Emily Dickinson's "A Bird Came Down the Walk": "abroad / head," "Crumb / Home," and "seam / swim." That device is called by a variety of terms: **imperfect rhyme, half-rhyme, off-rhyme,** and **slant rhyme**. Since the mid nineteenth century, half rhyme has been used by several poets as an alternative to perfect rhyme. Because imperfect rhyme does not fulfill the expectation of exactly chiming syllables that perfect rhyme would lead us to anticipate, it can create a disconcerting effect. Wilfred Owen's "Insensibility," a diatribe against those who are indifferent to the suffering caused by war, makes ingenious use of half rhyme, in such paired words as "killed / cold," "fooling / filling," and "red / rid." The final stanza contains a stinging denouncement:

> But cursed are dullards whom no cannon stuns,
> That they should be as stones.
> Wretched are they, and mean
> With paucity that never was simplicity.
> By choice they made themselves immune
> To pity and whatever moans in man.

The half rhyme of "stuns / stones" underlines the narrator's scorn of such "dullards," and the linking of "mean / immune / moan / man" implies the contrast between pettiness and indifference and the empathy for others' pain that is the essence of humane feeling. In SCANSION, eye rhymes and half rhymes are marked in the same way as perfect rhymes, with sequential letters of the alphabet.

Although half rhyme has been used as a minor device in English poetry from the earliest times, particularly in folk ballads, since the mid nineteenth century, it has been a prominent feature in the work

of several poets. In addition to Dickinson and Owen, other innovative users of half rhyme have included William Butler Yeats, W. H.
Auden, Adrienne Rich, and Seamus Heaney. Often, poets vary perfect with imperfect rhyme, as in the following poem, "Adam's
Curse,"[1] by William Butler Yeats. The NARRATOR, who is closely identified with the young Yeats, is talking with two women. At first,
their topic is the difficult and often unsung effort of writing poetry.
The narrator then changes the subject to an issue that preoccupied
Yeats, his passionate but unrequited love for one of the women present, Maud Gonne, the "you" in the final stanza. These are the closing stanzas of the poem:

> I said, "It's certain there is no fine thing
> Since Adam's fall but needs much labouring.
> There have been lovers who thought love should be
> so much compounded of high courtesy
> That they would sigh and quote with learned looks
> Precedents out of beautiful old books;
> Yet now it seems an idle trade enough."
>
> We sat grown quiet at the name of love;
> We saw the last embers of daylight die,
> And in the trembling blue-green of the sky
> A moon, worn as if it had been a shell
> Washed by time's waters as they rose and fell
> About the stars and broke in days and years.
>
> I had a thought for no one's but your ears;
> That you were beautiful, and that I strove
> To love you in the high old way of love;
> That it had all seemed happy, and yet we'd grown
> As weary-hearted as the hollow moon.

The RHYMES in the poem are, for the most part, perfect, fitting
for the passages in which the NARRATOR recalls ideal lovers "out of
beautiful old books." Then abruptly he turns flippant, dismissing the
depiction and the worship of such literary "precedents" as "an idle
trade enough." The shift in TONE is marked by the HALF RHYME of
"enough" and "love." Both romantic love and the writing of poetry

---

1. The title alludes to Genesis 3.17–19, the pronouncement of God's curse on Adam for
having broken his commandment not to eat of the tree of the knowledge of good and
evil in the Garden of Eden. Because Adam has given in to that temptation, offered him
by his wife, Eve, God banishes him from paradise and sentences him to a life of toil and
suffering.

that glorifies it are dismissed as mere "idle"—worthless—"trade"—
business. At that point the description of the SETTING, incipiently
romantic but disintegrating before the characters' eyes, reflects the
speaker's gradual disillusionment during the long years of futile love:
the "last embers of daylight die," the sky is a "trembling blue-green,"
and the moon is "worn" to a mere "shell" by the washing of "time's
waters." In a burst of renewed passion, he has an impulse to confide
in his beloved: to declare once more her surpassing beauty and his
own devotion and idealism, his long striving to "love [her] in the
old high way of love." Those factors had once "seemed" to him to
guarantee a "happy" outcome. The poem's conclusion, however,
expresses his deflating return to reality, marked by the half rhyme of
"grown" and "moon." That conventionally romantic heavenly body
is PERSONIFIED as having become as "hollow" and "weary-hearted" as
the rejected suitor. Like Adam, he has been cast out of paradise and
condemned to a life of thankless toil.

EXERCISE: Rhyme

For each of the following passages:

- Mark the RHYME SCHEME, both with letters of the alphabet at the ends
  of lines and with the rhyme pattern of the stanza—e.g., *abab.*
- Name the kind(s) of rhyme that the passage uses: PERFECT RHYME,
  HALF RHYME, or EYE RHYME.
- Mark any INTERNAL RHYMES by underlining the rhyming words.
- Specify whether each rhyme is MASCULINE or FEMININE.
- Describe the effects of the rhyme on the TONE and meaning of the
  passage.
  Note: Some passages may contain more than one kind of rhyme; in
  those cases, identify each kind and describe its effects.

1. I wander thro' each charter'd[1] street
   Near where the charter'd Thames does flow,
   And mark in every face I meet
   Marks of weakness, marks of woe.

   —WILLIAM BLAKE, "London"

2. If this be error and upon me proved,
   I never writ, nor no man ever loved.

   —WILLIAM SHAKESPEARE, Sonnet 116

---

1. Mapped; rented out.

▼

3. "Hope" is the thing with feathers—
   That perches in the soul—
   And sings the song without the words—
   And never stops—at all—

   —EMILY DICKINSON, " 'Hope' is the thing with feathers"

4. The splendor falls on castle walls
       And snowy summits old in story:
   The long light shakes across the lakes,
       And the wild cataract[2] leaps in glory.
   Blow, bugle, blow, set the wild echoes flying,   5
   Blow, bugle; answer, echoes, dying, dying, dying.

   —ALFRED, LORD TENNYSON, "The Splendor Falls"

5. It was in and about the Martinmas[3] time,
       When the green leaves were a falling,
   That Sir John Græme, in the West Country,
       Fell in love with Barbara Allan.

   —ANONYMOUS, "Bonny Barbara Allan"

6. Bald heads, forgetful of their sins,
   Old, learned, respectable bald heads
   Edit and annotate the lines
   That young men, tossing on their beds,
   Rhymed out in love's despair   5
   To flatter beauty's ignorant ear.

   —WILLIAM BUTLER YEATS, "The Scholars"

7. O, what can ail thee, Knight at arms,
       So haggard, and so woebegone?
   The squirrel's granary is full
       And the harvest's done.

   —JOHN KEATS, "La Belle Dame sans Merci"[4]

8. Nobody heard him, the dead man,
   But still he lay moaning:
   I was much further out than you thought
   And not waving but drowning.

   —STEVIE SMITH, "Not Waving but Drowning"

---

2. Waterfall.
3. November 11.
4. The beautiful, merciless lady.

9. Gather ye rosebuds while ye may,
        Old time is still a-flying;
    And this same flower that smiles today
        Tomorrow will be dying.
    The glorious lamp of heaven, the sun,   5
        The higher he's a getting,
    The sooner will his race be run,
        And nearer he's to setting.
                    —ROBERT HERRICK, "To the Virgins, to Make Much of Time"

10. My heart aches, and a drowsy numbness pains
        My sense, as though of hemlock[5] I had drunk,
    Or emptied some dull opiate to the drains
        One minute past, and Lethe-wards[6] had sunk:
    'Tis not through envy of thy happy lot,   5
        But being too happy in thine happiness—
            That thou, light wingèd Dryad[7] of the trees,
                In some melodious plot
    Of beechen green, and shadows numberless,
        Singest of summer in full-throated ease.   10
                    —JOHN KEATS, "Ode to a Nightingale"

SOUND AND SOUND PATTERNS

In addition to RHYME, several other recurrent patterns of sound may
be used to create unity and emphasis.

Alliteration

Alliteration, the repetition of sounds in nearby words or stressed
syllables, is frequent in both poetry and prose. Usually, the term
applies to consonants that appear at the beginnings of words. For
example, in Gwendolyn Brooks's "We Real Cool," the young delin-
quents who serve as the group of NARRATORS boast of their dangerous
lifestyle: "We / Lurk late. We / Strike straight." The **alliterated** *l* and
s sounds link the curt assertions and suggest the speakers' bravado

---

5. An opiate.
6. River in Hades that causes forgetfulness.
7. Nymph.

and their eagerness to promote their "cool" and threatening image. As with all patterns of sound, including RHYME, such effects depend on the combination of repetition of the sounds and of the meanings of the words in which the sounds occur. Alliteration was a major element of old English poetry, in which the lines, which were unrhymed, were linked by a pattern of alliteration of the stressed syllables. See ACCENTUAL METER.

Another effect of alliteration may be comic exaggeration. The title of Jane Austen's novel, *Pride and Prejudice*, uses alliteration to imply the cause and effect connection between the faults of character that the book will satirize. Shakespeare called attention to the intentionally comic effect of excessive alliteration in *A Midsummer Night's Dream*. In the final act, a group of dull-witted Athenian laborers stage a performance at court of a DOGGEREL tragedy. Their crude production, Shakespeare's ingenious parody of Elizabethan theater, contains such cacophonous passages as the following APOSTROPHE. The hero, believing that his love, whom he calls his "dainty duck," is dead, calls for the Fates to strike him, too:

> O Fates, come, come,
> Cut thread and thrum,[1]
> Quail,[2] crush, conclude, and quell[3]!

The humor lies in the relentlessness of the alliteration and the redundancy of the synonyms that it links. As this passage shows, alliteration depends on the way that words sound, not on their spelling: here, "cut" and "quail" **alliterate**. To take a second example, "gnaw," "know," and "new" alliterate, but "gnaw" and "get" do not. The reiterated sound may also occur within words, as in "conclude" above; in that case, it is called **internal alliteration**.

Used for serious purposes, alliteration may subtly create unity and influence TONE. In Walt Whitman's "A Noiseless, Patient Spider," the narrator describes the creature beginning to construct its web: "It launched forth filament, filament, filament, out of itself." The alliterated *f* suggests the step-by-step process of the venture, as well as the spider's determination. In William Butler Yeats's "The Lake Isle of Innisfree," the narrator uses alliteration to describe a beloved place: "I hear lake water lapping with low sounds by the shore." The repeated *l*, in linguistic terminology a "liquid" sound, suggests the tranquil atmosphere of the idyllic setting.

---

1. Weaving: loose end of thread.
2. Overpower.
3. Kill.

In Shakespeare's *Macbeth*, the protagonist reflects in an early
SOLILOQUY on his qualms about murdering kind old King Duncan,
who stands in the way of Macbeth's ambition for the throne of Scot-
land:

> If th'assassination
> Could trammel up[4] the consequence and catch
> With his surcease[5] success[6]—that but this blow
> Might be the be-all and the end-all!—here,   5
> But here, upon this bank and shoal[7] of time,
> We'd jump the life to come. But in these cases
> We still have judgment here, that we but teach
> Bloody instructions, which, being taught, return
> To plague th'inventor.   10

The alliterated s sounds, initial and internal, in lines 2–4 underline
the secrecy and egotism of Macbeth's impossible hope: that the
"assassination" could be done in a self-contained moment of time
and produce no further "consequence." The hissing s sound betrays
his recognition of his nefarious purpose, however, an effect underlined by the repeated b's that suggest the "blows" he plans to deal
his innocent victim. Macbeth's next step in the reasoning process is
the hyperbolic claim that were this freedom from consequences possible, he would be willing to sacrifice divine salvation—"the life to
come." The alliterated j of the colloquial verb "jump," however, con-
nects it to the somber noun "judgment." That link and the alliteration of hissing s and pointed t sounds in lines 7–10 show that the
aspiring regicide is all too aware of the ways that the malevolent
"instructions" he is about to "teach" will "return" against him.

Consonance

Consonance (CAHN-soh-nantz, from the Latin word for "to sound
together") is the repetition of consonant sounds in two or more successive words or stressed syllables that contain different vowel
sounds: "had / hid," "wonder / wander," "haven / heaven." In Shakespeare's *Twelfth Night*, the clown Feste uses consonance to taunt his

---

4. Trap in a net.
5. Duncan's death.
6. Victory; also, something that occurs afterwards.
7. Riverbank and shallows.

arch-enemy, the haughty Malvolio. Feste disguises himself as the curate Sir Topas and goes to visit Malvolio, who, in a cruel practical joke, has been declared mad and imprisoned. Malvolio, fooled by the clown's disguise, makes an earnest case for his sanity, to which "Sir Topas" responds imperiously: "leave thy vain bibble-babble." To label Malvolio's stolidly rational protests with the absurd consonance of "bibble-babble" is the ultimate insult.

Assonance

Assonance (ASS-oh-nantz, from the Latin word for "to sound in response to") is the repetition of identical or similar vowel sounds in nearby words or stressed syllables: "r*igh*t / t*i*me," "s*a*d / f*a*ct," "s*e*ven / *e*lves." It differs from RHYME, in which both the vowels and the consonants of nearby words match. As the examples above show, the **assonantal** sound may occur either at the beginning of words or in the middle. Like ALLITERATION and CONSONANCE, it can create subtle underlying harmony as well as provide coherence and emphasis. In the opening lines of John Keats's "Ode on a Grecian Urn," the narrator uses assonance in APOSTROPHIZING the work of art:

> Thou st*i*ll unrav*i*shed bride of quietness,
>   Thou foster child of silence and slow time.

The repetition of the short *i* sound in "still unravished" emphasizes the meaning of those words and suggests the speaker's first impression of wonder at the ancient urn's pristine state, while the long *i* that predominates suggests the serenity and self-possession that it exudes. Despite the metaphors of human relationship—the urn is compared to a "bride" and a "foster child"—the implication is that art is impervious to human passions. The bride is permanently virginal, and the child has been nurtured by abstract and serene forces.

Assonance conveys a very different tone in Tennyson's *In Memoriam*. The narrator, grieving over the death of a beloved friend, recalls waiting eagerly to take his hand, and then laments:

> A h*a*nd th*a*t c*a*n be cl*a*sped no more—
>   Behold m*e*, for I cannot sl*ee*p.

The repeated short *a* sounds, reinforced by the ALLITERATED *c*'s, like quick blows, imply the cruelty and permanence of the loss, while the long *e*'s suggest the reaction: a near wail of despair.

Onomatopoeia

Onomatopoeia (ah-noh-maht-oh-PEE-ah, Greek for "to coin names") has two meanings. Its most common definition is using a word or phrase that seems to imitate the sound it denotes; for example, *bang*, *creak*, *murmur*, *ding-dong*, or *plop*. As with CONSONANCE and ASSONANCE, that effect cannot come from the sound of the word alone: its meaning is involved as well. To illustrate, words whose sounds closely resemble those of some of the examples above—bank, creek, and plot—are not **onomatopoeic**. In "Piano," D. H. Lawrence uses onomatopoeia to echo the sounds that a small child hears as he sits under the piano while his mother plays, "in the *boom* of the *tingling* strings." The description implies that, with his ear so close to the sound box, the boy hears both the resonant "boom" of the music and the "tingling strings" of the keys that the musician presses to create it. Lewis Carroll makes clever use of onomatopoeia in "Jabberwocky," a nonsense poem about a boy who slays a dragon-like monster. Carroll's invention of "portmanteau" words, created by combining two conventional words, includes some that are onomatopoeic. For example, as the Jabberwock goes on the attack, it "burble[s]," a word that seems to be made up of "bubble" and "burp." Few young readers would likely be frightened by a creature that makes such a silly noise, or by the "snicker-snack" that describes the Jabberwock's quick and bloodless beheading. The light tone is sustained by the reaction of the boy's father, who "chortle[s]" (probably a combination of "chuckle" and "snort") his joyful congratulations.

 In its broader sense, onomatopoeia means using words in such a way that they seem to exemplify what they denote, not just in terms of sound but also of such qualities as pacing, force, touch, movement, or duration as well. For example, in the DRAMATIC MONOLOGUE "I felt a Funeral in my Brain" by Emily Dickinson, the narrator recounts the surreal experience of being conscious at her own funeral, using onomatopoeia to convey the sensations that she is experiencing:

> I felt a Funeral in my Brain,
> And Mourners to and fro
> Kept treading—treading—till it seemed
> That Sense was breaking through—
>
> And when they all were seated,
> A Service, like a Drum—

▼

Kept beating—beating—till I thought
My mind was going numb—

And then I heard them lift a Box
And creak across my Soul
With those same Boots of Lead again,
Then Space—began to toll,

As all the Heavens were a Bell,
And Being, but an Ear,
And I, and Silence, some strange Race
Wrecked, solitary, here—

And then a Plank in Reason, broke
And I dropped down, and down—
And hit a World, at every plunge,
And Finished knowing—then—

The poem begins by imitating the sound of the heavy footsteps of "Mourners," in the repetition of "treading, treading." The narrator compares the funeral service to a drum "beating, beating" so loudly that it threatens to "numb" her painfully acute "Mind." She next hears the "creak" of the wooden coffin and feels it being lifted off the bier, followed by the renewed tramp of feet, this time the "Boots of Lead" of the pallbearers. Next, the essence of "Being" is reduced to the capacity to hear the death knell "toll[ing]," a response denied the speaker, who is left "wrecked" and "solitary" at the graveside, with "Silence" her only companion. The final aspect of onomatopoeia is the kinesthetic movement of the last stanza: the "Plank" supporting the coffin and, metaphorically, the speaker's "Reason," collapses, and she "drop[s] down, and down" into the grave and the end of consciousness. The final rhyme, "down / then," unlike its predecessors, is partial rather than exact, a confirmation of the narrator's fading perception. Dickinson's deft use of onomatopoeia provides a hauntingly vivid depiction of the horror of a living death, culminating in the terrifying cessation of all movement and sensation.

As these examples show, the various sound patterns may coexist with one another, for example, onomatopoeia with ALLITERATION ("My mind was going numb") in the poem above. Also, it should be stressed again that none of these patterns depend solely on the sound of words: rather, their richness and force derive from the associations that they present between sound and meaning.

EXERCISES: Sound and Sound Patterns

I. For each of the following passages:

- Name the predominant SOUND PATTERN: ALLITERATION, ASSONANCE, CONSO-
  NANCE, or ONOMATOPOEIA.
- Underline the letters or words that display that SOUND PATTERN.
- Describe the effects of the SOUND PATTERN(s) on the meaning and the
  TONE of the passage.
  Note: Some passages may contain more than one sound pattern; in
  those cases, identify each kind and describe its effects.

1. He clasps the crag with crooked hands,
    Close to the sun in lonely lands.
    —ALFRED, LORD TENNYSON, "The Eagle"

2. A tap at the pane, the quick sharp scratch
    And blue spurt of a lighted match . . .
    —ROBERT BROWNING, "Meeting at Night"

3. In me thou see'st the twilight of such day
    As after sunset fadeth in the west;
    Which by and by black night doth take away,
    Death's second self, that seals up all in rest.
    —WILLIAM SHAKESPEARE, Sonnet 73

4. The hum of multitudes was there, but multitudes of lambs,
    Thousands of little boys & girls raising their innocent hands.
    —WILLIAM BLAKE, "Holy Thursday [I]"

5. And the silken, sad, uncertain rustling of each purple curtain
    Thrilled me—filled me with fantastic terrors never felt before.
    —EDGAR ALLAN POE, "The Raven"

6. By brooks too broad for leaping
    The lightfoot boys are laid;
    The rose-lipt girls are sleeping
    In fields where roses fade.
    —A. E. HOUSMAN, "With Rue My Heart Is Laden"

7. From camp to camp, through the foul womb of night,
    The hum of either army stilly[1] sounds,
    That the fixed sentinels almost receive
    The secret whispers of each other's watch.

    –WILLIAM SHAKESPEARE, *Henry V*

8. Generations have trod, have trod, have trod;
        And all is seared with trade; bleared, smeared with toil.

    –GERARD MANLEY HOPKINS, "God's Grandeur"

9. Beat! beat! drums!—blow! bugles! blow!
    Make no parley[2]—stop for no expostulation,
    Mind not the timid—mind not the weeper or prayer,
    Mind not the old man beseeching the young man,
    Let not the child's voice be heard, nor the mother's entreaties,   5
    Make even the trestles to shake the dead where they lie awaiting
        the hearses,
    So strong you thump O terrible drums—so loud you bugles blow.

    –WALT WHITMAN, "Beat! Beat! Drums!"

10. Full fathom five thy father lies;
        Of his bones are coral made;
    Those are pearls that were his eyes:
        Nothing of him that doth fade,
    But doth suffer a sea change   5
    Into something rich and strange.
    Sea nymphs hourly ring his knell:
        Ding-dong.
    Hark! now I hear them—Ding-dong, bell.

    –WILLIAM SHAKESPEARE, song from *The Tempest*

II. The following poem by Thomas Hardy, written on December 31,
    1900, uses several of the sound patterns described in this section:
    RHYME, HALF RHYME, ASSONANCE, CONSONANCE, and ONOMATOPOEIA. In a brief
    essay, focus on those that are most significant for the poem and
    explain how they affect its tone and contribute to its meaning.

        The Darkling[3] Thrush

    I leant upon a coppice gate[4]
        When Frost was spectre-grey,

---

1. Softly.
2. Conference with an enemy.
3. Appearing at dusk.
4. Leading to a small wood.

And Winter's dregs made desolate
    The weakening eye of day.
The tangled bine-stems[5] scored the sky   5
    Like strings of broken lyres,
And all mankind that haunted nigh
    Had sought their household fires.

The land's sharp features seemed to be
    The Century's corpse outleant,[6]   10
His crypt the cloudy canopy,
    The wind his death-lament.
The ancient pulse of germ[7] and birth
    Was shrunken hard and dry,
And every spirit upon earth   15
    Seemed fervourless as I.

At once a voice arose among
    The bleak twigs overhead
In a full-hearted evensong
    Of joy illimited;   20
An aged thrush, frail, gaunt, and small,
    In blast-beruffled plume,
Had chosen thus to fling his soul
    Upon the growing gloom.

So little cause for carolings   25
    Of such ecstatic sound
Was written on terrestrial things
    Afar or nigh around,
That I could think there trembled through
    His happy good-night air   30
Some blessed Hope, whereof he knew
    And I was unaware.

5. Stems of a climbing vine.
6. Leaning out of its coffin.
7. Seed.

Poetic Forms

The term **poetic form** indicates the way that a poem is structured by recurrent patterns of rhythms and words. In English poetry, there are three main types of structures: (1) STANZAS, which have a recurrent pattern of METER, line length, and RHYME; (2) BLANK VERSE, which has a recurrent pattern of METER and line length but without RHYME; and (3) FREE VERSE, which lacks both recurrent METER and RHYME but is structured by a variety of rhythmic and rhetorical patterns.

The REFRAIN, a word, phrase, line, or group of lines that is repeated at intervals, while not a separate poetic form, is a feature of some poetic STANZAS. Of the forms that describe the structure of an entire poem, only the most widely used, the SONNET, is dealt with in this book.

STANZAS

A **stanza** is a group of lines in a poem that share a common pattern of METER, line length, and RHYME. Some of the most common types of **stanzas** are discussed below.

Couplet

A **couplet** is a pair of rhymed lines of the same length and METER. This example, from Ben Jonson's short lyric "Still to Be Neat," is an IAMBIC TETRAMETER couplet:

> Give me a look, give me a face
> That makes simplicity a grace.

Rhymed pairs of lines in IAMBIC PENTAMETER (five feet of alternating unstressed and stressed syllables) are termed **heroic couplets**, so called because of their frequent use in epics and heroic plays, genres that depict the deeds of heroes. The heroic couplet was introduced into English poetry by Geoffrey Chaucer, most notably in *The Canterbury Tales*, written at the end of the fourteenth century.

Heroic couplets were the favorite poetic form of such eighteenth-century neoclassical poets as John Dryden and Alexander Pope. Poets of that era favored the **closed couplet**, that is, a pair of lines in which the end of the rhyme coincides with the end of the clause or sentence, as shown in Pope's "The Rape of the Lock":

> Bright as the sun, her eyes the gazers strike,
> And, like the sun, they shine on all alike.
> Yet graceful ease, and sweetness void of pride,
> Might hide her faults, if belles had faults to hide:
> If to her share some female errors fall,
> Look on her face, and you'll forget 'em all.

In order to maintain the closed form, poets made extensive use of END-STOPPED lines, CAESURAS, and MASCULINE line endings to put emphasis on the rhyming words. In contrast, **open couplets** are fluent, with the rhyme not insistent but subtly underlying the METER. One example is this excerpt from Robert Browning's DRAMATIC MONOLOGUE "My Last Duchess":

>   Sir, 'twas not
> Her husband's presence only called that spot
> Of joy into the Duchess' cheek: perhaps
> Frà Pandolf chanced to say "Her mantle laps
> Over my lady's wrist too much," or "Paint   5
> Must never hope to reproduce the faint
> Half-flush that dies along her throat": such stuff
> Was courtesy, she thought, and cause enough
> For calling up that spot of joy. She had
> A heart—how shall I say?—too soon made glad,   10
> Too easily impressed; she liked whate'er
> She looked on, and her looks went everywhere.

Here, the ENJAMBMENTS (the lengthy phrases and sentences, which run over the ends of the poetic lines) and the CAESURAS (which either end a long independent clause [lines 3, 7, and 9] or express incidental qualifications [lines 8 and 10]), give the poem an offhanded, conversational TONE. It comes as a surprise to realize that the monologue is written in couplets rather than in BLANK VERSE.

Tercet (Triplet)

A **tercet**, or **triplet**, is a group of three lines, usually sharing the same RHYME, as in Robert Herrick's "Upon Julia's Clothes":

> Whenas in silks my Julia goes,
> Then, then, methinks, how sweetly flows
> That liquefaction of her clothes.

The lines of a tercet may be the same length, as in Herrick's IAMBIC TETRAMETER, or their length may vary, as in Thomas Hardy's "The Convergence of the Twain":

> And as the smart ship grew
> In stature, grace, and hue,
> In shadowy silent distance grew the Iceberg too.

Here the third line of each STANZA, in IAMBIC HEXAMETER, is twice the length of the first two, which are in IAMBIC TRIMETER. The variation enhances the IRONIC contrast between the vanity of the PERSONIFIED ship and the grim fate awaiting it in the form of its nemesis, the iceberg destined to destroy it. The appearance of the lines on the page also suggests in each stanza the shape of the *Titanic*, whose sinking is the subject of the poem. Tercets may also form part of a larger poetic unit, as in the two tercets that make up the SESTET of an ITALIAN SONNET.

In **terza rima** (from the Italian for "third rhyme") the tercets are linked by a pattern of shared rhymes: the first and last lines of each STANZA rhyme, and the middle line rhymes with the first and third lines of the following tercet: *aba, bcb, cdc,* etc. The series ends with a final line (or sometimes two lines) that constitute a separate STANZA and rhymes with the middle line of the last tercet: *yzy, z(z)*. Terza rima was invented by Dante in his *Divine Comedy* (1310–14). It has not been used often in English poetry, since rhyming words occur much less frequently in English than in Italian. Some poets, though, such as John Milton in "On Time," T. S. Eliot in his unrhymed version at the end of Part II of "Little Gidding," and Robert Frost in "Acquainted with the Night," have used this demanding form to impressive effect. In one of the most famous examples, "Ode to the West Wind," Percy Bysshe Shelley used a complete terza rima pattern in each of the five sections:

> O wild West Wind, thou breath of autumn's being,
> Thou, from whose unseen presence the leaves dead
> Are driven, like ghosts from an enchanter fleeing,

Yellow, and black, and pale, and hectic red,
Pestilence-stricken multitudes: O thou,
Who chariotest to their dark wintry bed

The wingèd seeds, where they lie cold and low,
Each like a corpse within its grave, until
Thine azure sister of the Spring shall blow

Her clarion o'er the dreaming earth, and fill
(Driving sweet buds like flocks to feed in air)
With living hues and odors plain and hill:

Wild Spirit, which art moving everywhere;
Destroyer and preserver: hear, oh, hear!

Quatrain

The **quatrain**, consisting of four lines, is the most common STANZA
form in English poetry. A quatrain may use a variety of METERS and
RHYME SCHEMES. The most frequent RHYME SCHEME is that in which the
second and fourth lines rhyme (*abcb*), as in William Blake's "The
Garden of Love," in which the predominant meter is ANAPESTIC
TRIMETER:

I went to the Garden of Love,
And saw what I never had seen:
A Chapel was built in the midst,
Where I used to play on the green.

For his long elegy, *In Memoriam*, Tennyson devised a quatrain in
IAMBIC TETRAMETER that rhymed *abba*, which he used so deftly that it
has come to be known as the *In Memoriam* **stanza**:

Thy voice is on the rolling air;
    I hear thee where the waters run;
    Thou standest in the rising sun,
And in the setting thou art fair.

The OCTAVE of the ITALIAN SONNET consists of two quatrains, and the
SHAKESPEAREAN SONNET contains three quatrains and a COUPLET.

One of the most commonly used quatrains in English poetry is
ballad meter, alternating IAMBIC TETRAMETER and IAMBIC TRIMETER,
typically with the second and fourth lines rhyming. An example is
Samuel Taylor Coleridge's "The Rime of the Ancient Mariner":

> All in a hot and copper sky,
> The bloody Sun, at noon,
> Right up above the mast did stand,
> No bigger than the moon.

The term derives from the stanza's frequent use in folk songs, such as the anonymous "Sir Patrick Spens." Ballad meter is also typical in hymns, where it is called **common meter**. The form was a favorite with Emily Dickinson, who used it with striking innovation and variety:

> I felt a Funeral, in my Brain,
> And Mourners to and fro
> Kept treading—treading—till it seemed
> That Sense was breaking through—

Here, the HALF RHYME of the second and fourth lines aptly suggests the uneasiness evoked by the eerie situation.

Refrain

A **refrain** is a word, a phrase, a line, or a group of lines repeated at intervals in a poem. It is a common feature of folk ballads and of Elizabethan songs, such as the clown Feste's refrain in the song that concludes Shakespeare's *Twelfth Night*: "For the rain it raineth every day." Usually, as in that case, the refrain comes at the end of a STANZA. It may occur at other points in a poem, however, and it may contain variations on the original line. A striking use of that sort of variation occurs in Langston Hughes's "Song for a Dark Girl," a bitter LYRIC about the lynching of a young black man. The refrain occurs not at the end but the beginning of the three QUATRAINS, and in the first and last STANZA it is identical:

> Way Down South in Dixie
>   (Break the heart of me)

The middle STANZA, though, varies the second line of the refrain to describe the sight that the NARRATOR finds so heartbreaking: the tortured corpse of her lover:

> Way Down South in Dixie
>   (Bruised body high in air)

Sonnet

The **sonnet** (from the Italian word for "little song") is a LYRIC poem, written in a single STANZA that usually consists of fourteen lines of IAMBIC PENTAMETER. The RHYME SCHEME of the sonnet falls primarily into two types: the **Italian**, or **Petrarchan**, **sonnet** and the **English**, or **Shakespearean**, **sonnet**. The **Petrarchan sonnet**, named after Petrarch, the Italian poet who introduced the form in the early fourteenth century, is divided into an opening **octave**—a group of eight lines—and a concluding **sestet**—a six-line unit. The RHYME SCHEME of the octave is usually fixed—*abba abba*, but that of the sestet may vary: *cde cde*, or *cdc cdc*, or *cdc dcd*. The Petrarchan sonnet was introduced into English poetry by Sir Thomas Wyatt in the mid sixteenth century. It was given a major variation by his contemporary the Earl of Surrey, who changed the RHYME SCHEME to the format that has become known as the **English sonnet** or, after its most famous practitioner, the **Shakespearean**, **sonnet**: three QUATRAINS and a final COUPLET, which rhyme *abab cdcd efef gg*. Since the Shakespearean sonnet requires fewer rhymes on a single word than the Petrarchan form, it gives more leeway to writers in English, a language that contains fewer rhyming words than Italian.

The structure of the meaning in a sonnet follows the division of the parts. In the Petrarchan form, the octave usually describes a situation or a dilemma or poses a question, for which the sestet provides some sort of commentary or resolution. The **turn** (or **volta**, from the Italian for "turn") comes at the start of the sestet. Percy Bysshe Shelley's "Ozymandias," although highly irregular in its RHYME SCHEME, follows this typical division of the Petrarchan sonnet:

I met a traveler from an antique land
Who said: Two vast and trunkless legs of stone
Stand in the desert. . . . Near them, on the sand,
Half sunk, a shattered visage lies, whose frown,
And wrinkled lip, and sneer of cold command,
Tell that its sculptor well those passions read
Which yet survive, stamped on these lifeless things,
The hand that mocked them, and the heart that fed:
And on the pedestal these words appear:
"My name is Ozymandias, king of kings:
Look on my works, ye Mighty, and despair!"
Nothing beside remains. Round the decay
Of that colossal wreck, boundless and bare
The lone and level sands stretch far away.

Here, the speaker opens the octave with a description of a monument like the sphinx, which the pharaoh Ramses II, called Ozymandias in Greek, had constructed of himself. The ancient face, half ruined, still expresses a "sneer of cold command." The second QUATRAIN reveals that the sculptor "mocked" (in the double sense of "imitated" and "ridiculed") such imperious "passions" and the arrogant "heart" that "fed" them. The VOLTA comes in the first TERCET of the sestet, with the quotation of the inscription engraved on the statue's pedestal. It boasts of the monarch's "works" and asserts that even the "Mighty" can only "despair" at their supremacy. The sestet concludes, however, with an IRONIC description of the vast emptiness that now surrounds the "colossal wreck": the desert that has made a mockery of Ozymandias's vanity.

The structure of the Shakespearean sonnet fosters a different sort of internal logic than the Petrarchan. The three QUATRAINS usually present parallel images or variations on a theme. The TURN comes in the concluding COUPLET, which often either reverses the stance expressed earlier or provides a concise summary of it. A classic example is Shakespeare's Sonnet 30:

> When to the sessions[1] of sweet silent thought
> I summon up[2] remembrance of things past,
> I sigh the lack of many a thing I sought,
> And with old woes new wail my dear time's waste.
> Then can I drown an eye, unused to flow,
> For precious friends hid in death's dateless[3] night,
> And weep afresh love's long since cancelled woe,
> And moan the expense of many a vanished sight:
> Then can I grieve at grievances foregone,[4]
> And heavily from woe to woe tell[5] o'er
> The sad account[6] of fore-bemoanèd moan,
> Which I new pay as if not paid before.
> > But if the while I think on thee, dear friend,
> > All losses are restored and sorrows end.

In the first QUATRAIN the speaker begins by anticipating a pleasant, nostalgic recollection—"sweet silent thought"—of "things past." The ALLITERATED s sound is soothing, almost somnolent. Instead, his

---

1. Court hearings.
2. Call to court.
3. Endless.
4. Past.
5. Count up.
6. Financial tally.

conscience begins arraigning him for missed opportunities and wasted efforts. He compares the process to court "sessions" in which he "summon[s] up" painful memories and newly laments these long past "woes." The second QUATRAIN, which begins with the linking adverb "then," describes more specific sources of this anguished mood and shifts the metaphor to renewed accounts of past losses and debts. "Precious friends," now dead, the "woe" of an old, failed "love," and simply the "vanished sight" of other once valued things cause him to "moan" and "weep afresh." The third QUATRAIN, which opens with another "then," continues this "sad account" of past "grievances." The repeated words (for example, "grieve" and "griev-ances," "woe" and "woe," "pay" and "paid") reinforce the melan-choly tone. The largely END-STOPPED lines and the insistent stresses of the ENJAMBED line—"and heavily from woe to woe tell o'er / The sad account"—suggest the process of tallying past losses, with the speaker morosely counting up once more his "fore-bemoanèd moans." The final COUPLET, however, marks an abrupt shift in atti-tude, signaled by the word "but." The speaker's sudden recollection of a "dear friend," addressed by the tender pronoun "thee," totally alleviates his despair. Whether the beloved is deceased or just tem-porarily absent ("think on" is an ambiguous verb), the speaker is moved to the HYPERBOLIC assertion that his or her being constitutes restitution for "all losses" and cessation of all "sorrows."

John Keats's "Bright Star," which is discussed in the section on METER, is also a Shakespearean sonnet. Perhaps because the structure of the Shakespearean sonnet puts greater demands on the wit of the sonneteer or because the epigrammatic nature of the COUPLET can seem artificial, the Italian sonnet has been the preferred form in poetry written in English.

Except during the neoclassical period (1660–1785), when poets tended to favor the HEROIC COUPLET for most poetic purposes, the sonnet has proven a popular and enduring poetic form. It both allows for variety in its subject matter and provides a structure that can inspire the imagination. The critic Jon Stallworthy, himself a poet, calls the form "not a prison . . . but a theater." For Petrarch, who addressed his sonnets to an idealized lady, Laura, the focus was romantic love. A number of sonneteers have followed his example, both in his choice of subject matter and in writing a **sonnet sequence**, a series of poems on the same topic. Examples include Sir Phillip Sidney's *Astrophil and Stella*, Edmund Spenser's *Amoretti*, Shakespeare's own sonnets, and, in the nineteenth century, Elizabeth Barrett Browning's *Sonnets from the Portuguese*. Countless other poets have used the sonnet for single poems and for strikingly diverse subjects: a religious struggle, as in John Donne's *Holy Sonnets*; a social or political crisis, as in William Wordsworth's "The World Is Too Much With Us" and Paul Laurence Dunbar's "Douglass"; a personal agony, as in John Milton's sonnet on his blindness, "When I Consider How My Light Is Spent" and Keats's "When I Have Fears That I May Cease to Be"; or a mythological concept, as in William Butler Yeats's "Leda and the Swan" and Edna St. Vincent Millay's "I Dreamed I Moved Among the Elysian Fields."

Poets have also altered the conventional fourteen-line length of the sonnet. Shakespeare himself wrote a twelve-line sonnet, number 126; Gerard Manley Hopkins invented a ten-and-a-half-line form that he called a **curtal** (meaning "curtailed") **sonnet**, for example, "Pièd Beauty"; and George Meredith used a sixteen-line sonnet in his bitter SEQUENCE on the deterioration of a marriage, *Modern Love*. Recent poets have also done away with rhyme altogether and written sonnets in BLANK VERSE (Seamus Heaney's "The Haw Lantern"), or have dispensed with METER as well (Michael Palmer's FREE VERSE sonnet "Now I see them").

BLANK VERSE

Blank verse is unrhymed IAMBIC PENTAMETER; that is, it contains five FEET per line, each FOOT consisting of an UNSTRESSED followed by a STRESSED syllable. This METER was introduced into English poetry by Henry Howard, Earl of Surrey, in his translation of Virgil's *Aeneid* (1540). The verse is called "blank" because although it is in METER, it does not RHYME. Since blank verse is close to the rhythms of ordinary English speech, it is capable of an easy COLLOQUIALISM, but it can also rise to a FORMAL, ceremonial utterance. It also allows for a variety of RHYTHMIC effects. The PAUSES, or lack of them, in mid-line and at the ends of lines, and the emphases created by such choices, take on special significance in blank verse poems.

Robert Frost uses a COLLOQUIAL blank verse in his narrative "Mending Wall." In mid-poem, the NARRATOR and a cranky neighbor meet to repair the stone wall between their properties, which has been damaged by winter weather:

> We keep the wall between us as we go.
> To each the boulders that have fallen to each.
> And some are loaves and some so nearly balls
> We have to use a spell to make them balance:
> "Stay where you are until our backs are turned!"   5
> We wear our fingers rough with handling them.
> Oh, just another kind of outdoor game,

One on a side. It comes to little more:
There where it is we do not need the wall:
He is all pine and I am apple orchard.   10
My apple trees will never get across
And eat the cones under his pines, I tell him.
He only says, "Good fences make good neighbors."

The blank verse is so understated that a reader might at first mistake
the lines for prose. A more attentive look, however, shows Frost's
masterful use of the form. Here, the predominantly END-STOPPED
lines, most of which correspond to an INDEPENDENT CLAUSE, reflect
the neighbor's insistence on maintaining boundaries. The two sets of
ENJAMBED lines describe the rebellious boulders (3–4) and dismiss
the fanciful threat that the apple trees might graze the other farmer's
pine cones (11–12). By mocking the possibility that walls could be
breached by these inanimate objects, those lines suggest the narrator's wry conviction that walls between neighbors are futile and
counterproductive.

In contrast, John Milton's use of blank verse in his epic *Paradise
Lost* (1667) shows the FORMAL, magniloquent capabilities of this
poetic form. Here, for example, is the opening "Invocation" to the
Muse:

Of man's first disobedience, and the fruit
Of that forbidden tree[1] whose mortal taste
Brought death into the world, and all our woe,
With loss of Eden, till one greater Man[2]
Restore us, and regain the blissful seat,   5
Sing, Heavenly Muse, that, on the secret top
Of Oreb, or of Sinai, didst inspire
That shepherd[3] who first taught the chosen seed
In the beginning how the Heavens and Earth
Rose out of Chaos: or, if Sion hill   10
Delight thee more, or Siloa's brook that flowed
Fast by the oracle of God, I thence
Invoke thy aid to my adventurous song,
That with no middle flight intends to soar,
Above th'Aonian mount,[4] while it pursues   15
Things unattempted yet in prose or rhyme.
And chiefly thou, O Spirit, that dost prefer

---

1. By God's commandment to Adam and Eve (Genesis 2.17).
2. Jesus Christ.
3. Moses.
4. Home of the pagan Muses.

Before all temples th'upright heart and pure,
Instruct me, for thou know'st; thou from the first
Wast present, and with mighty wings outspread,   20
Dovelike sat'st brooding on the vast abyss,
And mad'st it pregnant: what in me is dark
Illumine; what is low, raise and support;
That, to the height of this great argument,[5]
I may assert Eternal Providence,   25
And justify the ways of God to men.

The narrator begins by announcing his grand THEME: the fall of man from God's grace, the "first disobedience" that resulted in Adam and Eve's expulsion from the Garden of Eden and, in Judeo-Christian doctrine, was the cause of all subsequent earthly suffering. His goal is to serve as the explicator of this great conflict, and "justify the ways of God to men." Milton used several means to elevate the style: extensive ENJAMBMENT—the opening sentence runs over sixteen lines, and the entire invocation consists of only two sentences; APOSTROPHES to both a classical Greek muse (line 6) and to a still higher "Spirit" that is depicted as having been "present" from the beginning of time, when it first created life out of "the vast abyss" (17–22); FORMAL, learned DICTION, including the antiquated SECOND PERSON singular pronoun to address a deity (for example, "thou, O Spirit, that dost prefer," 17); and abundant classical and biblical ALLUSIONS. The narrator himself defends his choice of blank verse as the medium for expressing "things unattempted yet in prose or rhyme" (16). As though that claim were not sufficient to stand on its own merits, Milton added a preface to the second edition of the EPIC, in which he termed his METER "English heroic verse" and cited the precedents of "Homer in Greek" and "Virgil in Latin" as inspiring examples of "liberty" from the "bondage of rhyming."

In addition to *Paradise Lost*, blank verse is used in other long poems, such as William Wordsworth's *The Prelude*, John Keats's *Hyperion*, Alfred, Lord Tennyson's *Idylls of the King*, Robert Browning's *The Ring and the Book*, and Seamus Heaney's *Station Island*, as well as in countless short narrative and meditative poems.

During the Elizabethan era, blank verse also became the predominant form in English DRAMA. It was first used in Thomas Sackville and Thomas Norton's tragedy *Gorboduc* (1561), later popularized by Christopher Marlowe in such plays as *Tamburlaine* and *Doctor Faustus*, and perfected by Shakespeare. He and his contemporaries rejected the tradition of writing in stiff, rather artificial

---

5. Theme.

COUPLETS that had been used by their immediate predecessors and developed a dramatic form that sounded much more naturalistic. At the same time, blank verse gave the dialogue greater formality and structure than could have been achieved with prose. While creating a more flexible line than RHYMED COUPLETS would allow, it elevated the style by suggesting that this was art, not real life.

Shakespeare's plays are not written entirely in blank verse; rather, they also include some passages in rhyme as well as others in prose. The rhyme tends to come in particular contexts: incantations, such as those of the fairy king Oberon in *A Midsummer Night's Dream* and the witches in *Macbeth*, and in contests of wit, such as that between Romeo and Benvolio (*Romeo and Juliet*) and between Desdemona's father Brabantio and the Duke of Venice (*Othello*). Shakespeare also often closes a scene or an act with a RHYMED COUPLET, as in the following conclusion to Hamlet's wish that night would come quickly, so that he might question the ghost about the suspicious circumstances of his father's death:

> Till then sit still, my soul. Foul deeds will rise
> Though all the earth o'erwhelm them to men's eyes.

In a theater so spare of set, the COUPLET could serve as a sort of verbal curtain on the action.

Shakespeare also included speeches in prose, ever more as he gained experience as a playwright and his style became more varied and fluid. Prose may indicate a difference in social class: servants and lower-class characters tend to speak in prose—for example, the sparring servingmen at the start of *Romeo and Juliet* and the Porter in *Macbeth*. That is not an absolute distinction, however. The aristocratic Mercutio signals his nonchalance about love by speaking prose, and some of Prince Hamlet's most famous speeches, such as his advice to the players and his bitter meditation on man as the mere "quintessence of dust," are in prose. Also, a shift from prose to verse, or vice versa, can signal a change of mood in the speaker, as in *Othello* when Iago goes from colloquial toying with the gullible Roderigo to the incisive SOLILOQUIES that reveal his nefarious schemes, and in *Twelfth Night* when the haughty Olivia ends her condescending dismissal of the disguised Viola's speeches and shifts to poetic wonder at the "boy's" eloquence. For the Elizabethan actor, often required to perform multiple roles in a single season, blank verse was a valuable aid to memorization since it created a kind of metronome that underlay the words. For modern actors, too, that recurrent RHYTHM is crucial. In fact, it is a commonplace that a Shakespearean actor who forgets his lines will tend to ad lib in blank verse.

Shakespeare's audience, many of whom were illiterate and for all of whom written materials were rare and precious commodities, were accustomed to taking in information aurally and would have been alert to speakers' shifts between prose and verse. To aid modern readers in seeing such contrasts, editors space prose passages as in novels: they extend the lines all the way to the right margins and capitalize words only at the beginnings of sentences, not of lines. In contrast, they indicate that a speech is in verse by capitalizing the word at the beginning of each line and by leaving a wide right margin, in keeping with the format for poetry. Editors also indent blank verse lines that are shared between two or more speakers and number them as one line, to show that the dialogue reflects a close meeting of the characters' minds. The reason for the shared line may be that the speakers are highly compatible, as in this exchange between Romeo and Juliet about plans for their secret wedding:

> JULIET Romeo!
> ROMEO   My nyas[6]?
> JULIET   What o'clock tomorrow
>   Shall I send to thee?
> ROMEO   By the hour of nine.

Here, "Romeo!" "My nyas?" and "What o'clock tomorrow" represent one blank verse line, and "Shall I send to thee?" and "By the hour of nine" another. These two shared lines, in which each lover responds without pause to the other's words, show how closely attuned Romeo and Juliet are to one another's thoughts and rhythms, almost as if their heartbeats are synchronized.

A shared line may also show that one character is dominating the thoughts of the other. In this dialogue from *Othello*, the distraught general is asking his subordinate, the devious Iago, questions about Cassio, his supposed rival for the affections of Desdemona:

> OTHELLO Is he not honest?[7]   1
> IAGO   Honest, my lord?
> OTHELLO   Honest. Ay, honest.
> IAGO My lord, for aught I know.
> OTHELLO What dost thou think?   3
> IAGO   Think, my lord?
> OTHELLO   Think, my lord?
>   By heaven, thou echo'st me
>   As if there were some monster in thy thought
>   Too hideous to be shown.

---

6. Nestling hawk.
7. Morally upright, trustworthy.

The two shared lines (1 and 3) show that Othello is quite literally hanging on Iago's words, while the villain has only to echo Othello's words and let the innuendoes plant the first seeds of "monstrous" jealousy. A further sign in the blank verse of how thoroughly Iago is dominating the conversation is the shortened line (2), which lacks the last two feet that would be needed to complete the IAMBIC PENTAMETER. That break in the METER signals a pause that shows how disconcerted Othello has become. Instead of the reassurance that he has sought from Iago, he has received further doubt. The only response that Othello can muster is another anxious question, which, again, Iago bandies back at him.

Blank verse has remained the preferred form for the relatively rare verse drama written in modern times, for example, T. S. Eliot's *Murder in the Cathedral* and Maxwell Anderson's *Winterset*.

FREE VERSE (OPEN FORM VERSE)

Free verse (from the French "vers libre"), also called **open form verse**, is distinguished from traditional versification in that its RHYTHMS are not organized into the regularity of METER; most free verse also lacks RHYME. The term should not be confused with BLANK VERSE, unrhymed IAMBIC PENTAMETER. What distinguishes free verse from prose? One of its main features is the deliberate division of the lines, which may consist of very long units or of single words, and which may be divided in mid-sentence or even mid-word. As with poems in METER, the arrangement of lines on the page, including choices about STANZA breaks, CAESURAS, and END-STOPPING and ENJAMB-MENT to emphasize certain sounds and words, are crucial to the meaning of free verse poems. Since METER and RHYME SCHEME do not control such choices, as they do in **closed form** poems, such as those discussed above, the poet must devise different means for creating coherence and emphasis.

The initial models for free verse poems were the psalms and the Song of Solomon in the King James Version of the Bible. While reproducing the Song of Solomon in English, the translators attempted to imitate the cadences of the original Hebrew:

> I am the rose of Sharon, and the lily of the valleys
> As the lily among the thorns, so is my love among the daughters.
> As the apple tree among the trees of the wood, so is my beloved
>   among the sons.
> I sat down under his shadow with great delight, and his fruit
>   was sweet to my taste.

> He brought me to the banqueting house, and his banner over
>   me was love.
> Stay me with flagons, comfort me with apples: for I am sick of
>   love.

The lengthy lines, full of ANTITHESIS and ANAPHORA, have inspired the
sonorous, extended form of such free verse works as Walt Whitman's "Song of Myself":

> I believe in you my soul, the other I am must not abase itself
>   to you,
> And you must not be abased to the other.
>
> Loafe with me on the grass, loose the stop from your throat,
> Not words, not music or rhyme I want, not custom or lecture,
>   not even the best,
> Only the lull I like, the hum of your valvèd voice.

Whitman's outlook, while decidedly more secular and solipsistic—he
is addressing not a lover who embodies the divine but his own
soul—echoes the biblical song's lyrical rhythms and sensuous
delights. Practitioners of this protracted free verse style, based on
biblical cadences, have included Allen Ginsberg and Carl Sandburg,
and, more recently, Paul Muldoon and Michael Longley.

An alternate style of free verse is the short, COLLOQUIAL, often
IRONIC form favored by such poets as E. E. Cummings, William Car-
los Williams, Elizabeth Bishop, and Langston Hughes. Here is the
beginning of Bishop's "The Fish":

> I caught a tremendous fish
> and held him beside the boat
> half out of water, with my hook
> fast in a corner of his mouth.
> He didn't fight.
> He hadn't fought at all.
> He hung a grunting weight,
> battered and venerable
> and homely. Here and there
> his brown skin hung in strips
> like ancient wallpaper, and its pattern of darker brown
> was like wallpaper:
> shapes like full-blown roses
> stained and lost through age.

The image of the fish at this point is decidedly unheroic, as suggested by the matter-of-fact tone and the "homely" SIMILE of dilapi-

dated wallpaper, with its leisurely line, longer than the rest, and its reiterated noun. In contrast, the earlier ANAPHORA, referring to the fish's lack of "fight," is emphasized by its IAMBIC beat and short, END-STOPPED line: "He didn't fight. / He hadn't fought at all." The fish is merely "a grunting weight," ready to be hauled in. As the poem continues, however, the narrator looks more closely at her captive and notices the remnants of previous struggles: "five big hooks" lodged in his mouth and several dangling lines that snapped when "he got away." This is the conclusion:

> Like medals with their ribbons
> frayed and wavering,
> a five-haired beard of wisdom
> trailing from his aching jaw.
> I stared and stared
> and victory filled up
> the little rented boat,
> where oil had spread a rainbow
> around the rusted engine
> to the bailer rusted orange,
> the sun-cracked thwarts,
> the oarlocks on their strings,
> the gunnels—until everything
> was rainbow, rainbow, rainbow!
> And I let the fish go.

Here the SIMILE and METAPHOR suggest the fish's heroism: the remnants of previous fights are pictured as combat "medals" and the snapped lines as signs of ancient "wisdom." The mundane details of the old "rented boat," listed in the long sentence that goes on for ten lines, get transformed by the narrator's awe at the fish's courage. In the triumphant final exclamation, the spilt oil becomes the "rainbow, rainbow, rainbow" of the fish's deification. The final line, to which the entire account builds, derives its power from its UNDERSTATEMENT and its contrast to the graphic objectivity of the opening lines.

Although the American poet Robert Frost famously dismissed writing in free verse as analogous to "playing tennis with the net down," and critics have occasionally called for a return to METRICS, free verse has become the most frequent poetic form in modern English poetry. It has been used with great effectiveness in distinguished works as diverse as Walt Whitman's "When Lilacs Last in the Dooryard Bloom'd," T. S. Eliot's "The Waste Land," and Ezra Pound's *The Cantos*. Indeed, numerous modern poets have mastered both CLOSED and OPEN FORMS—for example, D. H. Lawrence, T. S. Eliot, W. H. Auden, Sylvia Plath, and Adrienne Rich. Poets Mark Strand and Eavan Boland, in their book *The Making of a Poem*, argue that free verse represents not a "willful abandonment" of traditional models but a "passionate dialogue" with them. As with any poem, reading free verse aloud, pausing where the poet has indicated a line break or a punctuation mark, attending to striking *images* and reiterated *sounds*, may be the surest means of responding to the cadences.

EXERCISES: Poetic Forms

I. For each of the following passages:

- Name the STANZA pattern—COUPLET, TERCET, TERZA RIMA, QUATRAIN, BALLAD METER—or identify the REFRAIN.
- Explain why that term applies. *Note:* In some cases, more than one term may apply. If so, explain why both may be relevant.
- Describe how the STANZA pattern affects the TONE and the meaning of the passage.

1. I was angry with my friend:
   I told my wrath, my wrath did end.
   I was angry with my foe:
   I told it not, my wrath did grow.

   —WILLIAM BLAKE, "A Poison Tree"

2. Oh Galuppi, Baldassare, this is very sad to find!
   I can hardly misconceive you: it would prove me deaf and blind;
   But although I take your meaning, 'tis with such a heavy mind!

   Here you come with your old music, and here's all the good it
      brings.
   What, they lived once thus at Venice where the merchants were   5
      the kings,
   Where Saint Mark's is, where the Doges used to wed the sea with
      rings?

   —ROBERT BROWNING, "A Toccata of Galuppi's"

3. Does the road wind up-hill all the way?
      Yes, to the very end.
   Will the day's journey take the whole long day?
      From morn to night, my friend.

   —CHRISTINA ROSSETTI, "Up-hill"

4. This one was put in a jacket,
   This one was sent home,
   This one was given bread and meat
   But would eat none,
   And this one cried No No No No   5
   All day long.

   This one looked at the window
   As though it were a wall,
   This one saw things that were not there,
   This one things that were,   10
   And this one cried No No No No
   All day long.

   This one thought himself a bird,
   This one a dog,
   And this one thought himself a man,   15
   An ordinary man,
   And cried and cried No No No No
   All day long.

   —DONALD JUSTICE, "Counting the Mad"

5. Far off thou art, but ever nigh:
       I have thee still, and I rejoice;
       I prosper, circled with thy voice;
   I shall not lose thee though I die.

   —ALFRED, LORD TENNYSON, "In Memoriam"

6. Of all the causes which conspire to blind
   Man's erring judgment, and misguide the mind,
   What the weak head with strongest bias rules,
   Is pride, the never-failing vice of fools.

   —ALEXANDER POPE, "An Essay on Criticism"

7. Tell all the truth but tell it slant—
   Success in Circuit lies
   Too bright for our infirm Delight
   The Truth's superb surprise

   —EMILY DICKINSON, "Tell all the truth but tell it slant—"

8. The snow came down last night like moths
   Burned on the moon; it fell till dawn,
   Covered the town with simple cloths.

▼

Absolute snow lies rumpled on
What shellbursts scattered and deranged,   5
Entangled railings, crevassed lawn.

As if it did not know they'd changed,
Snow smoothly clasps the roofs of homes
Fear-gutted, trustless and estranged.

–RICHARD WILBUR, "First Snow in Alsace"

9. The old South Boston Aquarium stands
   in a Sahara of snow now. Its broken windows are boarded.
   The bronze weathervane cod has lost half its scales.
   The airy tanks are dry.

–ROBERT LOWELL, "For the Union Dead"

10. With blackest moss the flower-plots
        Were thickly crusted, one and all,
    The rusted nails fell from the knots
        That held the pear to the gable-wall.
    The broken sheds looked sad and strange: 5
        Unlifted was the clinking latch;
        Weeded and worn the ancient thatch
    Upon the lonely moated grange.
        She only said, "My life is dreary,
        He cometh not," she said;   10
        She said, "I am aweary, aweary,
            I would that I were dead!"

    Her tears fell with the dews at even;
        Her tears fell ere the dews were dried;
    She could not look on the sweet heaven,   15
        Either at morn or eventide.
    After the flitting of the bats,
        When thickest dark did trance the sky,
        She drew her casement curtain by,
    And glanced athwart the glooming flats.   20
        She only said, "The night is dreary,
            He cometh not," she said;
        She said, "I am aweary, aweary,
            I would that I were dead!"

–ALFRED, LORD TENNYSON, "Mariana"

▼

II. For each of the following poems or passages:

- Name the POETIC FORM exemplified—SONNET (PETRARCHAN or
  SHAKESPEAREAN), BLANK VERSE, or FREE VERSE.
- Identify the characteristics of the POETIC FORM.
- Explain how the POETIC FORM contributes to the TONE and meaning.

1. since feeling is first
   who pays any attention
   to the syntax of things
   will never wholly kiss you;

   wholly to be a fool   5
   while Spring is in the world

   my blood approves,
   and kisses are a better fate
   than wisdom
   lady I swear by all the flowers. Don't cry   10
   —the best gesture of my brain is less than
   your eyelids' flutter which says

   we are for each other: then
   laugh, leaning back in my arms
   for life's not a paragraph   15

   And death i think is no parenthesis

                              —E. E. CUMMINGS, "Since feeling is first"

2. Since there's no help, come let us kiss and part;   A
   Nay, I have done, you get no more of me,   B
   And I am glad, yea glad with all my heart   A
   That thus so cleanly I myself can free;   B
   Shake hands forever, cancel all our vows,   C
   And when we meet at any time again   D
   Be it not seen in either of our brows   C
   That we one jot of former love retain.   D
   Now at the last gasp of love's latest breath,   E
   When, his pulse failing, Passion speechless lies,   F
   When Faith is kneeling by his bed of death,   E
   And Innocence is closing up his eyes,   F
       Now if though wouldst, when all have given him over,   G
       From death to life thou mightst him yet recover.   G

                              —MICHAEL DRAYTON, "Since there's no help,
                                              come let us kiss and part"

(Handwritten annotations: "doomed characteristics:", "man ready to end relationship", "Hopeless", "Love is dying", "passion, innocence, faith = friends of love", "shakespearean", "couplet", "love can be saved?", "uncertainty")

3. This living hand, now warm and capable
    Of earnest grasping, would, if it were cold
    And in the icy silence of the tomb,
    So haunt thy days and chill thy dreaming nights
    That thou wouldst wish thine own heart dry of blood   5
    So in my veins red life might stream again,
    And thou be conscience-calmed—see here it is—
    I hold it towards you.

                              —JOHN KEATS, "This Living Hand"

4.

    LEAR   Where have I been? Where am I? Fair daylight?
       I am mightily abused. I should e'en die with pity
       To see another thus. I know not what to say.
       I will not swear these are my hands. Let's see—
       I feel this pin prick. Would I were assured
       Of my condition.
    CORDELIA   O, look upon me, sir,
       And hold your hand in benediction o'er me.
       You must not kneel.
    LEAR   Pray, do not mock me.
       I am a very foolish fond old man,
       Fourscore and upward, not an hour more nor less;
       And, to deal plainly,
       I fear I am not in my perfect mind.
       Methinks I should know you, and know this man;
       Yet I am doubtful, for I am mainly ignorant
       What place this is; and all the skill I have
       Remembers not these garments; nor I know not
       Where I did lodge last night. Do not laugh at me;
       For, as I am a man, I think this lady
       To be my child Cordelia.
    CORDELIA   And so I am! I am!

                              —WILLIAM SHAKESPEARE, *King Lear*

APPENDIX

MLA Style

Modern Language Association style calls for (1) brief in-text documentation and (2) complete documentation in a list of works cited at the end of your text. The models in this appendix draw on the *MLA Handbook for Writers of Research Papers*, 6th edition, by Joseph Gibaldi (2003). Additional information is available at www.mla.org.

MLA IN-TEXT DOCUMENTATION   249

1. Author named in a signal phrase   *249*
2. Author named in parentheses   *249*
3. Two or more works by the same author   *250*
4. Authors with the same last name   *250*
5. After a block quotation   *251*
6. Two or more authors   *251*
7. Organization or government as author   *251*
8. Author unknown   *251*
9. Literary works   *252*
10. Work in an anthology   *252*
11. Sacred text   *253*
12. Multivolume work   *253*
13. Two or more works cited together   *253*
14. Source quoted in another source   *253*
15. Work without page numbers   *253*
16. An entire work   *254*

NOTES   254

MLA LIST OF WORKS CITED   254

BOOKS   *255*

1. One author   *255*
2. Two or more works by the same author(s)   *255*
3. Two authors   *256*
4. Three authors   *256*
5. Four or more authors   *256*
6. Organization or government as author   *257*
7. Anthology   *257*

8. Work(s) in an anthology 257
9. Author and editor 257
10. No author or editor 258
11. Translation 258
12. Foreword, introduction, preface, or afterword 258
13. Multivolume work 258
14. Book in a series 259
15. Sacred text 259
16. Edition other than the first 259
17. Republished work 259

PERIODICALS 259
18. Article in a journal paginated by volume 260
19. Article in a journal paginated by issue 260
20. Article in a monthly magazine 260
21. Article in a weekly magazine 260
22. Article in a daily newspaper 260
23. Unsigned article 261
24. Editorial 261
25. Letter to the editor 261
26. Review 261

ELECTRONIC SOURCES 261
27. Professional Web site 262
28. Personal Web site 262
29. Home page for an academic department 262
30. Online book or part of a book 263
31. Article in an online periodical or database 263
32. Document accessed through AOL or other subscription service 263
33. Email 264
34. Posting to an electronic forum 264
35. CD-ROM 264

OTHER KINDS OF SOURCES 264
36. Advertisement 265
37. Art 265
38. Cartoon 265
39. Dissertation 266
40. Film, video, or DVD 266
41. Interview 266
42. Letter 267
43. Map 267
44. Musical composition 267

45. Music recording *267*
46. Oral presentation *268*
47. Paper from proceedings of a conference *268*
48. Performance *268*
49. Television or radio program *268*

SAMPLE RESEARCH PAPER, MLA STYLE *269*

MLA IN-TEXT DOCUMENTATION

Brief documentation in your text makes clear to your reader what you took from a source and where in the source you found the information.

In your text, you have three options for citing a source: quoting, paraphrasing, and summarizing. As you cite each source, you will need to decide whether or not to name the author in a signal phrase—"as Toni Morrison writes"—or in parentheses—"(Morrison 24)."

The first examples in this appendix show basic in-text citations of a work by one author. Variations on those examples follow. The examples also illustrate the MLA style of using quotation marks around titles of short works and underlining titles of long works. (Your instructor may prefer italics to underlining; find out if you're not sure.)

1. AUTHOR NAMED IN A SIGNAL PHRASE

If you mention the author in a signal phrase, put only the page number(s) in parentheses. Do not write *page* or *p*.

> McCullough describes John Adams as having "the hands of a man accustomed to pruning his own trees, cutting his own hay, and splitting his own firewood" (18).

> McCullough describes John Adams's hands as those of someone used to manual labor (18).

2. AUTHOR NAMED IN PARENTHESES

If you do not mention the author in a signal phrase, put his or her last name in parentheses along with the page number(s). Do not use punctuation between the name and the page number(s).

> Adams is said to have had "the hands of a man accustomed to pruning his own trees, cutting his own hay, and splitting his own firewood" (McCullough 18).

> One biographer describes John Adams as someone who was not a stranger to manual labor (McCullough 18).

Whether you use a signal phrase and parentheses or parentheses only, try to put the parenthetical citation at the end of the sentence or as close as possible to the material you've cited without awkwardly interrupting the sentence. Notice that in the first example above, the parenthetical reference comes after the closing quotation marks but before the period at the end of the sentence.

3. TWO OR MORE WORKS BY THE SAME AUTHOR

If you cite multiple works by one author, you have four choices. You can mention the author in a signal phrase and give the title and page reference in parentheses. Give the full title if it's brief; otherwise, give a short version.

> Kaplan insists that understanding power in the Near East requires "Western leaders who know when to intervene, and do so without illusions" (Eastward 330).

You can mention both author and title in a signal phrase and give only the page reference in parentheses.

> In Eastward to Tartary, Kaplan insists that understanding power in the Near East requires "Western leaders who know when to intervene, and do so without illusions" (330).

You can indicate author, title, and page reference only in parentheses, with a comma between author and title.

> Understanding power in the Near East requires "Western leaders who know when to intervene, and do so without illusions" (Kaplan, Eastward 330).

Or you can mention the title in a signal phrase and give the author and page reference in parentheses.

> Eastward to Tartary argues that understanding power in the Near East requires "Western leaders who know when to intervene, and do so without illusions" (Kaplan 330).

4. AUTHORS WITH THE SAME LAST NAME

If your works-cited list includes works by authors with the same last name, you need to give the author's first name in any signal phrase or the author's first initial in the parenthetical reference.

> Edmund Wilson uses the broader term imaginative, whereas Anne Wilson chooses the narrower adjective magical.

> Imaginative applies not only to modern literature (E. Wilson) but also to writing of all periods, whereas magical is often used in writing about Arthurian romances (A. Wilson).

5. AFTER A BLOCK QUOTATION

When quoting more than three lines of poetry, more than four lines of prose, or dialogue from a drama, set off the quotation from the rest of your text, indenting it one inch (or ten spaces) from the left margin. Do not use quotation marks. Place any parenthetical documentation *after* the final punctuation.

> In <u>Eastward to Tartary</u>, Kaplan captures ancient and contemporary Antioch for us:
>> At the height of its glory in the Roman-Byzantine age, when it had an amphitheater, public baths, aqueducts, and sewage pipes, half a million people lived in Antioch. Today the population is only 125,000. With sour relations between Turkey and Syria, and unstable politics throughout the Middle East, Antioch is now a backwater—seedy and tumbledown, with relatively few tourists. I found it altogether charming. (123)

6. TWO OR MORE AUTHORS

For a work by two or three authors, name all the authors, either in a signal phrase or in the parentheses.

> Carlson and Ventura's stated goal is to introduce Julio Cortázar, Marjorie Agosín, and other Latin American writers to an audience of English-speaking adolescents (v).

For a work with four or more authors, you have the option of mentioning all their names or just the name of the first author followed by *et al.*, which means "and others."

> One popular survey of American literature breaks the contents into sixteen thematic groupings (Anderson, Brinnin, Leggett, Arpin, and Toth A19–24).

> One popular survey of American literature breaks the contents into sixteen thematic groupings (Anderson et al. A19–24).

7. ORGANIZATION OR GOVERNMENT AS AUTHOR

If the author is an organization, cite the organization either in a signal phrase or in parentheses. It's acceptable to shorten long names.

> The U.S. government can be direct when it wants to be. For example, it sternly warns, "If you are overpaid, we will recover any payments not due you" (Social Security Administration 12).

8. AUTHOR UNKNOWN

If you don't know the author of a work, as you won't with many reference books and with most newspaper editorials, use the work's title or a shortened version of the title in the parentheses.

The explanatory notes at the front of the literature encyclopedia point out that writers known by pseudonyms are listed alphabetically under those pseudonyms (<u>Merriam-Webster's</u> vii).

A powerful editorial in last week's paper asserts that healthy liver donor Mike Hurewitz died because of "frightening" faulty post-operative care ("Every Patient's Nightmare").

9. LITERARY WORKS

When referring to literary works that are available in many different editions, cite the page numbers from the edition you are using, followed by information that will let readers of any edition locate the text you are citing.

NOVELS

Give the page and chapter number.

In <u>Pride and Prejudice</u>, Mrs. Bennet shows no warmth toward Jane and Elizabeth when they return from Netherfield (105; ch. 12).

VERSE PLAYS

Give the act, scene, and line numbers; separate them with periods.

Macbeth continues the vision theme when he addresses the Ghost with "Thou hast no speculation in those eyes / Which thou dost glare with" (3.3.96–97).

POEMS

Give the part and the line numbers (separated by periods). If a poem has only line numbers, use the word *line(s)* in the first reference.

Whitman sets up not only opposing adjectives but also opposing nouns in "Song of Myself" when he says, "I am of old and young, of the foolish as much as the wise, / . . . a child as well as a man" (16.330–32).

One description of the mere in <u>Beowulf</u> is "not a pleasant place!" (line 1372). Later, the label is "the awful place" (1378).

10. WORK IN AN ANTHOLOGY

If you're citing a work that is included in an anthology, name the author(s) of the work, not the editor of the anthology—either in a signal phrase or in parentheses.

"It is the teapots that truly shock," according to Cynthia Ozick in her essay on teapots as metaphor (70).

In <u>In Short: A Collection of Creative Nonfiction</u>, readers will find both an essay on Scottish tea (Hiestand) and a piece on teapots as metaphors (Ozick).

▼

11. SACRED TEXT

When citing sacred texts such as the Bible or the Qur'an, give the title of the edition used, and in parentheses give the book, chapter, and verse (or their equivalent), separated by periods. MLA style recommends that you abbreviate the names of the books of the Bible in parenthetical references.

> The wording from The New English Bible follows: "In the beginning of creation, when God made heaven and earth, the earth was without form and void, with darkness over the face of the abyss, and a mighty wind that swept over the surface of the waters" (Gen. 1.1–2).

12. MULTIVOLUME WORK

If you cite more than one volume of a multivolume work, each time you cite one of the volumes, give the volume *and* the page numbers in parentheses, separated by a colon.

> Sandburg concludes with the following sentence about those paying last respects to Lincoln: "All day long and through the night the unbroken line moved, the home town having its farewell" (4: 413).

If your works-cited list includes only a single volume of a multivolume work, the only number you need to give in your parenthetical reference is the page number.

13. TWO OR MORE WORKS CITED TOGETHER

If you're citing two or more works closely together, you will sometimes need to provide a parenthetical citation for each one.

> Tanner (7) and Smith (viii) have looked at works from a cultural perspective.

If the citation allows you to include both in the same parentheses, separate the references with a semicolon.

> Critics have looked at both Pride and Prejudice and Frankenstein from a cultural perspective (Tanner 7; Smith viii).

14. SOURCE QUOTED IN ANOTHER SOURCE

When you are quoting text that you found quoted in another source, use the abbreviation *qtd. in* in the parenthetical reference.

> Charlotte Brontë wrote to G. H. Lewes: "Why do you like Miss Austen so very much? I am puzzled on that point" (qtd. in Tanner 7).

15. WORK WITHOUT PAGE NUMBERS

For works without page numbers, give paragraph or section numbers, using the abbreviation *par.* or *sec.* If you are including the author's name in the parenthetical reference, add a comma.

▼

Russell's dismissals from Trinity College at Cambridge and from City College in New York City are seen as examples of the controversy that marked the philosopher's life (Irvine, par. 2).

16. AN ENTIRE WORK

If your text is referring to an entire work rather than a part of it, identify the author in a signal phrase or in parentheses. There's no need to include page numbers.

Kaplan considers Turkey and Central Asia explosive.

At least one observer considers Turkey and Central Asia explosive (Kaplan).

NOTES

Sometimes you may need to give information that doesn't fit into the text itself—to thank people who helped you, provide additional details, or refer readers to other sources not cited in your text. Such information can be given in a *footnote* (at the bottom of the page) or an *endnote* (on a separate page with the heading *Notes* just before your works-cited list). Put a superscript number at the appropriate point in your text, signaling to readers to look for the note with the corresponding number. If you have multiple notes, number them consecutively throughout your paper.

TEXT

This essay will argue that small liberal arts colleges should not recruit athletes and, more specifically, that giving student athletes preferential treatment undermines the larger educational goals.[1]

NOTE

[1] I want to thank all those who have contributed to my thinking on this topic, especially my classmates and my teachers Marian Johnson and Diane O'Connor.

MLA LIST OF WORKS CITED

A works-cited list provides full bibliographic information for every source cited in your text. The list should be alphabetized by authors' last names (or sometimes by editors' or translators' names). Works that do not have an identifiable author or editor are alphabetized by title. See page 274 for a sample works-cited list.

Books

BASIC FORMAT FOR A BOOK

For most books, you'll need to provide information about the author; the title and any subtitle; and the place of publication, publisher, and date. You'll find this information on the book's title page and copyright page.

> Greenblatt, Stephen. <u>Will in the World: How Shakespeare Became Shakespeare.</u> New York: Norton, 2004.

A FEW DETAILS TO NOTE

- TITLES: capitalize the first and last words of titles, subtitles, and all principal words. Do not capitalize *a*, *an*, *the*, *to*, or any prepositions or coordinating conjunctions unless they begin a title or subtitle.
- PLACE OF PUBLICATION: If more than one city is given, use only the first.
- PUBLISHER: Use a shortened form of the publisher's name (Norton for W. W. Norton & Company, Princeton UP for Princeton University Press).
- DATES: If more than one year is given, use the most recent one.

1. ONE AUTHOR

> Author's Last Name, First Name, <u>Title.</u> Publication City: Publisher, Year of publication.

> Miller, Susan. <u>Assuming the Positions: Cultural Pedagogy and the Politics of Commonplace Writing.</u> Pittsburgh: U of Pittsburgh P, 1998.

When the title of a book itself contains the title of another book (or other long work), do not underline that title.

> Walker, Roy. <u>Time Is Free: A Study of</u> Macbeth. London: Dakers, 1949.

Include the author's middle name or initials. When the title of a book contains the title of a short work, the title of the short work should be enclosed in quotation marks, and the entire title should be underlined.

> Thompson, Lawrance Roger. <u>"Fire and Ice": The Art and Thought of Robert Frost.</u> New York: Holt, 1942.

2. TWO OR MORE WORKS BY THE SAME AUTHOR(S)

Give the author's name in the first entry, and then use three hyphens in the author slot for each of the subsequent works, listing them alphabetically by the first important word of each title.

Author's Last Name, First Name. <u>Title That Comes First Alphabetically.</u> Publication City: Publisher, Year of publication.

---. <u>Title That Comes Next Alphabetically</u>. Publication City: Publisher, Year of publication.

Kaplan, Robert D. <u>The Coming Anarchy: Shattering the Dreams of the Post Cold War.</u> New York: Random, 2000.

---. <u>Eastward to Tartary: Travels in the Balkans, the Middle East, and the Caucasus</u>. New York: Random, 2000.

3. TWO AUTHORS

First Author's Last Name, First Name, and Second Author's First and Last Names. <u>Title</u>. Publication City: Publisher, Year of publication.

Malless, Stanley, and Jeffrey McQuain. <u>Coined by God: Words and Phrases That First Appear in the English Translations of the Bible</u>. New York: Norton, 2003.

4. THREE AUTHORS

First Author's Last Name, First Name, Second Author's First and Last Names, and Third Author's First and Last Names. <u>Title</u>. Publication City: Publisher, Year of publication.

Sebranek, Patrick, Verne Meyer, and Dave Kemper. <u>Writers INC: A Guide to Writing, Thinking, and Learning.</u> Burlington: Write Source, 1990.

5. FOUR OR MORE AUTHORS

You may give each author's name or the name of the first author only, followed by *et al.*, Latin for "and others."

First Author's Last Name, First Name, Second Author's First and Last Names, Third Author's First and Last Names, and Final Author's First and Last Names. <u>Title.</u> Publication City: Publisher, Year of publication.

Anderson, Robert, John Malcolm Brinnin, John Leggett, Gary Q. Arpin, and Susan Allen Toth. <u>Elements of Literature: Literature of the United States</u>. Austin: Holt, 1993.

First Author's Last Name, First Name, et al. <u>Title</u>. Publication City: Publisher, Year of publication.

Anderson, Robert, et al. <u>Elements of Literature: Literature of the United States</u>. Austin: Holt, 1993.

6. ORGANIZATION OR GOVERNMENT AS AUTHOR

Sometimes the author is a corporation or government organization.

> Organization Name. <u>Title</u>. Publication City: Publisher, Year of publication.

> Diagram Group. <u>The Macmillan Visual Desk Reference.</u> New York: Macmillan, 1993.

> National Assessment of Educational Progress. <u>The Civics Report Card.</u> Princeton: ETS, 1990.

7. ANTHOLOGY

> Editor's Last Name, First Name, ed. <u>Title.</u> Publication City: Publisher, Year of publication.

> Hall, Donald, ed. <u>The Oxford Book of Children's Verse in America.</u> New York: Oxford UP, 1985.

If there is more than one editor, list the first editor last-name-first and the others first-name-first.

> Kitchen, Judith, and Mary Paumier Jones, eds. <u>In Short: A Collection of Brief Creative Nonfiction.</u> New York: Norton, 1996.

8. WORK(S) IN AN ANTHOLOGY

> Author's Last Name, First Name. "Title of Work." <u>Title of Anthology.</u> Ed. Editor's First and Last Names. Publication City: Publisher, Year of publication. Pages.

> Achebe, Chinua. "Uncle Ben's Choice." <u>The Seagull Reader: Literature.</u> Ed. Joseph Kelly. New York: Norton, 2005. 23–27.

To document two or more selections from one anthology, list each selection by author and title, followed by a cross-reference to the anthology. In addition, include on your works-cited list an entry for the anthology itself (see no. 7, above).

> Author's Last Name, First Name. "Title of Work." Anthology Editor's Last Name. Pages.

> Hiestand, Emily. "Afternoon Tea." Kitchen and Jones. 65–67.

> Ozick, Cynthia. "The Shock of Teapots." Kitchen and Jones. 68–71.

9. AUTHOR AND EDITOR

Start with the author if you've cited the text itself.

> Author's Last Name, First Name. <u>Title.</u> Ed. Editor's First and Last Names. Publication City: Publisher, Year of publication.

> Austen, Jane. <u>Emma.</u> Ed. Stephen M. Parrish. New York: Norton, 2000.

▼

Start with the editor if you've cited his or her work.

> Editor's Last Name, First Name, ed. <u>Title.</u> By Author's First and Last Names. Publication City: Publisher, Year of publication.

> Parrish, Stephen M., ed. <u>Emma.</u> By Jane Austen. New York: Norton, 2000.

10. NO AUTHOR OR EDITOR

> Title. Publication City: Publisher, Year of publication.

> <u>2004 New York City Restaurants.</u> New York: Zagat, 2003.

11. TRANSLATION

Start with the author to emphasize the work itself.

> Author's Last Name, First Name. <u>Title.</u> Trans. Translator's First and Last Names. Publication City: Publisher, Year of publication.

> Dostoevsky, Fyodor. <u>Crime and Punishment.</u> Trans. Richard Pevear and Larissa Volokhonsky. New York: Vintage, 1993.

Start with the translator to emphasize the translation.

> Translator's Last Name, First Name, trans. <u>Title</u>. By Author's First and Last Names. Publication City: Publisher, Year of publication.

> Pevear, Richard, and Larissa Volokhonsky, trans. <u>Crime and Punishment.</u> By Fyodor Dostoevsky. New York: Vintage, 1993.

12. FOREWORD, INTRODUCTION, PREFACE, OR AFTERWORD

> Part Author's Last Name, First Name. Name of Part. <u>Title of Book.</u> By Author's First and Last Names. Publication City: Publisher, Year of publication. Pages.

> Tanner, Tony. Introduction. <u>Pride and Prejudice.</u> By Jane Austen. London: Penguin, 1972. 7–46.

13. MULTIVOLUME WORK

If you cite all the volumes of a multivolume work, give the number of volumes after the title.

> Author's Last Name, First Name. <u>Title of Complete Work.</u> Number of vols. Publication City: Publisher, Year of publication.

> Sandburg, Carl. <u>Abraham Lincoln: The War Years.</u> 4 vols. New York: Harcourt, 1939.

If you cite only one volume, give the volume number after the title.

> Sandburg, Carl. <u>Abraham Lincoln: The War Years.</u> Vol. 2. New York: Harcourt, 1939.

14. BOOK IN A SERIES

Editor's Last Name, First Name, ed. <u>Title of Book</u>. By Author's First and Last Names. Series Title abbreviated. Publication City: Publisher, Year of publication.

Hunter, J. Paul, ed. <u>Frankenstein.</u> By Mary Shelley. Norton Critical Ed. New York: Norton, 1996.

15. SACRED TEXT

If you have cited a specific edition of a religious text, you need to include it in your works-cited list.

<u>Title.</u> Editor's First and Last Names, ed. (if any) Publication City: Publisher, Year of publication.

<u>The New English Bible with the Apocrypha.</u> New York: Oxford UP, 1971.

<u>The Torah: A Modern Commentary.</u> W. Gunther Plaut, ed. New York: Union of American Hebrew Congregations, 1981.

16. EDITION OTHER THAN THE FIRST

Author's Last Name, First Name. <u>Title.</u> Name or number of ed. Publication City: Publisher, Year of publication.

Gibaldi, Joseph. <u>MLA Handbook for Writers of Research Papers.</u> 6th ed. New York: MLA, 2003.

Hirsch, E. D., Jr., ed. <u>What Your Second Grader Needs to Know: Fundamentals of a Good Second-Grade Education</u>. Rev. ed. New York: Doubleday, 1998.

17. REPUBLISHED WORK

Give the original publication date after the title, followed by the publication information of the republished edition.

Author's Last Name, First Name. <u>Title.</u> Year of original edition. Publication City: Current Publisher, Year of republication.

Bierce, Ambrose. <u>Civil War Stories.</u> 1909. New York: Dover, 1994.

Periodicals

BASIC FORMAT FOR AN ARTICLE

For most articles, you'll need to provide information about the author, the article title and any subtitle, the periodical title, any volume or issue number, the date, and inclusive page numbers.

Weinberger, Jerry. "Pious Princes and Red-Hot Lovers: The Politics of Shakespeare's <u>Romeo and Juliet</u>." <u>Journal of Politics</u> 65 (2003): 370–75.

▼

A FEW DETAILS TO NOTE

- AUTHORS: If there is more than one author, list the first author last-name-first and the others first-name-first.
- TITLES: Capitalize the first and last words of titles and subtitles and all principal words. Do not capitalize *a, an, the, to,* or any prepositions or coordinating conjunctions unless they begin a title or subtitle. For periodical titles, omit any initial *A, An,* or *The.*
- DATES: Abbreviate the names of months except for May, June, or July: Jan., Feb., Mar., Apr., Aug., Sept., Oct., Nov., Dec. Journals paginated by volume or issue call only for the year (in parentheses).
- PAGES: If an article does not fall on consecutive pages, give the first page with a plus sign (55+).

18. ARTICLE IN A JOURNAL PAGINATED BY VOLUME

Author's Last Name, First Name. "Title of Article." Title of Journal Volume (Year): Pages.

Bartley, William. "Imagining the Future in The Awakening." College English 62 (2000): 719–46.

19. ARTICLE IN A JOURNAL PAGINATED BY ISSUE

Author's Last Name, First Name. "Title of Article." Title of Journal Volume.Issue (Year): Pages.

Weaver, Constance, Carol McNally, and Sharon Moerman. "To Grammar or Not to Grammar: That Is Not the Question!" Voices from the Middle 8.3 (2001): 17–33.

20. ARTICLE IN A MONTHLY MAGAZINE

Author's Last Name, First Name. "Title of Article." Title of Magazine Month Year: Pages.

Fellman, Bruce. "Leading the Libraries." Yale Alumni Magazine Feb. 2002: 26–31.

21. ARTICLE IN A WEEKLY MAGAZINE

Author's Last Name, First Name. "Title of Article." Title of Magazine Day Month Year: Pages.

Cloud, John. "Should SATs Matter?" Time 12 Mar. 2001: 62+.

22. ARTICLE IN A DAILY NEWSPAPER

Author's Last Name, First Name. "Title of Article." Name of Newspaper Day Month Year: Pages.

Springer, Shira. "Celtics Reserves Are Whizzes vs. Wizards." Boston Globe 14 Mar. 2005: D4+.

If you are documenting a particular edition of a newspaper (indicated on the front page), specify the edition (late ed., natl. ed., etc.) in between the date and the section and page reference.

> Margulius, David L. "Smarter Call Centers: At Your Service?" <u>New York Times</u> 14 Mar. 2002, late ed.: G1+.

23. UNSIGNED ARTICLE

> "Title of Article." <u>Name of Publication</u> Day Month Year: Page(s).

> "Laura Bush Ponders Trip to Afghanistan." <u>New York Times</u> 2 Dec. 2003: A22.

24. EDITORIAL

> "Title." Editorial. <u>Name of Publication</u> Day Month Year: Page.

> "Gas, Cigarettes Are Safe to Tax." Editorial. <u>Lakeville Journal</u> 17 Feb. 2005: A10.

25. LETTER TO THE EDITOR

> Author's Last Name, First Name. "Title (if any)." Letter. <u>Name of Publication</u> Day Month Year: Page.

> Festa, Roger. "Social Security: Another Phony Crisis." Letter. <u>Lakeville Journal</u> 17 Feb. 2005: A10.

26. REVIEW

> Author's Last Name, First Name. "Title (if any) of Review." Rev. of <u>Title of Work</u>, by Author's First and Last Names. <u>Title of Periodical</u> Day Month Year: Pages.

> Lahr, John. "Night for Day." Rev. of <u>The Crucible</u>, by Arthur Miller. <u>New Yorker</u> 18 Mar. 2002: 149–51.

Electronic Sources

BASIC FORMAT FOR AN ELECTRONIC SOURCE

Not every electronic source gives you all the data that MLA would like to see in a works-cited entry. Ideally, you will be able to list the author's name, the title, any information about print publication, information about electronic publication (title of site, editor, date of first electronic publication and/or most recent revision, name of the sponsoring institution), date of access, and URL. Of those nine pieces of information, you will find seven in the following example.

> Johnson, Charles W. "How Our Laws Are Made." <u>Thomas: Legislative Information on the Internet</u> 31 Jan. 2000. Lib. of Congress. 5 Apr. 2005 <http://thomas.loc.gov/home/holam.txt>.

A FEW DETAILS TO NOTE

- AUTHORS: If there is more than one author, list the first author last-name-first and the others first-name-first.
- TITLES: Capitalize the first and last words of titles and subtitles, and all principal words. Do not capitalize *a, an, the, to,* or any prepositions or coordinating conjunctions unless they begin a title or subtitle. For periodical titles, omit any initial *A, An,* or *The.*
- DATES: Abbreviate the names of months except for May, June, or July: Jan., Feb., Mar., Apr., Aug., Sept., Oct., Nov., Dec. Although MLA asks for the date when materials were first posted or most recently updated, you won't always be able to find that information. You'll also find that it will vary—you may find only the year, not the day and month. The date you must include is the date on which you accessed the electronic source.
- URL: Give the address of the Web site in angle brackets. When a URL will not fit on one line, break it only after a slash (and do not add a hyphen). If a URL is very long, consider giving the URL of the site's home page or search page instead. Also, keep in mind that if you are accessing an online source through a library's subscription to a database provider (such as EBSCO), you may not see the URL itself. In that case, end your documentation with a period after your access date.

27. PROFESSIONAL WEB SITE

<u>Title of Site.</u> Ed. Editor's First and Last Names. Date posted or last updated. Sponsoring Institution. Day Month Year of access <URL>.

Stanford Encyclopedia of Philosophy. Ed. Edward N. Zalta. 2003. Metaphysics Research Lab, Center for the Study of Language and Information, Stanford U. 25 July 2004 <http:// plato.stanford.edu>.

28. PERSONAL WEB SITE

Author's Last Name, First Name. Home page. Date posted or last updated. Day Month Year of access <URL>.

Chomsky, Noam. Home page. 25 July 2004 <http://web.mit.edu/ linguistics/www.chomsky.home.html>.

29. HOME PAGE FOR AN ACADEMIC DEPARTMENT

Academic Department. Dept. home page. School. Day Month Year of access <URL>.

English Language and Literatures. Dept. home page. Wright State U College of Liberal Arts. 12 Mar. 2003 <http:// www.cola.wright.edu/Dept/ENG/Index.htm>.

30. ONLINE BOOK OR PART OF A BOOK

> Author's Last Name, First Name. "Title of Short Work." <u>Title of Long Work.</u> Original year of publication. <u>Database.</u> Date of electronic publication. Day Month Year of access <URL>.

> Anderson, Sherwood. "The Philosopher." <u>Winesburg, Ohio.</u> 1919. <u>Bartleby.com: Great Books Online.</u> 1999. 7 Apr. 2002 <http://www.bartleby.com/156/5.html>.

31. ARTICLE IN AN ONLINE PERIODICAL OR DATABASE

If a source does not number pages or paragraphs, follow the year with a period instead of a colon. Some periodicals have dates; others have volume and issue numbers instead—volume 10, issue 3 should be listed as 10.3, followed by the year (in parentheses). See the following examples.

FROM A PERIODICAL'S WEB SITE

> Author's Last Name, First Name. "Title of Article." <u>Title of Periodical</u> Date of Volume.Issue (Year): Pages or pars. Day Month Year of access <URL>.

> Landsburg, Steven E. "Putting All Your Potatoes in One Basket: The Economic Lessons of the Great Famine." <u>Slate</u> 13 Mar. 2001. 15 Mar. 2001 <http://slate.msn.com/Economics/01-03 13/Economics.asp>.

FROM A DATABASE PROVIDER

> Author's Last Name, First Name. "Title of Article." <u>Title of Periodical</u> Date or Volume.Issue (Year): Pages or pars. <u>Database</u>. Database provider. Library. Day Month Year of access <URL>.

> Bowman, James. "Moody Blues." <u>American Spectator</u> June 1999: 64–65. <u>Academic Search Premier.</u> EBSCO. Paul Laurence Dunbar Lib., Wright State U. 15 Mar. 2005 <http://epnet.com>.

32. DOCUMENT ACCESSED THROUGH AOL OR OTHER SUBSCRIPTION SERVICE

Note the *keyword* you used or the *path* you followed.

> Author's Last Name, First Name. "Title of Document." <u>Title of Longer Work.</u> Date of work. Service. Day Month Year of access. Keyword: Word.

> Stewart, Garrett. "Bloomsbury." <u>World Book Online.</u> 2003. America Online. 13 Mar. 2003. Keyword: Worldbook.

> Author's Last Name, First Name. "Title of Document." <u>Title of Longer Work.</u> Date of work. Service. Day Month Year of access. Path: Sequence of Topics.

▼

Hamashige, Hope. "New Pope's Election to Be Shrouded in Ritual, Secrecy." <u>National Geographic News.</u> 1 Apr. 2005. America Online. 25 Apr. 2005. Path: Research and Learning; History; History of Pope Selection.

33. EMAIL

Writer's Last Name, First Name. "Subject Line." Email to the author. Day Month Year of message.

Smith, William. "Teaching Grammar—Some Thoughts." Email to the author. 19 Nov. 2004.

34. POSTING TO AN ELECTRONIC FORUM

Writer's Last Name, First Name. "Title of Posting." Online posting. Day Month Year of posting. Name of Forum. Day Month Year of access <URL>.

Schafer, Judith Kelleher. "Re: Manumission." Online posting. 27 Jan. 2004. H-Net List on Slavery. 29 Jan. 2004 <http://h-net.msu.edu/cgi-bin/logbrowse.pl?trx=lm&list=H-Slavery>.

35. CD-ROM

FOR A SINGLE-ISSUE CD-ROM

<u>Title</u>. CD-ROM. Any pertinent information about the edition, release, or version. Publication City: Publisher, Year of publication.

<u>Othello</u>. CD-ROM. Princeton: Films for the Humanities and Sciences, 1998.

If you are citing only part of the CD-ROM, name the part as you would a part of a book.

"Snow Leopard." <u>Encarta Encyclopedia 1999</u>. CD-ROM. Seattle: Microsoft, 1998.

FOR A PERIODICAL ON A CD-ROM

Author's Last Name, First Name. "Title of Article." <u>Title of Periodical</u>. Date or Volume.Issue (Year): Page. <u>Database</u>. CD-ROM. Data-base provider. Month Year of CD-ROM.

Hwang, Suein L. "While Many Competitors See Sales Melt, Ben & Jerry's Scoops Out Solid Growth." <u>Wall Street Journal.</u> 25 May 1993: B1. <u>ABI-INFORM</u>. CD-ROM. Proquest. June 1993.

Other Kinds of Sources

This section shows how to prepare works-cited entries for categories other than books, periodicals, and writing found on the Web and

CD-ROMs. The categories are in alphabetical order. Two of them—art and cartoon—cover works that do not originate on the Web but make their way there. From these examples, you can figure out a documentation style for any texts that you may come across on the Web.

A FEW DETAILS TO NOTE

- AUTHORS: If there is more than one author, list the first author last-name-first and the others first-name-first. Do likewise if you begin an entry with performers, speakers, and so on.
- TITLES: Capitalize the first and last words of titles and subtitles, and all principal words. Do not capitalize *a, an, the, to,* or any prepositions or coordinating conjunctions unless they begin a title or subtitle. For periodical titles, omit any initial *A, An,* or *The.*
- DATES: Abbreviate the names of months except for May, June, or July: Jan., Feb., Mar., Apr., Aug., Sept., Oct., Nov., Dec. Journals paginated by volume or issue need only the year (in parentheses).

36. ADVERTISEMENT

Product or Company. Advertisement. Title of Periodical Date or
  Volume.Issue (Year): Page.

Empire BlueCross BlueShield. Advertisement. Fortune 8 Dec. 2003:
  208.

37. ART

Artist's Last Name, First Name. Title of Art. Year. Institution, City.

Van Gogh, Vincent. The Potato Eaters. 1885. Van Gogh Museum,
  Amsterdam.

ART ON THE WEB

Warhol, Andy. Self-Portrait. 1979. J. Paul Getty Museum, Los Angeles. 29 Mar. 2005 <http://getty.edu/art/collections/objects/
  oll4421.html>.

38. CARTOON

Artist's Last Name, First Name. "Title of Cartoon (if titled)." Cartoon.
  Title of Periodical Date or Volume.Issue (Year): Page.

Chast, Roz. "The Three Wise Men of Thanksgiving." Cartoon.
  New Yorker 1 Dec. 2003: 174.

CARTOON ON THE WEB

Fairington, Brian. Cartoon. Arizona Republic 6 Apr. 2002. 7 Apr.
  2002 <http://cagle.slate.msn.com/politicalcartoons/
  pccartoons/archives/fairington.asp???Action=Get!>.

39. DISSERTATION

Treat a published dissertation as you would a book, but after its title, add the abbreviation *Diss.*, the name of the institution, and the date of the dissertation. If the dissertation is published by University Microfilms International (UMI), include the order number, as in the example below.

> Author's Last Name, First Name. <u>Title</u>. Diss. Institution, Year. Publication City: Publisher, Year.

> Goggin, Peter N. <u>A New Literacy Map of Research and Scholarship in Computers and Writing</u>. Diss. Indiana U of Pennsylvania, 2000. Ann Arbor: UMI, 2001. 9985587.

For unpublished dissertations, put the title in quotation marks and end with the degree-granting institution and the year.

> Kim, Loel. "Students Respond to Teacher Comments: A Comparison of Online Written and Voice Modalities." Diss. Carnegie Mellon U, 1998.

40. FILM, VIDEO, OR DVD

> <u>Title</u>. Dir. Director's First and Last Names. Perf. Lead Actors' First and Last Names. Distributor, Year of release.

> <u>Casablanca</u>. Dir. Michael Curtiz. Perf. Humphrey Bogart, Ingrid Bergman, and Claude Rains. Warner, 1942.

If it's a video or DVD, give that information before the name of the distributor.

> <u>Easter Parade</u>. Dir. Charles Walters. Perf. Judy Garland and Fred Astaire. DVD. MGM, 1948.

41. INTERVIEW

BROADCAST INTERVIEW

> Subject's Last Name, First Name. Interview. <u>Title of Program</u>. Network. Station, City. Day Month Year.

> Gates, Henry Louis, Jr. Interview. <u>Fresh Air.</u> NPR. WNYC, New York. 9 Apr. 2002.

PUBLISHED INTERVIEW

> Subject's Last Name, First Name. Interview. or "Title of Interview." <u>Title of Periodical</u> Date or Volume.Issue (Year): Pages.

> Brzezinski, Zbigniew. "Against the Neocons." <u>American Prospect</u> Mar. 2005: 26–27.

> Stone, Oliver. Interview. <u>Esquire</u> Nov. 2004: 170.

PERSONAL INTERVIEW

Subject's Last Name, First Name. Personal interview. Day Month Year.

Berra, Yogi. Personal interview. 17 June 2001.

42. LETTER

UNPUBLISHED LETTER

Author's Last Name, First Name. Letter to the author. Day Month Year.

Quindlen, Anna. Letter to the author. 11 Apr. 2002.

PUBLISHED LETTER

Letter Writer's Last Name, First Name. Letter to First and Last Names. Day Month Year of letter. Title of Book. Ed. Editor's First and Last Names. Publication City: Publisher, Year of publication. Pages.

White, E. B. Letter to Carol Angell. 28 May 1970. Letters of E. B. White. Ed. Dorothy Lobarno Guth. New York: Harper, 1976. 600.

43. MAP

Title of Map. Map. Publication City: Publisher, Year of publication.

Toscana. Map. Milan: Touring Club Italiano, 1987.

44. MUSICAL COMPOSITION

Composer's Last Name, First Name. "Title of Short Composition." or Title of Long Composition. Year of composition (optional).

Ellington, Duke. "Mood Indigo." 1931.

If you are identifying a composition by form, number, key, and opus, do not underline that information or enclose it in quotation marks.

Beethoven, Ludwig van. String quartet no. 13 in B flat, op. 130. 1825.

45. MUSIC RECORDING

Artist's Last Name, First Name. Title of Long Work. Other pertinent details about the artists. Manufacturer, Year of release.

Beethoven, Ludwig van. Missa Solemnis. Perf. Westminster Choir and New York Philharmonic. Cond. Leonard Bernstein. Sony, 1992.

Whether you list the composer, conductor, or performer first depends on where you want to place the emphasis. If you are citing a specific song, put it in quotation marks before the name of the recording, which should be underlined.

Brown, Greg. "Canned Goods." The Live One. Red House, 1995.

▼

46. ORAL PRESENTATION

Speaker's Last Name, First Name. "Title of Lecture." Sponsoring Institution. Site, City. Day Month Year.

Cassin, Michael. "Nature in the Raw—The Art of Landscape Painting." Berkshire Institute for Lifetime Learning. Clark Art Institute, Williamstown. 24 Mar. 2005.

47. PAPER FROM PROCEEDINGS OF A CONFERENCE

Author's Last Name, First Name. "Title of Paper." Title of Conference Proceedings. Date, City. Ed. Editor's First and Last Names. Publication City: Publisher, Year. Pages.

Zolotow, Charlotte. "Passion in Publishing." A Sea of Upturned Faces: Proceedings of the Third Pacific Rim Conference on Children's Literature. 1986, Los Angeles. Ed. Winifred Ragsdale. Metuchen: Scarecrow P, 1989. 236–49.

48. PERFORMANCE

Title. By Author's First and Last Names. Other appropriate details about the performance. Site, City. Day Month Year.

Medea. By Euripedes. Dir. Jonathan Kent. Perf. Diana Rigg. Longacre Theatre, New Haven. 10 Apr. 1994.

49. TELEVISION OR RADIO PROGRAM

"Title of Episode." Title of Program. Other appropriate information about the writer, director, actors, etc. Network. Station, City. Day Month Year of broadcast.

"Stirred." The West Wing. Writ. Aaron Sorkin, Dir. Jeremy Kagan. Perf. Martin Sheen. NBC. WPTV, West Palm Beach. 3 Apr. 2002.

SAMPLE RESEARCH PAPER, MLA STYLE

Willow D. Crystal wrote the following essay. It is formatted according to the guidelines of the *MLA Handbook for Writers of Research Papers*, 6th edition (2003). The MLA guidelines are used widely in literature and other disciplines in the humanities.

Willow D. Crystal

Professor Akerley

English 1002

23 April 2006

"One of us . . . ": Concepts of the Private and
the Public in William Faulkner's "A Rose for Emily"

Throughout "A Rose for Emily," William Faulkner
introduces a tension between what is private, or belongs
to the individual, and what is public, or the possession
of the group. "When Miss Emily Grierson died," the tale
begins, "our whole town went to her funeral: the men
through a sort of respectful affection for a fallen monument, the women mostly out of curiosity to see the
inside of her house . . . " (594). The men of the small
town of Jefferson, Mississippi, are motivated to attend
Miss Emily's funeral for public reasons; the women, to
see "the inside of her house," that private realm which
has remained inaccessible for "at least ten years" (595).

This opposition of the private with the public has
intrigued critics of Faulkner's tale since the story was
first published. Distinctions between the private and the
public are central to Lawrence R. Rodgers's argument in
his essay "'We all said, "she will kill herself"': The Nar-
rator/Detective in William Faulkner's 'A Rose for
Emily.'" The very concept of the detective genre
demands that "there must be concealed facts that . . .
must become clear in the end" (119), private actions
which become public knowledge. In her feminist tribute, "A Rose for 'A Rose for Emily.'" Judith Fetterley
uses the private-public dichotomy to demonstrate the
"grotesque reality" (34) of the patriarchal social system
in Faulkner's story. According to Fetterley, Miss Emily's
"private life becomes a public document that the town
folk feel free to interpret at will" (36). Thus, while crit-

Center the title.

Double-space throughout.

Put page number of quotation inside the period.

Indent paragraphs ¹/₂ inch or 5 spaces.

If you name the author of a source in a signal phrase, give the page numbers in parentheses.

▼

The writer summarizes the effects of the critical points cited and then focuses on a critical distinction.

ics such as Rodgers and Fetterley offer convincing—if divergent—interpretations of "A Rose for Emily," it is necessary first to understand in Faulkner's eerie and enigmatic story the relationship between the public and the private, and the consequences of this relationship within the story and for the reader.

The most explicit illustration of the opposition between the public and the private occurs in the social and economic interactions between the town of Jefferson, represented by the narrator's "our" and "we," and the reclusive Miss Emily. "Alive," the narrator explains, "Miss Emily had been a tradition, a duty, and a care; a sort of hereditary obligation upon the town, dating from that day in 1894 when Colonel Sartoris, the mayor, . . . remitted her taxes, the dispensation dating from the death of her father on into perpetuity" (595). Ironically (and this is one of the prime examples of the complexity of the relationship of private and public in the story), the price of privacy for Miss Emily becomes the loss of that very privacy. Despite—or perhaps because of—her refusal to buy into the community, the citizens of Jefferson determine that it is their "duty," their "hereditary obligation," to oversee her activities. When, for example, Miss Emily's house begins to emit an unpleasant smell, the town officials decide to solve the problem by dusting her property with lime. When she refuses to say why she wants to buy poison, the druggist scrawls "For rats" (598) across the package, literally and protectively overwriting her silence.

The writer supports generalizations with brief, relevant quotations from the text.

Arguably, the townspeople's actions serve to protect Miss Emily's privacy—by preserving her perceived gentility—as much as they effectively destroy it with their intrusive zeal. But in this very act of protection they

▼

reaffirm the town's proprietary relation to the public "monument" that is Miss Emily and, consequently, reinforce her inability to make decisions for herself.

While the communal narrator and Miss Emily appear to be polar opposites—one stands for the public while the other fiercely defends her privacy—the two are united when an outsider such as Homer Barron appears in their midst. If Miss Emily serves as a representation—an icon, an inactive figure in a "tableau," an "idol"—of traditional antebellum southern values, then Homer represents all that is new and different. A "day laborer" (597) from the North, Homer comes to Jefferson to pave the sidewalks, a task which itself suggests the modernization of the town.

The writer summarizes a key contrast and then introduces a new element.

The secret and destructive union between these two representational figures implies a complex relationship between the private and the public. When Miss Emily kills Homer and confines his remains to a room in her attic, where, according to Rodgers, "she has been allowed to carry on her illicit love affair in post-mortem privacy" (119), this grotesque act ironically suggests that she has capitulated to the code of gentility that Jefferson imagines her to embody. This code demands the end of a romantic affair which some residents deemed "a disgrace to the town and a bad example to the young people" (598), thus placing traditions and the good of the community above Miss Emily's own wishes. Through its insistence on Miss Emily's symbolic relation to a bygone era, the town—via the narrator—becomes "an unknowing driving force behind Emily's crime" (Rodgers 120). Her private act is both the result of and a support for public norms and expectations.

The writer continues to develop the central terms, "private" and "public," and again cites a source mentioned earlier.

Give the author and page numbers in parentheses when no signal phrase is used.

At the same time, however, the act of murder also marks Miss Emily's corruption of that very code. By

▼

killing Homer in private, Miss Emily deliberately flouts public norms, and by eluding explicit detection until after her own death, she asserts the primacy of the private. The murder of the outsider in their midst thus leads Miss Emily to achieve paradoxically both a more complete privacy—a marriage of sorts without a husband—and a role in the preservation of the community.

The writer arrives at an important paradox in the interpretation of the key terms.

Yet the elaborate relationship between Jefferson and Miss Emily is not the only way in which Homer's murder may be understood as a casualty of the tension between the public and the private. When Miss Emily kills Homer, Rodgers contends, "from the town's point of view, it was the best thing. . . . Homer represents the kind of unwelcome resident and ineligible mate the town wants to repel if it is to preserve its traditional arrangements" (125). The people of Jefferson and Miss Emily join in a struggle to "repel" the outside and to ensure a private, inner order and tradition. This complicity creates intriguing parallels between the illicit, fatal union of Homer and Miss Emily and the reunion of the North and the South following the Civil War. In this reformulation of the private and the public, Miss Emily becomes, as Fetterley notes, a "metaphor and mirror for the town of Jefferson" (43). Miss Emily's honor is the townspeople's honor, her preservation their preservation.

Finally, the parallels between Miss Emily's secretive habits and the narrator's circuitous presentation of the story lead to a third dimension of the negotiations between the private and the public in "A Rose for Emily," a dimension in which Faulkner as author and the collective "we" as narrator confront their public consumers, the readers. Told by the anonymous narrator as if retrospectively, "A Rose for Emily" skips forward and back in time, omitting details and deferring revelations to such a degree that many critics have gone to extreme lengths to establish reliable chronologies for the tale. The much-debated "we" remains anonymous and unreachable throughout the tale—maintaining a virtually unbreachable privacy—even as it invites the public (the reader) to participate in the narrator's acts of detection and revelation. Rodgers observes:

> The dramatic distance on display here provides an ironic layer to the narrative. As the observers of the conflict between the teller-of-tale's desire to solve the curious mysteries that surround Emily's life—indeed, his complicity in shaping them—and his undetective-like detachment from her crimes, readers occupy the tantalizing position of having insight into unraveling the mystery which the narrator lacks. (120–21)

Set off quotations of four or more lines by indenting 1 inch (or 10 spaces).

Put parenthetical references after final punctuation in block quotations.

The reader is thus a member of the communal "we" party to the narrator's investigation and Jefferson's voyeuristic obsession with Miss Emily—but also apart, removed to a plane from which "insight" into and observation of the narrator's own actions and motives become possible. The reader, just like Miss Emily, Homer, and the town of Jefferson itself, becomes a crucial element in the tension between the public and the private.

The writer again explains the argument, to introduce the reader's role in the public/private issue.

Thus, public and private are, in the end, far from exclusive categories. And for all of its literal as well as figurative insistence on opposition and either/or structures, Faulkner's "A Rose for Emily" enacts the provocative idea of being "[o]ne of us" (600–601), of being both an individual and a member of a community, both a private entity and a participant in the public sphere.

The writer summarizes and resolves the debate (the seeming conflict).

▼

Center the heading.

Double-space.

Alphabetize the list by authors' last names or by title for works with no author.

Begin each entry at the left margin; indent subsequent lines ¹/₂ inch or 5 spaces.

Check to be sure that every source you use is on the list of works cited.

Works Cited

Faulkner, William. "A Rose for Emily." <u>The Norton Introduction to Literature</u>. 9th ed. Eds. Alison Booth, J. Paul Hunter, and Kelly J. Mays. New York: Norton, 2005. 595–601.

Fetterley, Judith. "A Rose for 'A Rose for Emily.'" <u>The Resisting Reader: A Feminist Approach to American Fiction</u>. Bloomington: Indiana UP, 1978. 34–45.

Moore, Gene M. "Of Time and Its Mathematical Progression: Problems of Chronology in Faulkner's 'A Rose for Emily.'" <u>Studies in Short Fiction</u> 29 (1992): 195–204.

Rodgers, Lawrence R. "'We all said, "she will kill herself"': The Narrator/Detective in William Faulkner's 'A Rose for Emily.'" <u>Clues: A Journal of Detection</u> 16 (1995): 117–29.

Permissions Acknowledgments

Index of Terms

abstract language:
   diction and, 70–74
   exercises, 80–82
   imagery and, 83
absurdist drama, 47, 152
accentual meter, 198, 218
accentual-syllabic meter, 198
adjective, 184
adverb, 184
allegory, 39, 86
alliteration:
   assonance and, 220
   exercises, 223–25
   internal, 218
   onomatopoeia and, 221
   overview, 217–19
   repetition and, 98
   in sonnet, 232
allusion:
   atmosphere and, 89
   blank verse and, 236
   exercises, 78–82
   imagery and, 83, 85
   overview, 74–76
   rhetorical strategy and, 68
   selection and order of details, 101
   stream of consciousness and,
      119–20
analogy:
   exercises, 78–82
   overview, 76–78
   rhetorical strategy and, 68
anapestic foot, 200, 203
anapestic trimeter, 229
anaphora:
   exercises, 66–67
   free verse and, 240–41
   overview, 64
   repetition and, 98
ancient Greek drama, 7
antagonist, 130–32
antinovel, 10
antithesis:
   exercises, 66–67

free verse and, 240
overview, 64–65
sentence variety and, 193
aphorism, 20
apostrophe:
   alliteration and, 218
   assonance and, 220
   blank verse and, 236
   exercises, 66–67
   invocation, 63
   meter and, 206
   overview, 62–63
   selection and order of details, 102
appositive, 185
aside, 140, 143–44
assonance:
   exercises, 223–25
   onomatopoeia and, 221
   overview, 220
   repetition and, 98
atmosphere:
   exercises, 92–97
   imagery and, 85
   overview, 89–92
   parallelism and, 189
   rhetorical strategy and, 68
   setting and, 150

ballad meter:
   exercises, 242–44
   in hymns, 230
   quatrains and, 229
   rhyme scheme, 212
   scansion in, 205
Bildungsroman, 10
blank verse:
   drama and, 2
   dramatic monologue and, 227
   exercises, 245–46
   free verse and, 239
   meter and, 226
   overview, 234–39
   repetition and, 98

blank verse (*continued*)
    rhyme and, 210–11
    soliloquy and, 142
    sonnets and, 234
    structure of, 167
    tone and, 157
    see also iambic pentameter

caesura:
    couplets and, 227
    defined, 205
    exercises, 209–10
    free verse and, 239
catalectic foot, 203
catalexis, 203
characterization:
    defined, 125
    dialogue and, 132, 137
    exercises, 127–29, 153
    flat vs. round characters, 126
    narration and, 113
    repetition and, 98
    showing vs. telling, 127
    stream of consciousness and, 120
    see also dialogue; narrator; point
      of view
chiasmus, 65–67
classical tragedy, 1, 4
closed couplet, 226–27
closed form poems, 239, 242
closet drama, 1
colloquial language:
    blank verse and, 234
    diction and, 68–70
    exercises, 80–82
    free verse and, 240
    lyric poetry and, 72
comedy:
    classical tragedy, 4
    farce, 3–4
    high, 3–4
    low, 3
    of manners, 4
    overview, 3–4
    romantic (*see* romantic comedy)
    subplot in, 175

    tragicomedy, 1, 5–6
    see also satire
comedy of manners, 4
comic exaggeration, 218
common meter, *see* ballad meter
complete predicate, 184
complete subject, 184
complex sentence:
    atmosphere and, 91
    defined, 186
    formal diction and, 69
    independent clause and, 188
    sentence variety and, 191, 193–94
    subordination, 187–86
compound sentence:
    colloquial diction and, 69–70
    coordination in, 186–87
    defined, 186
    loose, 187, 192, 194–95
    sentence variety, 192
concrete diction:
    atmosphere and, 91
    exercises, 80–82
    imagery and, 83–84
    overview, 68–73
consonance:
    assonance and, 220
    exercises, 223–25
    onomatopoeia and, 221
    overview, 219–20
    repetition and, 98
coordinating conjunction, 186–88
coordination, 186–87, 195–96
cosmic irony, 44, 46–47
couplets:
    blank verse and, 237
    closed, 226–27
    exercises, 242–44
    heroic, 2, 19, 226, 233
    iambic pentameter, 2, 226
    iambic tetrameter in, 226–27
    inversion of, 190
    open, 227
    rhymed, 2, 142, 237
    rhyme scheme, 212
    Shakespearean sonnet and,
      229–31

couplets (*continued*)
  sonnets and, 233
  trochaic tetrameter in, 89
  turn in, 232
cumulative sentence, 189–90
curtal sonnet, 234

dactylic foot, 200, 202–203
dactylic tetrameter, 202
deity, second-person pronoun for,
  236
dependent clause, 184, 187
details, selection and order of, *see*
  selection and order of details
dialogue:
  aside, 143
  atmosphere and, 89–90
  characterization and, 127
  in drama, 1–2, 132, 138–139, 140
  exercises, 144–49
  narration and, 112, 132–49
  objective narrator and, 117
  overview, 132–43
  in short story, 11, 137
  soliloquy, 141–43
  tone in, 136
  understatement in, 55
diction:
  abstract (*see* abstract language)
  atmosphere and, 89–90
  colloquial (*see* colloquial language)
  concrete (*see* concrete diction)
  exercises, 78–82, 162, 166
  formal (*see* formal diction)
  informal, 158
  Latinate, 194
  poetic, 72–74, 80–82
  rhetorical strategy and, 68
  tone and, 156–57
dimeter, 200
direct discourse, 139
direct object, 184
direct satire, 21–22, 24
discourse, 139
doggerel tragedy, 218
domestic tragedy, 5

drama:
  absurdist, 47, 152
  ancient Greek, 7
  blank verse and, 236
  categories of, 1
  characterization in, 125, 127
  closet, 1
  comedy (*see* comedy)
  dialogue in, 1–2, 132, 136–37,
    140
  eighteenth-century, 7
  Elizabethan (*see* Elizabethan
    drama)
  English medieval, 7
  exercises, 132, 154, 166, 183
  flashback and, 169
  Jacobean (*see* Jacobean drama)
  in medias res, 170
  modern, 7
  novel and, 11
  omniscient narrator in, 117
  overview, 1–3
  periods of, 7
  plot and, 129
  poetry and, 13
  protagonist in, 129, 132
  repartee in, 140
  repetition and, 98
  Restoration, 7
  Roman, 7
  setting in, 150
  theater of the absurd, 6
  tone in, 156
  tragedy (*see* tragedy)
  tragicomedy, 1, 5–6
  see also aside; narration; soliloquy
dramatic irony:
  dialogue and, 136
  exercises, 47
  imagery and, 85
  overview, 46
  tone and, 156
  as type of irony, 44
dramatic monologue:
  exercises, 16–19, 111
  onomatopoeia and, 221–22
  open couplet and, 227

dramatic monologue (*continued*)
  overview, 15–16
  voice of, 112
  see also unreliable narrator
dramatic poetry, 1, 13–14

eighteenth-century drama, 7
Elizabethan drama:
  in blank verse, 2
  overview, 7
  revenge tragedy, 4–5
  tragicomedy, 5
end rhyme, 211–12
  see also poetic forms
end-stopped lines:
  blank verse and, 235
  couplets and, 227
  defined, 204
  exercises, 209–10
  free verse and, 239, 241
  in sonnets, 233
English medieval drama, 7
English sonnet, *see* Shakespearean
    sonnet
enjambed lines (enjambments):
  blank verse and, 235–36
  couplets and, 227
  defined, 204
  exercises, 209–10
  free verse and, 239
  in sonnets, 233
  structure and, 167
epic poetry (epics):
  blank verse and, 236
  defined, 1, 14
  exercises, 132
  heroic couplets in, 226
  in medias res, 167–68
  as narrative form, 112
  overview, 13–14
  protagonist in, 132
epigram, 19–21
epiphany:
  exercises, 104–11
  overview, 102–4
  rhetorical strategy and, 68

epistolary novel, 8, 10
equivoque, 60
exposition, 168–69, 181–82
extended metaphor, 35–38
eye rhyme, 213–17

farce, 3–4
feet, *see* metrical feet
feminine ending, 203, 211, 215–17
fiction:
  atmosphere and, 90
  characterization in, 125
  dialogue in, 132, 138–39
  epiphany and, 102–3
  exercises, 154
  flashback and, 168
  genres of, 1, 8
  in medias res, 169
  metafiction, 10, 121
  as narrative form, 1
  nonfiction and, 8
  novel (*see* novel)
  novella (*see* novella)
  plot and, 129
  poetry and, 13
  prose (*see* prose fiction)
  protagonist in, 129
  repartee in, 140
  repetition and, 98
  selection and order of details,
    99
  setting in, 150
  short story (*see* short story)
  voice of, 112
fictional narrator, 15
figurative language:
  atmosphere and, 91
  defined, 32
  diction and, 68, 73
  exercises, 36, 42, 53
  imagery and, 85
  poetry and, 1
  setting and, 151
  see also figures of speech; figures
    of thought
figurative terms, 69

figures of speech:
    anaphora, 64–67
    antithesis, 64–67
    apostrophe, 62–63, 65–67
    categories of, 62
    chiasmus, 65–67
    exercises, 66–67
    as figurative language, 32
    rhetorical question, 63, 66–67
figures of thought:
    categories of, 32
    exercises, 36, 42, 60–62
    hyperbole, 54, 60–62
    irony, 44–54
    litotes, 57–58, 60–62
    metaphor, 33–38
    metonymy, 41–43
    oxymoron, 57, 60–62
    paradox, 56–57, 60–62
    pathetic fallacy, 40–43, 86
    personification, 38–40, 42–43
    pun, 59–62
    simile, 32–33, 36–38
    synecdoche, 41–43
    understatement, 55–56, 60–62
first-person point of view, 173
    atmosphere and, 91
    defined, 113
    dialogue and, 133
    direct satire and, 21
    exercises, 122–25
    overview, 113–14
    parenthetical observation, 173
    second-person point of view and,
        121–22
    selection and order of details,
        100
    soliloquy and, 143
    tone and, 157
    unreliable narrator and, 157
flashback, 168, 181–82
flat (two-dimensional) characters:
    defined, 125
    exercises, 127–29
    foil as, 131
    repetition and, 98–99
    round characters vs., 126

foil character:
    exercises, 132
    overview, 129, 131
formal diction:
    blank verse and, 234–36
    exercises, 80–82
    overview, 68–70
    sentence variety and, 194
formality:
    dialogue and, 138
    parallelism and, 189
formal satire, 21–22, 24
free verse:
    defined, 198
    exercises, 245–48
    meter and, 226
    overview, 239–42
    rhyme and, 210–11, 226
    sonnets and, 234

half rhyme:
    exercises, 215–17, 224–25
    overview, 213–14
    in quatrains, 230
heptameter, 201
hero, 129–30
heroic couplets:
    defined, 226
    in epigrams, 19
    sonnets and, 233
    in tragedies, 2
heroine, 129–30
hexameter, 201, 228
high comedy, 3–4
historical novel, 10
homonyms, 59
Horatian satire, 22, 24
hubris, 4
hyperbole:
    exercises, 60–62
    overview, 54
    sentence variety and, 193–94
    in sonnets, 233
    tone and, 159
    understatement and, 54–55

iambic foot:
 defined, 199
 example, 201
 free verse and, 241
 rhymed iambic pentameter
   couplets, 2
 trochee and, 202
 unrhymed iambic pentameter, 2,
   167
iambic hexameter, 228
iambic pentameter:
 ballad meter, 205
 common substitutions,
   202–3
 in couplets, 2, 226
 dramas and, 2
 free verse and, 239
 overview, 201, 234–39
 rhymed couplets, 2
 scansion, 206
 sonnet and, 231
 structure of, 167
 tercet and, 228
 unrhymed, 2, 167
 see also blank verse
iambic tetrameter:
 ballad meter, 205, 229
 couplets, 226–27
 quatrains and, 229
iambic trimeter, 228–29
 ballad meter, 205, 229
imagery:
 abstract vs. concrete language,
   70–71
 atmosphere and, 91
 epiphany and, 103
 exercises, 92–97
 overview, 83–86
 repetition and, 98
 rhetorical strategy and, 68
imperfect rhyme, 213–15
independent clause:
 blank verse and, 235
 complex sentence and, 188
 compound sentence and, 186
 defined, 184

parallelism and, 189
 subordinate clause and, 186
indirect discourse, 139
indirect object, 185
indirect satire, 22, 24
informal diction, 157
informal style, 189
in medias res, 167–70, 178
internal alliteration, 218
internal rhyme, 211–12, 215–17
intrusive third-person narrator:
 exercises, 122
 exposition and, 168
 indirect satire, 22
 overview, 115–16
 tone and, 160
inversion:
 exercises, 195–96
 overview, 190–91
 sentence variety and, 193–94
invocation, 63
irony:
 allusion and, 74
 cosmic, 44, 46–47
 dramatic (*see* dramatic irony)
 exercises, 47–54
 free verse and, 240
 narrator and, 116, 176, 187
 pathetic fallacy and, 40
 structural, 44–45, 47
 tragic, 44, 46–47, 54
 understatement and, 55–56
 verbal, 44–45, 47, 160
Italian sonnet:
 exercises, 245–46
 octave of, 167, 206, 229, 231
 rhyme scheme of, 231
 sestet of, 167, 206, 228, 231

Jacobean drama:
 in blank verse, 2
 overview, 7
 revenge tragedy, 4–5
 tragicomedy, 5
Juvenalian satire, 22–24

Latinate diction, 194
Latinate periphrasis, 69
limited point of view, *see* third-person limited point of view
lines:
  closed couplet, 226–27
  end rhyme, 211
  end-stopped (*see* end-stopped lines)
  enjambed (*see* enjambed lines)
  internal rhyme, 211–12
  number of feet in, 200–1
  refrain and, 226
  run-on, 204
  scansion, 205–7
literal language:
  defined, 32
  diction and, 68, 73
  exercises, 92
  symbolism and, 87
literary form:
  drama (*see* drama)
  dramatic monologue (*see* dramatic monologue)
  epigram, 19–21
  fiction (*see* fiction)
  poetry (*see* poetry)
  specialized, 15–31
litotes:
  exercises, 60–62
  overview, 57–58
  as understatement, 55, 57–58
loose compound sentence, 187, 192, 194–95
low comedy, 3
lyric poetry:
  as category, 1, 13
  colloquial language and, 72
  overview, 14
  sonnet as (*see* sonnet)
lyrics, 14

masculine ending:
  couplets and, 227
  defined, 203

end rhyme and, 211
exercises, 215–17
metafiction, 10, 121
metaphor:
  analogy and, 78
  atmosphere and, 91
  exercises, 36–38, 92
  extended, 35–38
  figurative terms, 69
  free verse and, 241
  imagery and, 83, 85
  mixed, 34–35
  setting and, 151
  subtext, 36
  tenor, 33–34
  vehicle, 33–34
  see also metonymy; pathetic fallacy; simile; synecdoche
meter:
  accentual, 198, 218
  accentual-syllabic, 198
  ballad (*see* ballad meter)
  blank verse and, 226, 234, 236, 239
  common substitutions, 202–3
  exercises, 207–10
  free verse and, 226–39
  metrical feet (*see* metrical feet)
  naming the, 201–2
  number of feet in a line, 200–1
  open couplet and, 227
  overview, 198–99
  pauses in verse, 204–5
  quantitative, 198
  quatrain and, 229
  repetition and, 98
  rhyme and, 210
  scansion, 198, 205–6
  sonnets and, 233
  stanza and, 226
  syllabic, 198
  see also prosody
metonymy, 41–43
metrical feet:
  blank verse and, 234
  exercises, 207–9

metrical feet (*continued*)
  naming the meter, 202–3
  number of feet in a line, 200–1
  scansion, 205–7
  types of, 199–200
mixed metaphor, 34–35
MLA (Modern Language Association) style:
  books cited, 255–59
  electronic sources, 261–64
  in-text documentation, 249–54
  list of works cited, 254
  notes, 254
  other sources cited, 264–68
  periodicals cited, 259–61
  sample research paper, 268–74
modern drama, 7
monometer, 200
morality plays, 7
mystery plays, 7

narration:
  characterization, 112, 125–29
  defined, 112
  dialogue, 112, 132–49
  exercises, 196–97
  point of view, 112–25
  roles in the plot, 112, 129–32
  setting, 112, 150–54
  theme, 112, 155–56, 162–66
  tone, 112, 156–66
  voice, 112–13
narrative:
  exercises, 144
  fiction as, 1
  forms of, 112
  narration and, 112
narrative pace:
  defined, 112, 167
  exercises, 183
  overview, 170–72
narrative poetry:
  characterization in, 125
  comedy and, 3
  dialogue in, 132
  exercises, 154, 178

  plot and, 129
  protagonist in, 129
  setting in, 150
  tone in, 156
narrator:
  blank verse and, 234
  characterization and, 127
  defined, 112
  dialogue and, 132–33, 136
  drama and, 1
  in dramatic monologues, 15–16
  exercises, 97, 108–10
  fictional, 15
  first-person (*see* first-person point of view)
  flat vs. round characters, 126
  intrusive third-person (*see* intrusive third-person narrator)
  irony and, 116, 176, 187
  in medias res, 168
  narrative pace, 170–72
  objective, 116–17, 122, 160
  objective third-person, 116–17, 122, 160
  omniscient (*see* third-person omniscient point of view)
  point of view and, 113
  refrain and, 230
  rhyme and, 214
  in satire, 21–23
  selection and order of details, 100, 102
  sentence fragments, 185
  sentence variety, 192
  setting and, 151
  structure and, 168
  third-person (*see* third-person narrator)
  third-person limited (*see* third-person limited point of view)
  third-person omniscient (*see* third-person omniscient point of view)
  tone and, 157
  understatement and, 55
  unreliable, 45, 157

nonfiction, 8
noun, 184–85
noun phrase, 185
novel:
  antinovel, 10
  of character, 9
  characterization in, 127
  defined, 1, 8
  dialogue in, 135–37
  epiphany and, 102–3
  epistolary, 8, 10
  exercises, 94, 132, 152, 166, 178,
    183
  historical, 10
  of incident, 9
  metafiction, 10
  as narrative form, 112
  narrative pace, 171
  novella (see novella)
  overview, 8–11
  protagonist in, 8–9, 132
  realistic, 9
  romance, 9–10, 12
  subplot in, 176
  third-person limited point of
    view, 120
  voice of, 112
novella:
  allusion and, 75
  analogy and, 76–77
  defined, 1, 8
  dialogue in, 137
  as narrative form, 112
  overview, 12
  third-person limited point of
    view, 120
  voice of, 112
novel of character, 9
novel of incident, 9

object, 189–90
objective third-person narrator:
  exercises, 122
  overview, 116–17
  tone and, 160
octave (Italian sonnet):
  defined, 231
  quatrains and, 229
  structure, 167
off-rhyme, 213
omniscient point of view, see third-
    person omniscient point of
    view
onomatopoeia, 221–25
open couplets, 227
open form poems, 242
open form verse, see free verse
order of details, see selection and
    order of details
oxymoron, 57, 60–62

pace, see narrative pace
paradox:
  atmosphere and, 89
  exercises, 60–62
  overview, 56–57
  oxymoron as, 57
parallel clause, 188–89, 193
parallelism:
  exercises, 195–96
  metonymy and, 41
  overview, 188–89
  sentence variety and, 193
parenthetical observation, 172–74,
    183
pathetic fallacy, 40–43, 86
pathos, 23, 161–62
pauses in verse, 204–5, 234
pentameter, 201
  see also iambic pentameter
perfect rhyme, 213–17
periodic sentence, 190, 193–95
periphrasis:
  diction and, 73
  exercises, 60–62
  formal diction and, 69
  Latinate, 69
  overview, 58–59
personification:
  allegory, 39
  epiphany and, 104
  exercises, 42–43

personification (*continued*)
  imagery and, 85
  overview, 38–40
  pathetic fallacy, 40–41
  sentence variety and, 193
Petrarchan sonnet, *see* Italian sonnet
phrase, 184
plays:
  exercises, 94, 153–54, 178
  indirect satire in, 22
  morality, 7
  mystery, 7
  omniscient narrator in, 117
  selection and order of details, 99
  in verse, 2
plot:
  dialogue and, 132
  in fiction, 8
  flat vs. round characters, 126
  narration and, 112
  roles in the, 112, 129–32
  see also subplot
poems:
  closed form, 239
  epiphany and, 102–4
  meter and, 198
  selection and order of details, 99
  see also poetry
poetic diction, 72–74, 80–82
poetic forms:
  blank verse (*see* blank verse)
  defined, 226
  exercises, 242–46
  free verse (*see* free verse)
  stanza (*see* stanza)
poetry:
  accentual meter, 198
  accentual-syllabic meter, 198
  categories of, 1
  dramatic, 1, 13–14
  epic (*see* epic poetry)
  figurative language in, 32
  free verse in, 241–42
  inversion in, 190
  lyric, 1, 13–14, 72
  meter in, 198–210
  narrative (*see* narrative poetry)
  novel and, 11
  overview, 13–14
  quantitative meter, 198
  repetition and, 98
  scansion, 205–7
  syllabic meter, 198
  voice of, 112
  see also poems; rhyme
point of view:
  characterization and, 127
  exercises, 53, 122–25, 162, 166
  in fiction, 8
  first-person (*see* first-person point
    of view)
  narration and, 112–25
  overview, 113
  second-person (*see* second-person
    point of view)
  third-person (*see* third-person
    point of view)
  third-person limited (*see* third-
    person limited point of view)
  third-person omniscient (*see*
    third-person omniscient point
    of view)
  tone and, 156–57
predicate:
  defined, 184
  sentence fragments and, 185
  subordinate clause and, 186
prepositional phrase, 185
pronoun, 184–85
prose fiction:
  comedy in, 3
  dialogue in, 135
  figurative language in, 32
  indirect satire in, 22
  tone in, 156
prosody:
  defined, 198
  meter (*see* meter)
  rhyme (*see* rhyme)
  sound patterns (*see* sound
    patterns)
protagonist:
  allusion and, 75
  antagonist and, 130

▼

protagonist (*continued*)
  atmosphere and, 92
  dialogue and, 133, 136
  epiphany and, 103
  exercises, 132, 152–54, 197
  flashback and, 168
  flat vs. round characters, 126
  foil and, 131
  in medias res, 168, 170
  narrative pace, 170–72
  in novel, 8–9, 132
  overview, 129–30
  rhetorical strategy and, 68
  second-person point of view, 121
  in short story, 11, 132
  soliloquy and, 141
  theater of the absurd, 6
  in tragedy, 4
  in tragicomedy, 5
  understatement and, 55–56
pun:
  atmosphere and, 92
  equivoque, 60
  in foil, 131

quantitative meter, 198
quatrain:
  exercises, 242–44
  overview, 229–31
  sonnet and, 231–33

realistic novel, 9
refrain:
  defined, 226, 230
  exercises, 242–44
  repetition and, 98
reliability, 143
repartee:
  in drama, 140
  exercises, 144
  in fiction, 140
  in high comedy, 3
  in satire, 23
repetition:
  exercises, 104–11
  overview, 98–99

rhetorical strategy and, 68
selection and order of details,
  100, 102
Restoration drama, 7
revenge tragedy, 4–5
rhetorical question, 63, 66–67
rhetorical strategy:
  allusion, 68, 74–76, 78–82
  analogy, 68, 76–82
  atmosphere, 68, 89–97
  categories of, 68
  defined, 68
  diction, 68–74, 78–82
  epiphany, 68, 102–11
  exercises, 78–80
  imagery (*see* imagery)
  repetition, 68, 98–99, 104–11
  selection and order of details, 68,
    99–102, 104–11
  symbolism, 68, 86–89, 92–97
rhyme:
  blank verse and, 226, 234
  end, 211–12
  exercises, 215–17, 224–25
  eye, 213–17
  free verse and, 226, 239
  half (*see* half rhyme)
  imperfect, 213–15
  internal, 211–12, 215–17
  off-, 213
  overview, 210–11
  perfect, 213–17
  poetry and, 198
  repetition and, 98
  rhyme scheme (*see* rhyme scheme)
  slant, 213
  sound patterns and, 218
rhymed couplet:
  blank verse and, 237
  iambic pentameter, 2
  soliloquy and, 142
rhyme scheme:
  exercises, 215–17
  free verse, 239
  overview, 212–13
  quatrain and, 229
  of sonnets, 231

rhythm:
    blank verse and, 237
    free verse and, 239
    poetry and, 1
roles in the plot:
    antagonist, 130–31
    exercises, 132
    foil character, 131
    narration and, 112
    overview, 129
    protagonist, 129–30
romance, 9–10, 12
Roman drama, 7
romantic comedy:
    overview, 4
    setting in, 150
    as subcategory, 1
    subplot in, 23
round (three-dimensional) characters:
    defined, 125
    exercises, 127–29
    flat characters vs., 126
    repetition and, 99
    stream of consciousness and, 120
run-on lines, 204

sarcasm, 44–45
satire:
    alliteration and, 218
    direct, 21–22, 24
    epigrams and, 19
    example of, 9
    exercises, 24–31
    formal, 21–22, 24
    Horatian, 22, 24
    indirect, 22, 24
    Juvenalian, 22–24
scansion:
    defined, 198
    overview, 205–7
    rhyme scheme, 212–13
schemes, *see* figures of speech
second-person point of view:
    defined, 113
    exercises, 122–25
    first-person point of view and, 121–22
    metafiction, 121
    overview, 120–22
    third-person point of view and, 116, 121
selection and order of details:
    atmosphere and, 89–90
    exercises, 104–11, 160, 163
    overview, 99–102
    rhetorical strategy and, 68
    tone and, 156
    see also concrete diction;
        dialogue; imagery; symbolism
Senecan tragedy, 4
sentence:
    complex (*see* complex sentence)
    compound (*see* compound sentence)
    cumulative, 189–90
    defined, 184
    kinds of, 186
    periodic, 190, 193–95
    simple (*see* simple sentence)
sentence fragments, 185–86, 189, 194–95
second-person pronoun for deity, 236
sequence, sonnet, 233–34
sestet (Italian sonnet):
    caesura, 206
    defined, 231
    structure, 167
    tercet and, 228
setting:
    exercises, 152–54
    narration and, 112, 150–54
    in novel, 8
    overview, 150–54
    parallelism and, 189
    in short story, 11
    see also atmosphere; pathetic fallacy
Shakespearean sonnet, 229, 231, 245–46
shift in style, 174–76

short story:
  atmosphere and, 90
  characterization in, 127
  defined, 1, 8
  dialogue in, 11, 136
  epiphany and, 102
  exercises, 94, 132, 153, 166, 178, 183
  in medias res, 169–70
  as narrative form, 112
  novel and, 8
  overview, 11–12
  protagonist in, 11, 132
  selection and order of details, 99–100
  soliloquy and, 143
  third-person limited point of view, 120
  understated tone, 187
  voice of, 112
showing, 125, 127
simile:
  analogy and, 78
  epiphany and, 104
  exercises, 36–38, 92
  free verse and, 210–11
  imagery and, 83, 85
  metaphor and, 33
  overview, 32–33
  selection and order of details, 100
simple predicate, 184
simple sentence:
  colloquial diction and, 69–70
  defined, 186
  sentence variety and, 191–92
simple subject, 184
slant rhyme, 213
soliloquy:
  alliteration and, 219
  allusion and, 74–75
  blank verse and, 237
  dialogue and, 138, 140
  exercises, 144
  imagery and, 85
  overview, 141–43
  parenthetical observation, 173

sonnet:
  curtal, 234
  English (see Shakespearean sonnet)
  Italian (see Italian sonnet)
  meter in, 206
  overview, 231–34
  Petrarchan (see Italian sonnet)
  as poetic form, 226
  rhyme scheme, 212
  Shakespearean (see Shakespearean sonnet)
sonnet sequence, 233–34
sound patterns:
  alliteration, 217–19, 223–24
  assonance, 220, 223–25
  consonance, 219–20, 223–25
  exercises, 223–24
  onomatopoeia, 221–23
  repetition and, 98
speech headings, 136, 144
spondaic foot (spondee), 202, 206
stage directions:
  dialogue and, 132, 136
  drama, 1
  exercises, 144, 152
  theater of the absurd, 6
  tragedy, 2
  tragicomedy, 6
stanza:
  couplet (see couplets)
  defined, 226
  exercises, 242–44
  free verse and, 239
  meter and, 226
  quatrain (see quatrain)
  refrain (see refrain)
  rhyme scheme, 212
  sonnet (see sonnet)
  tercet (see tercet)
stock characters, 4
stream of consciousness, 118–19, 122
stressed syllables:
  alliteration, 217–18
  assonance, 220
  blank verse and, 234

stressed syllables (*continued*)
common substitutions and,
212–13
consonance, 219
couplets, 226
defined, 198
end rhyme, 211
exercises, 207–9
metrical feet and, 199–200
rhyme and, 210
scansion, 205–6
in verse, 199
see also prosody
structural irony, 44–45, 47
structure:
exercises, 178–82
in medias res, 167–70, 178
narrative pace, 167, 170–72, 183
overview, 167
parenthetical observation,
172–74, 183
shift in style, 176–78
subplot, 167, 174–76, 183
style, shift in, 176–78
subject:
cumulative sentence, 189
defined, 184
inversion, 190, 194
sentence fragments and, 185
subordinate clause and, 186
subordinate clause, 186, 188
subordination, 187–88, 195–96
subplot:
analogy and, 78
defined, 167
exercises, 183
overview, 174–76
in romantic comedy, 23
substitution:
common, 202–203
exercises, 208–10
of metrical feet, 205–6
subtext, 36
syllabic meter, 198
symbolism:
exercises, 92–97
overview, 86–89
repetition and, 98

rhetorical strategy and, 68
setting and, 151
synecdoche, 41–43
syntax:
colloquial diction and, 69
cumulative sentence, 190
exercises, 162, 165, 194–97
figures of speech and, 62
kinds of sentences, 186
means of linkage, 186–89
overview, 184–85
parallelism in, 189
periodic sentence, 190
poetry and, 1
sentence fragments, 185–86
sentence variety, 191–94
syntactical order, 189–91
tone and, 157–58
see also diction

telling:
characterization and, 125, 127
defined, 127
exposition and, 169
in medias res, 170
tenor, 33–34, 36
tercet (triplet):
exercises, 242–44
overview, 228–29
terza rima, 228, 242–44
tetrameter:
dactylic tetrameter, 202
defined, 201
iambic tetrameter, 205, 226–27,
229
trochaic tetrameter, 89
theater of the absurd, 6
theme:
blank verse and, 236
exercises, 162–66
narration and, 112, 154–55,
162–66
narrative pace, 172
overview, 154–55
third-person limited point of view:
atmosphere and, 92
exercises, 122–25

third-person limited point of view
(*continued*)
in medias res, 170
narrative pace, 172
overview, 114, 118–20
second-person point of view and,
121
tone and, 160
third-person narrator:
intrusive (*see* intrusive third-
person narrator)
objective, 116–17, 122, 159
see also third-person point of view
third-person omniscient point of
view:
dialogue and, 133, 138
in drama, 117
exercises, 122–25
exposition and, 168
metafiction and, 121
overview, 114–18
second-person point of view and,
121
setting and, 151
tone and, 160
understatement and, 56
third-person point of view:
defined, 113
dialogue and, 139
limited (*see* third-person limited
point of view)
objective, 116–17, 122, 160
omniscient (*see* third-person
omniscient point of view)
overview, 114–20
second-person point of view and,
116, 121
see also third-person narrator
three-dimensional (round)
characters:
defined, 125
exercises, 127–29
flat characters vs., 126
repetition and, 99
stream of consciousness and, 120
tone:
alliteration and, 218
assonance and, 220

atmosphere and, 89
in comedy, 3–4
cumulative sentence, 190
dialogue and, 132
exercises, 108, 162–66, 178–83,
208–9, 223–25
flat vs. round characters, 126
inversion and, 191
meter and, 199
narration and, 112, 157–66
overview, 157–61
rhetorical strategy and, 68
rhyme and, 210–11, 213
scansion and, 207
selection and order of details,
100–101
sentence variety and, 194
shifts in style, 176
in simile, 33
theme and, 155
in tragedy, 4
understated, 187
understatement and, 56
see also first-person point of view;
irony; structural irony;
unreliable narrator
tragedy:
classical, 1, 4
doggerel, 218
domestic, 5
exercises, 153
overview, 4–5
revenge, 4–5
Senecan, 4
stage directions, 2
subcategories of, 1
subplot in, 175
tragicomedy, 1, 5–6
tragic irony:
exercises, 47
hyperbole and, 54
overview, 44, 46
tragicomedy, 1, 5–6
trimeter:
anapestic trimeter, 229
defined, 201
iambic trimeter, 228–29
trochaic trimeter, 202

triplet (tercet), 228–29
trochaic foot (trochee):
    defined, 200, 202
    example, 202–3
    trochaic tetrameter couplets,
      89
trochaic tetrameter, 89
trochaic trimeter, 202
tropes, 62
    see also figures of thought
turn (volta), 231–32
two-dimensional characters, see flat
    characters

understated tone, 187
understatement:
    exercises, 60–62
    free verse and, 241
    hyperbole and, 54–55
    litotes as, 55, 57–58
    overview, 55–56
    pathos and, 161
unreliable narrator, 45, 157
unrhymed iambic pentameter, 2,
    167
unstressed syllables:
    blank verse and, 234
    common substitutions and,
      202–3
    couplets, 226
    defined, 198
    end rhyme, 211

    exercises, 207–9
    metrical feet and, 199–200
    scansion, 205–6
    in verse, 199
    see also prosody

vehicle:
    defined, 33–34
    exercises, 36, 92
    imagery and, 83
verb:
    cumulative sentence, 189
    inversion, 190
    parallelism and, 189
    simple predicate, 184
verbal irony, 44–45, 47, 160
verisimilitude, 136
verse:
    blank (see blank verse)
    fiction in, 1
    figurative language, 32
    free (see free verse)
    meter and, 195
    open form (see free verse)
    pauses in, 204–5, 234
    plays in, 2
    poetry and, 13
    scansion, 205–7
    stress in (see stressed syllables)
villain, 130
voice, 112–13, 169
volta (turn), 231–32